Revisiting "Social Factors"

Revisiting "Social Factors":

Advancing Research into People and Place

Edited by

Georgia Lindsay and Lusi Morhayim

Cambridge
Scholars
Publishing

Revisiting "Social Factors": Advancing Research into People and Place

Edited by Georgia Lindsay and Lusi Morhayim

This book first published 2015

Cambridge Scholars Publishing

Lady Stephenson Library, Newcastle upon Tyne, NE6 2PA, UK

British Library Cataloguing in Publication Data
A catalogue record for this book is available from the British Library

ISBN (10): 1-4438-7734-4
ISBN (13): 978-1-4438-7734-3

TABLE OF CONTENTS

LIST OF ILLUSTRATIONS

LIST OF TABLES

FOREWORD

GALEN CRANZ

After thirty-six years at the University of California, Berkeley teaching social and cultural perspectives on architectural design, three of my students—Lusi Morhayim, Georgia Lindsay, and Jonathan Bean—held a conference in the spring of 2011. It felt like a celebration of a generation's work in that field. The presentations—and this edited collection of research articles that grew from them—demonstrate that a focus on the social nature of architecture continues to be an essential and growing part of architectural education and research. The chapters in this book show how social considerations are involved at every scale, in every setting, and accordingly, they draw from an extensive toolkit of research methods, both qualitative and quantitative.

In a sense, this trans-disciplinary research presages the recent changes in criteria for accreditation of architecture departments by the National Architectural Accreditation Board (NAAB). NAAB recognizes that social concerns touch every area of architectural decision-making and accordingly created categories that presume social research and decision-making throughout architectural curriculum (and, by implication, practice). The 2014 NAAB conditions for accreditation state that graduates

"must be able to build abstract relationships and understand the impact of ideas based on the study and analysis of multiple theoretical, social, political, economic, cultural, and environmental contexts. ...Student learning aspirations for this realm include being broadly educated, valuing lifelong inquisitiveness, communicating graphically in a range of media, assessing evidence, comprehending people, place, and context, recognizing the disparate needs of client, community, and society."

Of these six goals, two are overtly social, but all require an understanding of human interactions: representation too assumes cultural knowledge of how to communicate with others.

NAAB confirms the importance of research "to inform the design process." That is, graduates must demonstrate the "ability to raise clear and precise questions, use abstract ideas to interpret information, consider diverse points of view, reach well-reasoned conclusions, and test alternative outcomes . . ." (NAAB 2014) and the investigative skills "to gather, assess, record, and comparatively evaluate relevant information and performance . . ." (NAAB 2014). These skills belong as much if not more to the social basis of design than its formal basis. The goal of understanding "the parallel and divergent histories of architecture and the cultural norms of a variety of indigenous, vernacular, local, and regional settings in terms of their political, economic, social, ecological, and technological factors" is even more explicitly social/cultural. Finally, understanding "the diverse needs, values, behavioral norms, physical abilities, and social and spatial patterns that characterize different cultures and individuals and the responsibility of the architect to ensure equity of access to sites, buildings, and structures" requires profound social-cultural knowledge.

In this book, research is marshaled to help establish criteria for the decision-making process in design. For example, Dominic Fisher shows how park design now benefits from observation research as it did thirty years ago (Whyte 1980). Heyligen shows how autobiographies, interviews, and video observations combine subjective and objective perspectives on the experience of disability to help able-bodied designers create supportive environments. Golembiewski and Schuette detail the quantitative and qualitative research approaches of a large commercial architectural practice. Bodelmann et al. compare preschool playgrounds (regarding size, shade, and vegetation) in North Carolina and Sweden regarding adequate access to vitamin D, sun protection, and adequate physical activity to promote kids' health as measured by their attention, activity, and sleep. L'Heureux documents the process of rebuilding three different buildings with an eye to sustainability after a tornado decimated a small Kansas community, leading to an evaluation of sustainability, LEED standards, and participatory design strategies. Perez et al. also document and evaluate participation, in the context of inter-cultural communication strategies between Berkeley students and the Pinoleville Pomo Nation in northern California. These chapters all implicate the human context as a necessary component to design, and merge the boundaries between research and practice.

Social research in architecture continues to grow, professionally and critically

A postmodern backlash against the modern interest in research was based on the (mistaken) idea that user-oriented research was naive and a constraint on artistic freedom (Cupers 2014). Some high-style architects and theorists have turned to versions of literary theory rather than empirical readings of reality. Despite this turn to theory in architectural discourse, the amount of empirical research about users and design has grown by leaps and bounds. The Environmental Design Research Association (EDRA) is the chief professional association of architects and social scientists of all stripes and it continues to grow since it started in 1969. It is bigger, and more active, than ever. Several journals specialize in social research on building issues (among them *Environment & Behavior, Journal of Architectural Planning and Research,* and *Environmental Psychology*). Based on my observations over the last forty years from the Princeton study of the energy use in a Planned Unit Development (Twin Rivers) in 1971 to the work of Berkeley's Center for the Built Environment in 2014, I would estimate that approximately half the research in building science entails social variables, like user comfort, user regulation of thermostats, etc. Further, I note that social theory (by Giddens, Bourdieu, LaTour, etc.) has worked its way into the teaching of architectural history and theory.

Social research is directly tied to both professional service and cultural criticism. Social research in a professional school often focuses on serving the profession, but it can also serve as a form of cultural criticism in the tradition of the humanities (Franck and Lepori 2007; Cranz 1982; 1998). Professionally, social research is part of the design process at the beginning in the programming stage, and also towards the end of the cycle after a building has been planned, constructed, and inhabited in what is known as Post Occupancy Evaluation (POE) research. POEs have become a recognized specialty in architectural and planning practice (Mallory-Hill et al. 2012; Zimring 2001). And, some practitioners recognize that programming should not only list the square-footage assigned to functions, but also include more socially- psychologically- and culturally-informed performance criteria (Pena and Parsall 2001; Cherry 2003). These criteria, usually based on close observations of reality, can inspire new designs and refine existing building types in a cycle of thinking, designing, constructing, and evaluating that parallels the scientific process of hypothesis formulation, testing against reality, and revision.

At the same time, social research as a form of criticism can give us the distance to stand back and observe what society is producing through its architecture and to comment on the wisdom or folly entailed. By analyzing the way something was created, there is the implicit suggestion that it could be re-created a different way. Each scholar has to combine the roles of servant and critic in their own proportions. Similarly, each architect needs to find a balance between performing as an employee with obligation to the paying client and as a professional with an obligation to the welfare of society. When archeologists dig our built environment they will find clues about our way of life, so architects may want to challenge themselves to consider what values they are manifesting in the built environment. Our field helps by providing theoretical, conceptual, and empirical tools to do so.

All levels of analysis, aka systems thinking

One of the theoretical tools that we offer both professionals and cultural critics is systems thinking, and the idea that architecture works at different levels of analysis. The field of person-environment studies now includes (1) behavioral, (2) organizational, (3) institutional, (4) societal, and (5) cultural levels of analysis. For example, at the *behavioral* level a lawyer needs to use forms and books, address the judge, etc. Supporting these activities in the design of the office would require workstation design like that of other office workers but perhaps with particular emphasis on settings for private conversation, a way to read large books that is comfortable from an ergonomic point of view, secure storage, etc. At the *organizational* level the design requirements are different; obligations to colleagues, the kind of law practice, and the managerial style might require conference space, thoughtfulness about the visual messages communicated in the public reception area, etc. The *institution* of the law upholds the importance of law versus force in resolving social conflicts. What is needed to reinforce the institution is different from what is needed to run the organization or meet face-to-face with a client. In this regard, courthouses often have columns, grand stairs, flags, and other common symbols of "civilization" drawn from historical contexts. Such symbols and rituals help clients, practitioners, and other members of a society remember that very general social norms are being enacted through the institution of the law. At the levels of US *society and culture*, the institution of law shares with other institutions commitment to a range of values, including fair play, equality of opportunity, legitimate power, etc. These general values are often symbolized through site selection (central locations) and architectural form (such as large size and distinctive shape), material choice, symbolism, and decoration.

At first, much of the social factors research in the US emphasized the behavioral level of analysis, but it has expanded over the last forty-five years to include these other levels. This breadth is partly how the role of the architectural sociologist-researcher expands to cultural critic. Not only do we describe and analyze, but also we can challenge the status quo by asking if these are the right values, and if these institutions and organizations are the best ways to pursue them.

Both qualitative and quantitative methods

As the research field has expanded, methods have expanded correspondingly. Because studies can be behavioral, organizational, institutional, or societal and cultural, methods are correspondingly varied. Some researchers in the social aspects of architecture use qualitative, interpretive, and critical approaches to describe, analyze, understand, critique, and even reform, while others use quantitative and behavioral with reformist motivations to "fix" or help resolve social-environmental problems—in housing, schools, professional offices, hospitals, commercial outlets, other workplaces, and recreational settings.

A significant methodological challenge remains. How do we measure the *relationship* between humans and their environments? How do we measure the hyphen in person-environment relations? Most scientists in the 20th century have been content to assume that persons and environments are the two units of analysis. The behaviorist legacy of Skinner and others emphasizes input and output, without regard for the transformational process that connects the two. In contrast (according to philosopher Richard Rorty), three 20th Century philosophers—Heidegger, Wittgenstein, and Dewey—have emphasized the transactional quality between people and their environments. Also, Barker's "behavior settings" (1968) and Alexander's "patterns" (1977) are attempts to couple people and their settings. If people are defined in relation to their environments, the unit of analysis is the person-in-environment, harder to measure than either person or environment.

Social research can differ from historical research for four main reasons. First, social researchers often seek to move beyond description to generalization, sometimes sacrificing minor differences among cases in order to focus attention on their commonalities. This, in turn, is motivated by the second difference, namely, attention to contemporary life, especially current problems and policy issues. The third difference concerns data collection techniques. Observation, interviews, questionnaires, participant observation, and photo elicitation lend themselves to study of contemporary behavior. Content analysis of text, drawings, and other visual media lend themselves to the study of organizational decision-making, institutional development, and social and cultural values in the present or in the past. Here is where social history and social science are most likely to converge. Further convergence occurs when historians use social theory, and when social researchers study the present by including the historical past. A fourth difference is that social research follows a scientific model, while history follows a humanities model. However, social research does not have to subscribe to this dichotomous way of thinking—primarily because interpretive social science is widely recognized as one of the humanities. Furthermore, we can view science itself as one of the humanities. That is, science is a way that humans have constructed in order to know things.

Let us remind ourselves of the ultimate creativity and imagination that science entails. The familiar dualisms of art versus science, Romantic versus Classical reasoning, feeling versus fact are transcended by creativity. We want to use both sides of these polarities freely, appropriately, and robustly. Pirsig's (1974) novel *Zen and the Art of Motorcycle Maintenance* demonstrated philosophically that art and science share the common wellspring of creativity, and can serve as an introductory text for architecture students who need to integrate both the art and science of their chosen profession. The building has to stand up and use energy as modestly as possible, which requires knowledge of engineering and building science, *and* it should look good, which requires artistic training. Architecture is both an art, as emphasized by the French Beaux-Arts tradition, and a practical science as emphasized by the Germanic architectural tradition. We need the research techniques that come from each tradition.

We use qualitative case studies especially when we need to describe, usually the first phase of science, also sometimes called *discovery science* as distinguished from *hypothesis science*. This means we as students of space often work *inductively* rather than *deductively*. Anslem Strauss called this grounded theory, and Paolo Friere also insisted on learning about people's problems as they themselves described them and only then seeking commonalities among the problems to develop generalizations and theories about the causes of the problems. In environmental design our studies are often site-specific, so we too need to start from careful description of a unique situation, rather than testing an existing hypothesis. Our use of case studies is similar to many of the studies in history, unique to the site, but in our case with an eye to the possibility of comparisons with other such cases and developing generalizations that can be applied elsewhere. We generate and use quantitative information *after* we have identified the range of opinions, preferences, and needs, and want to know how many fall into each of those qualitative categories. In this collection three chapters are qualitative, one is quantitative, and four combine both.

Understanding the relationship among qualities may be as or more important than quantitative measures. A correlation may be adequate statistically, but we need theory to explain its meaning, and why it might hold true, and for what reasons. In other words, in the language of the philosophy of science, "validity" (measures mean what you think they mean) is as important as "reliability" (the likelihood that two or more observers get the same result). And *vice versa*: that is, we can make a good argument for something and still need to find out if it is true in fact. For example, we can make the argument that a space will create community, but until we find out what we mean by community and then measure to see if there is more or less of it, our claims can be no more than wishful thinking, ideological propaganda, or current fashion in architectural thought and discourse.

While social research in architecture uses many levels of analysis, many environmental psychologists often start with behavioral and attitudinal analyses. There *is* a psychological bias in this field and in American thought generally. (The nineteenth-century French sociologist Durkheim worked hard to explain that sociology is different from psychology by showing how to analyze suicide—extremely personal, yes, but then why do its rates vary by nation and events?) This field also works at the levels of complex organizations (work place, hospitals, schools)— Sommer, *Hard Architecture and How to Humanize It*—institutions—King, *Buildings and Society,* Cranz, *The Politics of Park Design*, Henn, *Moving Targets*: *Managing Inter-Institutional Relations in Building Design and Construction*—and societies and culture—Hall, *Hidden Dimension*, L'Heureux, *Ideology and Architecture in Estonia*. EDRA's European counterpart International Association for Person-Environment Studies (IAPS) tends to use a more institutional level of analysis. Architectural historians work at this higher level of analysis, too. The idea that social-cultural researchers work on many levels, not just behavioral, needs wider circulation and this new volume demonstrates the multiple methods at work in the field.

In this book several authors use individual behavior and experiences as the primary unit of analysis: Fisher's observation of behavior in parks, Heylighen's focus on experience of disability, Golembiewski and

Schuette's aggregated individual data to establish patterns, Bodelmann's comparison of children's health in terms their attention, activity, and sleep.

Other authors move up to the organizational, institutional, and societal levels of analysis. L'Heureux's documentation of rebuilding three different buildings led to evaluation of emerging institutional practices regarding sustainability, LEED standards, and participatory design strategies. Perez et al. also documented and evaluated participation, which is being institutionalized unevenly in design practice.

Ethnography is valuable in our field because it requires the researcher to take the user's point of view (literally the subjective point of view), aids description and induction, and brings qualitative categories to the fore. Cognitive or semantic ethnography focuses on what people can *tell* you about their culture, so it is particularly practical for architects who would not always be able to travel to a site before designing a building. Ideally, one should observe and talk to people, but the fact is that architects' budgets often treat fieldwork as a luxury. Therefore, a method that teaches them how to get as much information as possible from *at least* phone conversations seemed practical and theoretically in line with our commitment to a user perspective. Semantic ethnography has a particularly powerful tool to offer, namely, the taxonomy. This simple device allows us to see that the same term in a different context has very different meanings. Listening for the specialized vocabulary and underlying logical structure that another person uses to organize his or her world is a skill not taught in many societies or universities. This orientation is valuable not only as a professional skill, but also as a needed part of liberal arts education. Who teaches us how to listen actively, accurately, and creatively? (Cranz, 2014, under review). In this volume, Fischer, Golembiewski and Schuette, L'Heureux, and Perez use qualitative methods and an ethnographic approach. Heylighen's focus on experience of disability involves both objective and subjective measures.

What's in a name?

It is almost a truism that architecture has three parts: structural, social, and aesthetic. The social aspects were foregrounded in the late 1960s when the National Science Foundation funded sociological research in architecture at Rutgers, Princeton, and Berkeley, and when environmental psychologists and architects formed the Environmental Design Research Association in 1969. Sociologist Suzanne Keller at Princeton in 1971 used the term social factors. Some still call our field social factors; others call it environmental psychology, person-environment relations, or human factors. None seem exactly right because the social is intimately embedded with the aesthetic and the structural; what we perceive as beautiful varies culturally, and our structural decisions (e.g., big span or small?) ultimately depend on how we want to live (in large or small groups or both?). The philosophical and methodological difficulties of finding a way to name the ever-shifting network of people making and being influenced by built forms have stayed with us more than forty-five years after the field began. The anthropologist Hilda Geertz once said in conversation that social science might be better called social studies. But of course the term sounds like a high school subject and the culture at large is still enamored with "science," so we continue to use the term social science to legitimate what we do. Karen Franck discusses the words we use in the field of social research in architecture in more depth in her chapter.

A factor is not a relationship; in contrast, the "use of space" embeds people with environment. Mechanism assumes that one part can be exchanged for another without consequences for the remaining parts of a system. For example, designers once thought that people can be moved from a slum neighborhood to better housing without grief or loss of supportive networks. Determinism is the belief that social life can be explained by one underlying force, for example, economic determinism, or architectural determinism. For over fifty years determinism has been in disrepute.

In contrast to determinism, symbolic interactionism is appropriate for environmental design research as sociologist Ron Smith (2006) has demonstrated in his paper on architecture and symbolic interactionism. For example, Frederick Law Olmsted described how an attractive and respectable public setting could be a place where a man could take his wife and children with the fortunate by-product of seeing himself as others saw him—as the head of the household. Seeing himself in others' eyes, he would resolve not to spend his income in the saloon or brothel, but rather on his family. Whether or not that turned out to be true in practice is another story, but Olmsted's intentions show how an environment might interact with self-conception. One can enfold symbolic interactionism into a communication model, and thereby side-step both physical and social determinism.

Today the term "Evidence-based design," copied from medicine, is positivistic in that there is the belief that more information will yield better decisions. Positivism is a philosophic idea from the 19th century French sociologist August Compte that society evolves upward and that science makes progress inevitable. The idea is discredited, but sometimes scientific research does indeed improve social policies. For example,

Zeisel et al (2003) have demonstrated that appropriate environmental design can be as effective as drugs on several dimensions for those with Alzheimer's disease. The environmental psychologist Ulrich demonstrated that patients in a hospital recovering from surgery left the hospital faster if they had a view of a tree rather than a brick wall (Ulrich 1984). Social research in environmental design does not inevitably lead to improvements, but it can be used to help mobilize people to enact social change. Social science and social studies are neither a prison, nor a guarantee of progress, but rather a springboard.

The future of social research in environmental design

How might the field continue to grow? I see several options. The most important issue for continuing research relates to learning to live sustainably on earth with its finite resources.

The ultimate goal of our research and design proposals is to improve the quality of the environment, so perhaps we need to bring our work to the attention of the broader public, not just to other design professionals. Radio, TV, and New Media come to mind. Roman Mars has a radio program called 99% Invisible about the effects of design decisions on our everyday lives; Kim Dovey has a radio show in Australia; Nezar Alsayyad has produced a film on earth houses; Elefterios Pavlides writes letters to the editor of the *NY Times*. We need a television program to advocate serviceable, beautiful, and sustainable environments. And how about some TED talks online?

Professionally and pedagogically, we might search for a "brand" that is somewhat less mechanistic than the term "social factors." Karen Franck and I have independently proposed "social use of space." As suggested earlier, we might want to find a term that brackets persons and environments as inseparable rather than independent variables that can be "factored" into a design equation or not.

Paying close attention to social practices can inspire architectural innovation. Social patterns are not a "straight jacket," but rather a muse. We want to help students and practitioners in the design community become better artistically by helping them *feel* and interpret social forces. Fortunately, design education tends to be learning-centered, rather than teaching-centered, so those who teach social research in design can also emphasize experiential learning in the classroom. Design education is one way to bring the unified self of body and mind back into the classroom and workplace. The unity of art and science is what may keep us alive as a species as we face the burgeoning ecological crisis. Using the hand and mind brings sensate experience and cognitive order together. Here, cultural criticism and service are seamless. To critique, advocate, and create is to serve.

References

Alexander, Chrisotpher. 1977. *A Pattern Language: Towns, Buildings, Construction.* New York: Oxford University Press.

Barker, R. G. 1968. *Ecological Psychology.* Palo Alto, CA: Stanford University Press.

Cherry, Edith. 1998. *Programming for Design: From Theory to Practice.* Hoboken, NJ: Wiley.

Cranz, Galen. 1982. *The Politics of Park Design: A History of Urban Parks in America* Cambridge, MA: MIT Press.

—. 1998. *The Chair: Rethinking Culture, Body and Design.* New York: WW Norton.

—. 2014 under review. *Ethnography for Architects.*

Cupers, Kenny. 2014. "Where Is the Social Project?" *Journal of Architectural Education*, 68:1, 6-8, DOI: 10.1080/10464883.2014.864892.

Franck, Karen and Lepori, Bianca. 2007. *Architecture from the Inside Out: From the Body, the Senses, the Site and the Community.* Hoboken, NJ: Wiley.

Friere, Paulo. 2006. *Pedagogy of the Oppressed. 30th Anniversary ed.* English translation 1970. New York: Continuum.

Glaser, Barney G. and Strauss, Anselm L. 1967. *The discovery of Grounded Theory: Strategies for Qualitative Research.* Chicago: Aldine.

Gutman, Robert. 1972. *People and Buildings.* New York: Basic Books.

Hall, Edward T. 1990. *The Hidden Dimension.* New York: Anchor Books.

Henn, Rebecca. 2013. *Moving Targets: Managing Inter-Institutional Relations in Building Design and Construction.* Ann Arbor: University of Michigan.

King, Anthony D. 1984, 2005. *Buildings and Society.* London: Taylor & Francis.

L'Heureux, Marie-Alice. 2003. "Ideology and Architecture in Estonia." PhD diss, University of California at Berkeley.

Mallory-Hill, Shauna and Wolfgang P.E. Preiser, Christopher G. Watson eds. 2012. *Enhancing Building and Environmental Performance.* Hoboken, NJ: Wiley-Blackwell.

National Architectural Accrediting Board, Inc. 2014. *2014 Conditions for*

Accreditation. Washington DC: NAAB.

Peña, William M. and Steven A. Parshall. 2001. *Problem Seeking: An Architectural Programming Primer.* Hoboken, NJ: Wiley.

Pirsig, Robert. 1974. *Zen and the Art of Motorcycle Maintenance: An Inquiry into Values.* New York: William Morrow.

Smith, Ron and Valerie Bugni. 2006. "Symbolic Interaction Theory and Architecture." *Symbolic Interaction* 29 (2).

Sommer, Robert. 1974. *Tight Spaces: Hard Architecture and How to Humanize It.* Englewood Cliffs, N.J: Prentice-Hall.

Ulrich, Roger B. 1984. "View through a Window May Influence Recovery from Surgery." *Science* April 27, 224: 420-422.

Whyte, William H. 1980. *The Social Life of Small Urban Spaces.* Washington DC: Conservation Fdn.

Zeisel, John and Nina M. Silverstein, Joan Hyde, Sue Levkoff, M. Powell Lawton, William Holmes. 2003. "Environmental Correlates to Behavioral Health Outcomes in Alxheimer's Special Care Units." *Gerontologist* 43(5): 697-711.

Zimring, Craig. 2001. "Post-occupancy Evaluations and Organizational Learning." In *Learning from Our Buildings: A State-of-the-practice Summary of Post-occupancy Evaluation.* Federal Facilities Council Technical Report No. 145. Washington, D.C.: National Academy Press.)

PREFACE

GEORGIA LINDSAY AND LUSI MORHAYIM

Between April 29 and May 1 2011, researchers and practitioners interested in spatial and social studies and design gathered at the University of California, Berkeley's College of Environmental Design for *The Death and Life of "Social Factors": A Conference Reexamining Behavioral and Cultural Research in Environmental Design.*[i] The conference brought together researchers and practitioners from a variety of disciplinary backgrounds, methodological stances, and countries of origin to stimulate discussion on what constitutes research into the social impacts of design. Around 200 participants from thirty-five countries attended for three days of panels, paper presentations, special sessions, workshops, and posters. Over 100 paper presentations indicated continued lively interest in research regarding the relationship between culture, individuals, and the built environment. The conference questioned the boundaries, the status, and the future of social and behavioral research in environmental design.

The positive and international response to the conference call for papers demonstrates that there is still strong interest in the field that has at various times been called *social factors*, *man-environment relations*, and *environment and behavior research*. One of many of our goals with this conference was to create an international platform for the discussion and critique of social factors research; it was time to take a close look at the past and future of our field. Paper sessions covered topics including special needs populations, design for health, sustainability, perception, place identity, theoretical explorations within the field, and the practice of socially conscious architecture.

Given the variety and the dynamism within this field, the conference aimed to start a dialogue about the present and future of social research in environmental design. From its early days, where there was an alignment with behavioral determinism, to more recent approaches such as anthropological studies of space, social factors has been a diverse—and divisive—topic. Interest in "the social" has moved beyond "social factors" researchers within the environmental design field, and methods have shifted in response to the adoption of participatory design and the influence of post-modern and post-structuralist modes of inquiry. Moreover, other fields such as geography, history, and sociology have also staked a claim to the analysis of social issues related to space. In this conference, we asked how contemporary research addresses the idea of "the social" in space, not only from those in our field, but also from those in emerging fields of research, to understand how we might address critiques such as the disconnect with design practice and our use of social science methods. Thus, we aimed to connect researchers across dispersed fields, and to provide a platform for working together to define a common set of interests, research questions, and set a new direction for our field. In short, we sought the rebirth and redefinition of social factors.

The conference yielded a variety of published research. The Journal of Urban Design collected articles working at the urban scale in a special issue (Volume 17 Number 4, November 2012). And this book presents innovative research into people and space, divided into two broad topics: (1) History and future outlook and (2) Perspectives on the user.

Notes

[i] The conference was organized by Lusi Morhayim, Georgia Lindsay, and Jonathan Bean, together with the help of the advising committee, consisting of Professor Galen Cranz, Professor Margaret Crawford, and Professor Michael Southworth. The conference was generously funded by The College of Environmental Design, the Draper Fund, the Student Opportunity Fund and the Intellectual Community Fund of the Associated Students of the University of California, and University of California's Graduate Student Assembly.

INTRODUCTION

GEORGIA LINDSAY AND LUSI MORHAYIM

The interaction between people and the built environment can be studied at multiple scales, from rooms to cities, and is comprised of many layers that interest researchers from multiple disciplines and interdisciplinary areas. A reaction to modernism in architecture—which disregarded the depth and diversity of human experiences—and a deep curiosity about the significant relationship between society, culture, body, and space, combined to give birth to the research field which is referred to as social factors in architecture and urban design. Now, this field of social factors is expanding, with vibrant interest from the Middle East, Europe, Australia, and across the US.

Understanding this area of research starts with understanding the way it is referenced. The field is called many different names, including human factors, social factors, environment and behavior, and social and cultural processes. In Chapter 1, Karen A. Franck addresses some of the words used to describe the field; for the purposes of this introduction, we will persist with the commonly used, but not unproblematic, "social factors."

Concomitant with confusion over the name comes a blurring of the edges of the field. If a geographer writes on the importance of space, is she doing the work of social factors? If an architect designs a town and claims it fosters community, is he working within the field? Should a dissertation on the totalizing nature of the neoliberal state that focuses on the spatial characteristics of urban spaces count towards a PhD in Architecture? The chapters presented in this book offer a resounding answer to these questions—all in the affirmative. In this book we revisit research into people and space: chapter topics range from new media and technological solutions to the problem of co-design from far away, to meditations on the question of physical ability and inclusive design, to measurements of sun exposure and playground design's impact on health. In doing so, we help define a way forward, based on the history of social factors.

The origins of social factors research date back to the late 1960s. The birth of the Environmental Design Research Association (or EDRA) and the journal *Environment and Behavior* marked a consensus among researchers that the study of the meanings and uses of space is a distinctive field worthy of its own journal and conferences. The field developed as researchers from varied disciplines such as psychology, sociology, and anthropology started to pay special attention to the importance of the interaction between people and the environment. In Chapter 2, Susanne Cowan and Ayda Melika present interviews from many key individuals who defined the field in the United States, exploring how the history of the field of social factors unfolded.

The early period in social factors research gave birth to fundamental concepts in the field such as proxemics, density, and crowding, reflecting society's concerns over living in high-density urban environments and an interest in the cultural aspects of space. For example, anthropologist Edward T. Hall invented the study of proxemics, investigating appropriate personal and social distances across cultures as well as describing cultural differences in the conceptualization of time and space (Hall 1966; Hall 1959). Such cross-cultural comparisons made visible subtle norms that had previously gone unnoticed, and formed the foundations of understanding human and cultural factors in the context of spatial relations. Housing, identity, and public space were other common topics that defined the early stages of the field (Cranz 1982; Marcus 1988; Rapoport 1969). Robert Sommer uncovered the inhumane aspects of prison designs and schools, among other institutional buildings (Sommer 1974). Clare Cooper Marcus demonstrated that architects may overlook at basic human principles even at the most simple and common building type, housing (Marcus 1988).

Researchers' interests and demand from students of late 1960s and early 1970s made social factors an essential part of architecture and planning. The field attracted not only social scientists but also architects and planners who wanted to use science as a tool to better understand the human aspects of the built environment. Oscar Newman's defensible space research—in which observations and architectural analysis were used to develop guidelines to design apartment buildings in which people have better control over the safety of their physical surroundings—illustrates the point (Newman 1976). The methods of sociology and anthropology gave architects and planners tools to study cross-cultural differences. Some architects, such as Rem Koolhaas, began research not only at the architectural scale, but also at the urban scale (Koolhaas 1978). Landscape architect Lawrence Halprin worked with his wife, a dancer, to develop a system for understanding outdoor spaces as performance spaces, based on observations of people in motion (Halprin 1970). Kevin Lynch pioneered a method, mental maps, for understanding how people categorize urban spaces they move through (Lynch 1960).

The planning profession had been using surveys since the post-war period to legitimate their decisions (Cowan 2010), but in the 1970s, planners recognized the need for more genuine participation. The tools and guidelines developed by landscape architect Randy Hester's for participatory planning were largely adopted by designers and planners actively shaping our cities (Hester 1999).

Sometimes a profession's interest in social factors blossomed into a productive partnership between researchers and architects. Evidence of such partnerships includes the design of Parc de la Villette in Paris by avant-garde architect Bernard Tschumi in collaboration with sociologist Galen Cranz. The application of social science methods to spatial problems developed traction even in the minds of policy makers and legislators. It was during this period that William Whyte (1980) observed New Yorkers taking lunch breaks in urban plazas, changing building codes and creating a legacy for generations. No longer could policy to help people lack the evidence to back up. In Chapter 3, Dominic Fischer returns to public parks in New York City, investigating if the same precepts Whyte found hold true today.

Not only does social factors influence designers and researchers in design, but it has also impacted thinking in other academic fields, such as with the influence that Christopher Alexander's *A Pattern Language* (Alexander, Ishikawa, and Silverstein 1977) has had in computer science and object-oriented programming.

In addition to public spaces and public housing, the field of social factors helps understand how people of different cultures, ethnicities, genders, and physical abilities interact with and understand the same spaces. For example, women use plaza places differently than men do (Mozingo 1989) and Hispanic families use parks differently than white men (Hutchinson 1987). Likewise, Chapter 4 by Ann Heylighen demonstrates that people with lower sight abilities would notice subtle temperature changes, whereas in the same space fully-sighted people would be preoccupied with differences in materials. That is, social factors researchers study not only generalizations of people in space, but the particularities of a person in space as well.

Some of the richest work in social factors is about understanding how design impacts behavior. Post-occupancy evaluations (POE) in institutional buildings lead the way in providing concrete information to designers to create more successfully functioning buildings (Zimring and Reizenstein 1980). Evidence-based design (EBD) in healthcare settings uses research to direct inform practice, improving health and providing cost-savings at the same time. For instance, Robert Ulrich's research (1984) demonstrated that being able to see a natural view from a hospital window cut down on the length of hospital stay length and recovery time. Since then, EBD in healthcare has become a subfield with its own accreditation and certification. This approach has expanded to a variety of building types, including learning environments, performance spaces, and retail, among others (Hamilton and Watkins 2009). Another thread of POE focuses on office buildings and workplace strategy, to create a better fit between organizational cultures. POE in workplaces is a growing field in practice existing both as a subdepartment in large design firms and as specialized stand-alone companies. In Chapter 5, Emily Golembiewski describes methods used by architecture and strategy firms to gather such evidence for spaces and organizations at a variety of scales.

Sustainability, health, and culture are strongly intertwined topics. Although, many researchers focus on the technical aspects of sustainability, such as energy-efficient design, scholars in social factors continue to explain that without the "social"—for instance demand from users, attention to user health, respect to culture and indigenous knowledge—technology's contribution to solving environmental problems will remain limited. In Chapter 8, Yael Perez et al. delve into the ways in which new media and other innovative participation techniques can be called upon to make the behavioral and cultural needs of an American Indian community part of the design process for sustainable housing design. Cecilia Boldemann et al. in Chapter 6 focus on a particular user group—children—to compare health outcomes in preschool outdoor environment design based on sun exposure and play time, and discuss different policy approaches in Europe and United States. Likewise, Marie-Alice L'Heureux, in Chapter 7, demonstrates how users and architectural education are integral parts of creating sustainable, functional, and user-friendly architecture: energy-efficiency is not a solution on its own.

This book reasserts the importance of paying attention to the social in design, to the user in space, and to the cultural particularities of place by highlighting new research in two fundamental areas: (1) the history and future outlook of the field, and (2) perspectives on the user.

Part 1: History and future outlook

Because the field is broad, complex and contentious, uncovering its origins and scrutinizing contemporary practices help expose the fundamentals of the field. The chapters in this part also assert the potential for social impact inherent in the study of people in space.

In "The Words We Choose," Karen Frank conducts a deep analysis of two words that define the field, drawing on her lifetime of scholarship in the field. She uncovers how the word *environment*, while useful in its generality, in fact implies a separation between people and the spaces they inhabit. Similarly general, and useful because of its application to a wide variety of actions people might take, *behavior* unfortunately limits what we can study, since it abrogates people's experience of space. Drawn from the study of psychology, *behavior* limits researchers to what they can see. Taken together, the two terms often imply causality and separation, instead of propagating the interconnectedness of people and the places they inhabit. Franck proposes that instead, our field in fact studies how people *use space*, with those words implying a more symbiotic relationship.

Susanne Cowan and Ayda Melika, in "Design as a Social Act," explore the history of social factors through archival research and interviews with the people who generated many of the seminal works of the field. Cowan and Melika begin with the social upheaval of the 1960s and investigate how that time of change combined with the perceived failure of modernists led many researchers and practitioners to people-focused approaches in environmental design. The authors discuss the place of social factors in practice, research, and architecture and planning schools in the past and today. Cowan and Melika's chapter speaks to the continuing importance of research into the meaning and use of space, as many of the issues that galvanized earlier researchers are still alive in design today.

Dominic Fischer uses research from the early days of the field as a point of departure for his own research on pocket parks. William Whyte's seminal study on how people use public space in New York City is thirty years old. "Reassessing Small Urban Spaces" updates that research by focusing how people use two New York City pocket parks today. Foremost in Fischer's study is the question of how to sustain the use and viability of street corner parks as the character of the neighborhood changes and the parks themselves change. Fischer finds that as the socio-economic vitality of the neighborhood, pedestrian activity on the street, and conditions that determine ways to access to the park changes, so does the vitality of these small parks. He concludes that there is no "one-size-fits-all" design for pocket parks; land-use, density, and resident enthusiasm, in addition to the design, matter deeply to how and to what extent a park is used.

Part 2: Perspectives on the user

In spite of the complexity of the field of social factors, the importance of the user remains foundational to research in the field. The chapters in the second part assume the user perspective, with human responses and needs as the unit of measurement, whether the topic is health-promoting design, the social aspects of sustainability, energy-efficient technologies, embodied experience, or inter-cultural communication.

Building codes demand that designers of the built environment rarely take disabled-bodies' spatial experiences into account. Ann Heylighen, in "Enacting the Socio-material," rather than taking disability as an absolute concept, accepts a socio-material model of disability and offers an insightful analysis on how disability experience can provide new meanings about space that is often unconsidered by the abled-bodied. The chapter includes an analysis of spatial experiences of visually impaired people, wheelchair users, and people with dementia and autism. The experiences of disabled bodies gathered through multiple mediums such as autobiographies, interviews, and video recording of observations reveal a variety of boundaries that are less detectable to able-bodied users. The chapter illustrates the fact that one's experience may be considered "disabled" because of spatial design, not necessarily because of biological limitations per se.

Emily Golembiewski, in "The Algorithmic vs. the Messy," gives insights into strategic programming and ways to customize the design process to clients' needs, whether it is for the design of a new building or for remodeling an existing one. Based on extensive experience working in space planning, design and strategy firms, Golembiewski details three approaches which vary from using mostly quantitative data, to mostly qualitative data, to a mix, in order to create building programs that are primarily built upon the needs of users and clients. She proposes a way forward to design firms in order to incorporate the user perspective in the overall design process.

In "The Health-Promoting Potential of Preschool Outdoor Environments," Cecilia Boldemann et al. present an interdisciplinary collaborative research effort, comparing the health potential of preschool environments in the United States and Sweden. The chapter points to the much-needed balance between providing children adequate access to vitamin D, protecting them from unhealthy solar exposure, and supporting adequate physical activity for healthy development. The authors test the qualities required in preschool outdoor environments to achieve that balance, qualities such as the size of the outdoor area, the proportion of shaded areas accessible to children, and the integration of play areas and vegetation. These qualities are tested against children's ultra-violet exposure, physical activity levels, attention, and sleep. Policy comparisons from the United States and Sweden noting best practices that might be implemented in other parts of the world complement this empirical study.

In "Making Sense of Sustainability," Marie-Alice L'Heureux argues that sustainable design requires comprehensive attention to the user needs and not just to energy efficiency. A small Kansas community decided, after a tornado decimated much of the town, to rebuild with an eye on sustainability. Using two case studies that were part of this rebuilding, she examines the challenges of sustainable design and the role of education in creating sustainable built environments. L'Heureux weaves together ideas on sustainability, LEED standards, and participatory design strategies; she documents the dilemma that many architects face such as quickly designing for buildings to be aesthetically pleasing, affordable, and sustainable, while simultaneously considering the community.

Yael Perez et al., in "Social Factors in the Age of Social Media," detail co-design methodologies varying from design charrettes, face-to-face communication and to the use of social media employed in designing homes for a Native American Community. A design site and a community that is not easily accessible to the team of architects and engineers can present extra challenges to a design process in which community knowledge and the culture of the client is an integral component, such as in a co-design approach. The case study stems from a work that a group of University of California, Berkeley faculty and students completed, designing for the Pinoleville Pomo Nation. The chapter higlights the advantages and disadvantages of various technologies which were tested in the process of trying to involve all stakeholders in the design, enrich the cultural understanding of the designers, and incorporate sustainable features into the building.

Taken together, these eight chapters in two parts constitute a cross-section of the issues and ideas alive today in the study of people and place.

References

Alexander, Christopher, Sara Ishikawa, and Murray Silverstein. 1977. *A Pattern Language: Towns, Buildings, Construction.* New York: Oxford University Press.

Childress, Herb. 2000. *Landscapes of Betrayal, Landscapes of Joy: Curtisville in the Lives of Its Teenagers.* SUNY Press.

Cowan, Susanne Elizabeth. 2010. "Democracy, Technocracy and Publicity: Public Consultation and British Planning, 1939--1951." Ph.D., United States -- California: University of California, Berkeley. http://0-search.proquest.com.libraries.colorado.edu/docview/8592475 85/abstract/DAF3096AB6A84DCBPQ/1?accountid=14503.

Cranz, Galen. 1982. *The Politics of Park Design : A History of Urban Parks in America.* Cambridge: MIT Press.

Gehl, Jan. 1987. *Life between Buildings: Using Public Space.* New York: Van Nostrand Reinhold.

Hall, Edward Twitchell. 1959. *The Silent Language.* 1st ed. Garden City, N.Y: Doubleday.

—. 1966. *The Hidden Dimension.* 1st ed. Garden City, N.Y: Doubleday.

Halprin, Lawrence. 1970. *The RSVP Cycles: Creative Processes in the Human Environment.* 1st edition. New York: George Braziller.

Hamilton, D. Kirk and David H. Watkins. 2009. *Evidence-Based Design for Multiple Building Types.* Hoboken, N.J: Wiley.

Hester, Randolph T. Jr. 1999. "A Refrain with a View [Participation with a View]." *Places* 12 (2). http://escholarship.org/uc/item/87c2d02w.

Hutchinson, R. 1987. "Ethnicity and Urban Recreation: Whites, Blacks, and Hispanics in Chicago's Public Parks." *Journal of Leisure Research* 19 (3): 205–22.

Koolhaas, Rem. 1978. *Delirious New York: A Retroactive Manifesto for Manhattan.* New York: Oxford University Press.

Lynch, Kevin. 1960. *The Image of the City.* Cambridge [Mass.]: Technology Press.

Marcus, Clare Cooper. 1988. *Housing as If People Mattered: Site Design Guidelines for Medium-Density Family Housing.* University of California Press.

Mozingo, Louise. 1989. "Women and Downtown Open Space." *Places* 6: 38–47.

Newman, Oscar. 1976. "Design Guidelines for Creating Defensible Space.," April. http://eric.ed.gov/?id=ED133823.

Rapoport, Amos. 1969. "House Form and Culture." http://www.bcin.ca/Interface/openbcin.cgi?submit=submit&Chinkey=7 3461.

Rosenzweig, Roy, and Elizabeth Blackmar. 1992. *The Park and the People: A History of Central Park.* Ithaca, N.Y: Cornell University Press.

Sommer, Robert. 1974. *Tight Spaces; Hard Architecture and How to Humanize It.* Englewood Cliffs, N.J: Prentice-Hall.

Ulrich, Roger. 1984. "View through a window may influence recovery." *Science* 224, no. 4647: 224-225.

Whyte, William Hollingsworth. 1980. *The Social Life of Small Urban Spaces*. Washington, D.C: Conservation Foundation.

Zimring, Craig M., and Janet E. Reizenstein. 1980. "Post-Occupancy Evaluation An Overview." *Environment and Behavior* 12 (4): 429–50. doi:10.1177/0013916580124002.

PART 1:

HISTORY AND FUTURE OUTLOOK

CHAPTER ONE

THE WORDS WE CHOOSE: REVISITING "ENVIRONMENT" AND "BEHAVIOR"

KAREN A. FRANCK

The words we use in theorizing, researching, writing, and teaching matter enormously. Nouns in particular, in any field, identify important topics and concepts; when used repeatedly they shape entire attitudes and approaches to research and to understanding the world. These nouns direct, often without our realizing how much, the ways we think and the research we do and then the ways our readers and students think. The explicit and implicit meanings they convey set the agenda for what is included—what is assumed to be important—and what is excluded. And so, they serve both as *magnets,* drawing other ideas and assumptions to them, and as *boundaries* that delimit fields of inquiry. The terms employed and the ways they are employed are extremely useful precisely because of the directions they seem to carry with them. And the implicit associations they hold may also work to the advantage of researchers and theorists who employ them. At the same time, however, the words may have consequences that remain hidden; some or even many of these consequences may be limitations.

No words could be more frequent, or more significant, in the field of environmental design research than "environment" and "behavior." They consistently appear in book titles, journal articles and conference papers and for some they name the field ("ebs" or "environment behavior studies"). They point to the central subject matter of environmental design research and do so simply and directly. The goal of this essay is to explore the advantages and disadvantages of these two terms, to suggest two alternatives that possess other advantages, and to point out several properties that any concepts we choose might well possess. My intention is to suggest what some readers may not have considered, to invite them to examine their own word choices carefully and to encourage us all to make future choices in a reflective and self-conscious manner. The end goal is not to urge a replacement of "environment" and "behavior" but rather to raise our collective awareness of their limitations and to encourage us all to consider what terms might better serve our particular individual, or shared, research interests and goals. The essay draws from my own experiences and observations rather than from a thorough examination of the field of environmental design research and its history. A future historical analysis of the evolution of the terms and their adoption in environmental design research would be valuable to the field, as would a sustained and systematic analysis of their various meanings in particular fields, much as Doreen Massey (1992, 2005) has pursued for space.

Two very common terms

Environment refers to the surroundings or the milieu of human and non-human organisms. With its connection to biology and ecology, environment emphasizes the dependency of the organism upon those surroundings, which can be supportive and life giving as well as harmful. Gestalt psychologist Kurt Koffka (1935) used the term environment and distinguished between one environment that is geographical or physical and one that is behavioral or perceived, showing interest only in the latter, as did Kurt Lewin (1951). Among Gestalt psychologists it was James Gibson who first showed an interest in one environment, one external to people, that surrounds them and to which they are closely bound: "…animal and environment make an inseparable pair. Each term implies the other" (1979, 8). In establishing a new branch of psychology in the 1960s to explore what had previously been excluded from the field—the possible importance of physical settings—psychologists adopted the term environment in the Gibsonian sense.

"Environment" continues to be both general and inclusive enough to refer to nearly any condition in our surroundings, from characteristics of climate, wind, or air pollution to characteristics of cities, neighborhoods, buildings, rooms, or furniture. These characteristics may be social as well as physical or ambient (such as light, shadow, temperature). Focusing on physical environments, this inclusiveness allows for a tremendous range of distinctions among different kinds of settings: built, designed, and natural; urban, rural and suburban; learning, work, school, health, consumer, and food. It can be applied across scales as well: home, neighborhood, municipality, and region. This inclusiveness comes with vagueness as well, which can be confusing. (In the 1970s, when I told people I was studying environmental psychology at the Graduate Center at the City University of New York (CUNY), people's responses would often be: "In

New York, what a perfect place to study that!" or "How can you study
environmental psychology in New York? There is no environment there.")

   With this inclusiveness, members of a great variety of fields—social
scientists of different types, architects, landscape architects, interior
designers, urban designers, and planners—could find common interests in
research, education and professional organizations, such as the
Environmental Design Research Association established in 1968.
Similarly, the desire to bring together faculty in architecture, landscape
architecture and planning had been one reason for establishing the College
of Environmental Design at Berkeley in 1959, and naming it that way
(Sachs 2009). The term environment also captured the progressive spirit of
the 1960s, suggesting conditions that were problematic and that deserved
empirical attention from researchers as a way to ameliorate those
conditions. Semantically it was useful since it easily became an adjective:
environmental design, environmental psychology, environmental
sociology.
   Despite the assertions of Gibson and others to the contrary, as both a
term and a concept, environment suggests surroundings that are separate
from the people who occupy them and the manner in which they are
occupied. Intrinsic to the term environment, and apparently unavoidably
so, is an assumed separation between it and the people or behavior which
it contains. Although the separation of self from environment is a key
achievement in early child development and is also prevalent throughout
Western thought, it is a misleading and problematic conceptualization
(Ittelson 1976). It sets apart what is defined as human from what is
assumed to be nonhuman, such as environment, thereby creating an
underlying distinction rather than any connection or overlap. Jane Bennett
makes this point in arguing for the concept of "materiality" over
environment since the former "… draws human attention sideways, away
from an ontologically ranked Great Chain of Meaning and toward a greater
appreciation of the complex entanglements of humans and nonhumans"
(2010, 112).
   Despite its key meaning as surroundings and not a single object, the
term environment has strong connotations of object-hood, of being a
unified *whole* or *totality* rather than a complex array of different aspects
that come together in different ways and that allow for a perceived unity.
In addition, environment tends to imply what is unchanging; yet, in fact,
environments are continually created and modified. Indeed, the processes by
which environments are created and how they change over time receives far
less attention than the consequences given, static environments have for

people. And the assumed immobility of environments requires an explicit effort to distinguish what is impermanent from what is permanent as in Amos Rapport's (1977) delineation of non-fixed, semi-fixed, and fixed features of the environment. But viewed over a longer time period, no features of the environment are "fixed." Kim Dovey (2013) makes a similar critique of the conceptualization of place: that it privileges stability and rootedness over processes of becoming.

Behavior is the term commonly used in environmental design research to refer in an inclusive manner to people's actions, perceptions and experiences. It made imminent sense for environmental psychologists to adopt this term when they established their field, coming as they were from psychology. "Behavior" entered the vocabulary of psychology early in the 20th century with the work of psychologist John Watson who developed the concept of "behaviorism" to found a branch of psychology that would eschew any ideas of consciousness or mental states and would pursue a more scientific approach than psychology previously had (Watson 1913). The goal was to study the relationships between stimuli and behavior in order to be able to predict and control the latter, as evident in the later work of B.F. Skinner. The importance of stimuli in relation to the term behavior is apparent in many dictionary definitions of behavior that point to it as a "response" to "stimuli."

Behavior also implies what is described or observed by an outsider. Indeed, the observability of something called "behavior" by a so-called objective researcher was one of the reasons for promoting behaviorism in psychology, namely to make research more scientific. Only what could be seen or manipulated would be acceptable, nothing would be inferred. The continued use of the term behavior represents environmental design research's links to psychology and still carries with it associations with behaviorism, and accordingly, the possibility, even the desirability, of manipulating behavior through the promulgation of particular stimuli. As a term and with its associated history of behaviorism, "behavior" neglects the agency and creativity of people. And, I would argue, carries an earlier intention of the goal of being able to manipulate behavior through social engineering. Even though, counter to Watson's intentions, the term is now used to refer to perceptions and mental states, this is not always an easy or obvious inclusion.

In psychology and biology and in its dictionary definitions, behavior is generally viewed as a response to internal and external stimuli. With good reason, William Ittelson noted that behavior is often assumed to be "the resultant" of environment (1973, 53). And so the implication for environmental design research is that behavior is a response to environment. In fact, this notion of environment influencing behavior is often explicitly stated as the topic of environmental psychology. For instance:

> As environmental psychologists, we are concerned with the ways in which physical and social features of the environment influence people's transactions with their everyday surroundings (Clitheroe *et al.* 1998, 103).

In environmental design research there is far more interest in how environment influences behavior and much less in how environments are, also, the outcomes of behavior. Consequently the environment is considered largely as a site of human action and not an object of human action, implicitly treated as always already there rather than as invented, constructed and changing.

At the same time the very idea that the environment may well influence behavior often generates concern about ascribing too much significance to the built environment and thereby subscribing to environmental determinism. This concern poses a dilemma for the field: how can we study the environment if we are so unsure about its possible importance and so paranoid about implying it is important at all for fear of being labeled physical determinists (Franck 1984)? It may be this same fear that has hindered sufficient theorizing of the many roles the environment fulfills, including understanding how environments are tools of human action, how they actually possess a certain degree of agency (Gieryn 2002) rather than being only inert backgrounds.

Environmental design researchers have made concerted efforts over many years to overcome the tendency to treat environment and behavior as separate, independent entities, with the environment as the source of stimuli and people as subjects of those stimuli. In establishing the field of environmental psychology, William Ittelson, Leanne Rivlin and their colleagues at CUNY (1974) often emphasized the interdependence of people and the environment, saying for example,

> We experience neither an environment independent of ourselves as participants nor ourselves independent of the situation in which we are participating, but rather we experience ourselves in and of an environment (104).

Proponents of transactionalism took this point further by positing that people and environments mutually define each other and constitute integral and inseparable units (Altman and Rogoff 1986). This is a valuable theoretical framing but the collection and analysis of data often require a splitting of people (and their behavior/experience) from the environment. Roger Barker (1963) avoids this empirical splitting by connecting components of recurring patterns of behavior to components of a physical structure at a particular time and place with a single concept—a behavior setting.

The very choice of the terms "environment" and "behavior" may have burdened environmental design researchers with two nouns that, by dictionary definitions, commonsense connotations, and their history in psychology are consistently assumed to refer to separate and independent entities where the latter results from the former. No wonder we then entered such a tricky territory of trying to theorize and demonstrate how these two *things* are related to each other. In *Social Logic of Space* Bill Hillier and Julienne Hanson (1984) identify this problem as the "man-environment paradigm" that is separating out a human subject from an environmental object and then trying to understand what the relation could be between the two. And in this dividing of people/behavior from environment, were we not also subscribing to a long Western tradition of creating dichotomous opposites such as objective/subjective, mind/body, culture/nature, men/women?

Two other possibilities

Here is an important question all researchers might well pose to themselves: "What words do I wish to use to identify key concepts in my teaching, research and writing and why?" In developing the themes for this essay and holding a symposium at the 2011 annual conference of the Environmental Design Research Association, "The Words We Use in Environmental Design Research," with David Seamon, Lynda Schneekloth, and Sanjoy Mazumdar, it became clear to me that our choices of terms emerge from our respective disciplinary backgrounds, theoretical positions, and values, as well as from our current teaching and research interests. It is very likely that my choices arise from: my long-term teaching position in a school of architecture; my research interests in how design choices are made, and how people, through their patterns of use and appropriation, help produce the spaces they occupy; and from my more general theoretical sensibility that recognizes the agency of both people and settings—that people are active and inventive and that environments are in flux. It is very likely that the research I have pursued in connection to design has guided my choice of "space" over "environment" and "use" over "behavior." Notably, space appears in the title of three books I have published—*Ordering Space: Types in*

Architecture and Design (Franck and Schneekloth 1994) *Loose Space: Diversity and Possibility in Urban Life* (Franck and Stevens 2007) and *Memorials as Spaces of Engagement: Memorial Design, Use and Meaning* (Stevens and Franck 2015).

Space

As a reference in design research to locations people occupy, "space" comes from the twentieth-century discourse in modern architecture as described by Adrian Forty (2000), who identifies the word as the English version of the German word *raum*, which, unlike space, refers to both a material enclosure (room) and a philosophical concept. As Forty puts it, space is both a physical property that architects and others can manipulate as well as a mental construct with which we perceive and represent the world. Forty distinguishes between space as enclosure, space as continuum (inside and outside space being continuous) and space as extension of the body.

"Space" can refer to a setting separate from its occupants that is already there and precedes their entry into it (as an auditorium, an apartment for rent) or it can refer to a setting people create through their own actions or their modifications to the surroundings and their relationships with each other (a cocktail party or moving the chairs for a discussion group) or a combination of both. A particular type of "space" may be created by fixed features of the built surroundings or by movable features such as chairs and tables or, as importantly, by the ways in which people themselves occupy the space: e.g. people standing in a line or standing in a group, facing each other, holding drinks.

And so as a term and a concept "space" captures multiples qualities: of a background, of a product of human action, and of an extension of the human body. Unlike "environment" it is less likely to suggest what is separate and independent of people. As a malleable medium and not a fixed thing, the term space avoids the connotations of object-hood that come with the term environment. Nor does it tend to fix the relationship between place and action as independent and dependent variables. Instead it captures what people create through their own actions, over both the short and the long term. Using the example of the cloister, Henri Lefevbre (1991) writes: "Bodies themselves generate spaces, which are produced by and for their gestures" (217). The body can be considered a constituent of space and also, through the body's actions and use of objects; space can be considered as an extension of the body. Rather than *surrounding*, space *extends*.

Like environment, space crosses scales but it appears to do so more easily since it does not suggest what surrounds but rather, at least in the abstract, what is continuous and a medium that is fluid, changing and changeable. Space is both what is already there and what is continually being created. What Lefevbre calls "social space" refers both to a field of action *and* a basis of action, to what is actual and given *and* to what is potential and a locus of possibilities (191). And so space can be orderly and predictable or surprising and unexpected; "the spatial has *both* an element of order *and* an element of chaos" (Massey 1995, 81).

As a term, space is now commonly used in great variety of fields: sociology, geography, philosophy, environmental psychology, urban studies, architecture, landscape architecture, urban design, and interior design. That those in social science and the humanities are now concerned with space is often referred to as "the spatial turn." Many concepts in design research and related areas incorporate the word: urban space, open space, public space and then more specialized concepts including Edward Hall's personal space, Robert Sommer's sociofugal and sociopetal space as well as his tight space, Oscar Newman's defensible space, Henri Lefevbre's perceived, conceived, and lived space, Edward Soja's first, second, and third space, Jeffrey Hou's insurgent space, Franck and Stevens's loose space. Space easily takes on all these characterizations while the concepts themselves suggest the many ways that space is conceived and regulated, already there as well as continually created, recreated or modified.

Use

Architects, other designers and design researchers all employ the term "use." It also appears in other formulations—adaptive re-use, land use, and mixed use. Its history in architecture may be traced to the term "user," which Forty dates to the introduction of welfare programs in the UK after 1945. "User" now seems abstract and slightly disembodied, and carries connotations of drug addiction but "use" has important advantages over "behavior." As a common, colloquial word, it comes with none of the disciplinary or the historical and ideological connotations of "behavior." It is, in those respects, more neutral, more open to newer connotations and associations.

Conveniently enough, "use" is a noun, a verb, and a transitive verb. People use, or employ, some thing or some space. A connection between people and a thing or place is built into the term, and the middle term—the using—is an action. "Use" gives people both agency and creativity in a way "behavior" does not. In architecture and environmental design research, use immediately implies a connection between people and the space or building they are using, where people are the subject and the space or building is the object. People are always present; some object of their action is always present and the connection between the two is present. Use suggests both bodily presence and engagement with something. Unlike behavior, use gives some direction to what one might observe in a space. Behavior can refer to almost any activity, which may or may not have any relationship to the space where it occurs which leaves us with the puzzle of how environment and behavior may be related. "Use" when paired with "space" immediately implies a relationship of some kind between the two.

This instrumental aspect of the concept of use is invaluable. An identified space or building fulfills some purpose; it is not only a backdrop but also a tool that serves particular goals with lesser or greater success (Gieryn 2002). The built-in connection between space and use, and the instrumental connotations of use, encourage design researchers to think about how the space can help people fulfill daily tasks or how they can or could manipulate the space in their own way to meet their needs. In this regard it is notable that Jane Jacobs chose the term "uses": the entire first section *of Death and Life of the Great American City* is precisely on that topic, with chapters on the *uses* of sidewalks, the *uses* of neighborhood parks, and the *uses* of city neighborhoods.

Use as a concept is open: it may refer to activities and patterns of activities the designer of the space intended or those invented by those who are doing the using or some combination of both. This is essential: use suggests the possibility of choice, creativity, and improvisation on the part of people. Use incorporates the possibility that people appropriate spaces or objects for their own, possibly unanticipated and surprising purposes. People's ways of *using* a space are often a matter of choice, variety, and change. Use may be intended or unintended and suggests the possibility of quick change, possibly with few or minor physical interventions or adaptations.

Researchers' consideration of ongoing or future uses of space generates a kind of specificity and a grounded orientation that reference to behavior does not. Concern with use seems to focus attention on the precise and embodied ways in which people pursue activities, how the design of spaces and objects aids or hinders those activities, how people create adaptations, and how patterns of use can change further, possibly with changes in design or through the everyday creativity of people. People's ingenuity, creativity, and determination in appropriating space, in inventing new uses and new objects is gaining more attention in a variety of fields: in architecture (Nishat et al 2011), in the design of objects (Perra and Gandolfi 2010, Perra et al., 2012) and in studies of public space (Franck and Stevens 2007, Hou 2010, Franck and Huang 2011). In so many ways use implies the agency and creativity of people—both their reliance on space and their ability to create and manipulate it. With the term and concept of use one is a long way from the social engineering connotations of behavior where it is more the observer than the observed that has agency and, moreover, freedom of choice.

Conceived as ...

In calling particular phenomena "environment" or "space," "behavior" or "use," we are naming a concept that helps us describe and understand the phenomena of concern. We are not identifying what is there in the world (as we might use words to identify a cat or a dog, a chair or a table). Bruno Latour (2005) makes this point regarding the term network: "… a concept, not a thing out there. It is a tool to help describe something, not what is being described" (131). Latour's actor network theory is more abstract than the terms I have discussed here and provides more of a theoretical and methodological tool: "…you can provide an actor-network account of topics which have in no way the shape of network—symphony, legislation" (131). Nonetheless we can apply the same logic to other key terms: that is, we can recognize that whatever terms we choose are ways of treating phenomena *as* what is named rather than assuming the phenomenon actually *is* what is named. The name then becomes a means of characterizing rather than defining. Given that understanding, it makes sense to explore the advantages and disadvantages of particular terms for guiding thinking and research. Kim Dovey (2013) makes a similar point regarding the concept of "assemblage" adopted from the writings of Giles Deleuze: "What is at stake is not truth but usefulness—how does it enable us to think" (132).

I have presented the concepts of space and use as possible alternatives to environment and behavior because with them we avoid some of the weaknesses inherent in the latter but also because they are useful for the kinds of research and writing I do. Certainly others will have different preferences. Whatever choices we make, however, we might well keep in mind several important features the concepts we select should possess regardless of the particular words we choose. Can we define and think of x (environment, space behavior, use, place and possibly the relationships between the concepts) *as* multiple, relational and alive?

Multiple

The terms environment and behavior suggest two entities distinct and separate from each other with environment taking on the quality of an object-like, unified whole. The implicit dualism of these two entities is reminiscent of other dualisms prevalent in Western thought. One alternative approach to dualistic thinking is the addition of a third or what Edward Soja calls "thirding," as seen in Lefevbre's delineation of perceived, conceived, and lived. Doreen Massey also calls into question dualistic thinking, referring to the work of many feminists who have long made such a critique. But in many cases adding a third term may not be sufficiently useful for thinking and understanding. Another possible approach is to treat entities, which might otherwise be treated as organic totalities or unities (or collections of such entities), as "assemblies" (Latour 2000) or "assemblages" (Deleuze and Guittari 1987; De Landa 2007), which emphasize the interactions between the constituent parts that make up the wholes and the process by which those wholes come about. Such a view dissolves many divides, such as that between culture and nature (De Landa 2007). Kim Dovey (2010) recommends treating a place as an assemblage, or a "coherent multiplicity of parts," and in doing so points to the ideas of Christopher Alexander who "argued that a building is not a thing, that what we call form is the product of a pattern of forces," forces that are spatial, material, social and aesthetic in character (27).

Relational

As noted earlier, one of the drawbacks of the terms "environment" and "behavior" is that they carry connotations of being fully separate, if not independent, entities, a connotation many find problematic. The concept of assemblage avoids this dilemma since an assemblage is a whole defined by its constituent parts and also by the connections between those parts. Moreover, the interrelations between parts are so key in creating or changing an assemblage that the introduction of new parts will change it. And an element from one assemblage found in another will not have the same properties since it is partly defined by its interaction with the other parts of the second assemblage (De Landa 2007).

Relationality is a key characteristic of other concepts relevant to environmental design research, such as Doreen Massey's (1992) explication of space:

'Space' is created out of the vast intricacies, the incredible complexities of the interlocking and the non-interlocking, and the networks of relations at every scale from local to global (80).

Indeed, a *network of relations* is also central to Hillier and Hanson's (1984) concept, and tool, of spatial syntax, and to my concept of place type as a web of connections between aspects of form, use, and meaning (Franck 1994b). All these concepts describe multiplicity and the interrelations between constituent parts rather than singular, seamless wholes. It appears that in many disciplines there is a concerted effort to conceptualize the phenomenon of interest as a series of connections rather than as a solid whole.

Dynamic

The term environment seems to suggest what is already there, static and unchanging. One reason for adopting the term space instead is that it suggests what is continually created and modified and so is dynamic and changing—in process. As a consequence of its relationality, space is always in process:

> Precisely because space on this reading is a product of relations-between, relations which are necessarily embedded in material practice which have to be carried out, it is always in the process of being made. It is never finished; never closed… (Massey 2005, 9).

Fluidity, continually "becoming," is another property of assemblage in contrast to place, which is more frequently treated as consistently stable (Dovey 2013). And it is the property of interconnectedness of its parts that gives an assemblage this fluid character:

> Allowing the possibility of complex interactions between component parts is crucial to define mechanisms of emergence, but this possibility disappears if the parts are fused together into a seamless web (De Landa 2007, 10).

Alive

Yet another distinction between environment and behavior is that the former is frequently treated as inert while the latter as animate. Doreen Massey (2005) suggests that some characterizations of space, including by Foucault, also portray it as "dead," whereas she argues for its "liveliness"

(12). In describing the importance of the sensory experiences of architecture, Bianca Lepori and I (2007) point to the "animism of architecture." Jane Bennett, in proposing "an ecology of matter" (2004) or "a political ecology of things" (2010), also advocates for the liveliness or vibrancy of matter, arguing that focusing on materiality breaks down the distinctions between "inorganic and organic, passive object and active subject" (2004, 353).

Bennett also refers to assemblage and networks:

> This is not a world… of subjects and objects, but of various materialities constantly engaged in a network of relations. It is a world populated less by individuals than by groupings or compositions that shift over time (354).

Proposing what she calls "thing-power" and drawing from the philosophies of Spinoza and Guattari, Bennett suggests that this power arises from how one thing works in relation to another: that "thing power, as a kind of agency, *is the property of an assemblage*" (354). And drawing upon the ideas of Bruno Latour, she describes agency as power differentially possessed by all material bodies. From her ecological perspective the human and the nonhuman are all within the same web of intimate connections, with power arising from those connections. Could we not conceive of environment and behavior, or space and use or whatever concepts we choose to employ in this same way—as parts of a network or an assemblage and as multiple, interrelational, dynamic and in different ways alive?

References

Altman, Irwin and Barbara Rogoff. 1987. "World Views in Psychology: Trait, Interactional, Organismic and Transactional Perspectives." In *Handbook of Environmental Psychology* edited by Daniel Stokols and Irwin Altman,1-40. New York: Wiley.

Awan, Nishat, Tatjana Schneider and Jeremy Till. 2011. *Spatial Agency: Other Ways of Doing Architecture*. Abingdon, Oxon: Routledge.

Barker, Roger G. (ed). 1963. *The Stream of Behavior*. New York: Appleton-Century Crofts.

Bennett, Jane. 2004. "The Force of Things: Steps toward an Ecology of Matter." *Political Theory* 32(3): 342-372.

—. 2010. *Vibrant Matter: A Political Ecology of Things*. Durham, NC: Duke University Press.

Clitheroe, H.C., Daniel Stokols and Mary Zmuidzinas. 1998. "Conceptualizing the Context of Environment and Behavior." *Journal of Environmental Psychology* 18: 103-112.

De Landa, Manuel. 2007. *A New Philosophy of Society: Assemblage Theory and Social Complexity*. London: Continuum.

Deleuze, Giles, and Felix Guattari.1987. *A Thousand Plateaus: Capitalism and Schizophrenia*. Translated by Brian Massumi. Minneapolis: University of Minnesota Press.

Dovey, Kim. 2010. *Becoming Places: Urbanism/Architecture/Identity/ Power*. London: Routledge.

—. 2013. "Assembling Architecture." In *Deleuze and Architecture,* edited by Helene Frichot and Stephen Loo. Edinburgh: University of Edinburgh Press.

Forty, Adrian. 2000. *Words and Buildings: A Vocabulary of Modern Architecture*. London: Thames & Hudson.

Franck, Karen A. 1984. "Exorcising the Ghost of Physical Determinism." *Environment and Behavior* 16: 411-435.

Franck, Karen A., and Lynda Schneekloth (eds). 1994a. *Ordering Space: Types in Architecture and Design*. New York: Van Nostrand Reinhold.

Franck, Karen A. 1994b. "Types are Us." In *Ordering Space: Types in Architecture and Design,* edited by Karen A. Franck and Lynda Schneekloth, 345-370. New York: Van Nostrand Reinhold.

Franck, Karen A., and Bianca Lepori. 2007. *Architecture from the Inside Out: From the Body, the Senses, the Site and the Community*. London: Wiley-Academy

Franck, Karen A., and Quentin Stevens (eds). 2007. *Loose Space: Possibility and Diversity in Urban Life*. London: Routledge.

Franck, Karen A., and Te-Sheng Huang. 2012. In *Beyond Zuccotti Park: Freedom of Assembly and the Occupation of Public Space,* edited by Ron Shiffman, Rick Bell, Lance Jay Brown and Lynne Elizabeth, 3-20. Oakland, CA: New Village Press.

Gibson, James J. 1979. *The Ecological Approach to Visual Perception*. Hillsdale, NJ: Lawrence Erlbaum Associates.

Gieryn,Thomas F. 2002. "What Buildings Do." *Theory and Society* 31: 35-75.

Hall, Edward T. 1966. *The Hidden Dimension*. New York: Anchor Books.

Hillier, Bill and Julienne Hanson. 1984. *The Social Logic of Space*. Cambridge: Cambridge University Press.

Hou, Jeffrey, ed. 2010. *Insurgent Space*: *Guerilla Urbanism and the Remaking of Contemporary Cities*. London: Routledge.

Ittelson, William H. 1976. "Some Issues Facing a Theory of Environment and Behavior." In *Environmental Psychology: People and their Physical Settings* (2nd edition), edited by Harold M. Proshansky, William H. Ittelson and Leanne G. Rivlin, 51-59. New York: Holt Rinehart and Winston.

Ittelson, William H., and Harold M. Proshansky, Leanne G. Rivlin and Gary H. Winkel. 1974. *An Introduction to Environmental Psychology.* New York: Holt, Rinehart and Winston.

Jacobs, Jane. 1961. *Death and Life of Great American Cities.* New York: Random House.

Koffka, Kurt. 1935. *Principles of Gestalt Psychology.* New York: Harcourt Brace.

Lang, Jon. 1987. *Creating Architectural Theory: The Role of the Behavioral Sciences in Environmental Design.* New York: Van Nostrand Reinhold.

Latour, Bruno. 2000. "When Things Strike Back." *British Journal of Sociology* 51(1):107-123.

—. 2005. *Reassembling the Social: An Introduction to Actor-Network-Theory.* Oxford: Oxford University Press.

Lefevbre, Henri. 1991. *The Production of Space.* Translated by Donald Nicholson-Smith. Oxford: Blackwell Publishing

Lewin, Kurt. 1951. "Field Theory and Learning." In *Field Theory in Social Science: Selected Theoretical Papers by Kurt Lewin*, edited by Dorwin Cartwright, 60-86. New York: Harper and Row.

Massey, Doreen. 1992. "Politics and Space/Time." *New Left Review.* 196:65-84.

—. 2005. *For Space.* London: Sage.

Newman, Oscar. 1972. *Defensible Space: Crime Prevention through Urban Design.* New York: MacMillan.

Perra, Danielle Pario and Emiliano Gandolfi. 2010. Vol.1. Milan: Silvano Editoriale.

Rapoport, Amos. 1977. *Human Aspects of Urban Form: Towards a Man Environment Approach to Urban Form and Design.* Oxford: Pergamon Press.

Perra, Danielle Pario, Lucia Babina, Pier Francisco Frillici and Emilian Gandolfi. 2012. *Low Cost Design,* Vol.2. Milan: Silvano Editoriale.

Sachs, Avigail. 2009. "The Postwar Legacy of Architectural Research." *Journal of Architectural Education* 62 (3) 53-64.

Soja, Edward J. 2000. "Thirdspace: Expanding the Scope of the Geographical Imagination." In *Architecturally Speaking: Practices of*

Art, Architecture and the Everyday edited by Alan Read, 13-30. London: Routledge.

Sommer, Robert. 1974. *Tight Spaces: Hard Architecture and How to Humanize It.* 1974. Englewood Cliffs, NJ: Prentice-Hall.

—. 1967. "Sociofugal Space." *American Journal of Sociology* 72 (6): 657-660.

CHAPTER TWO

DESIGN AS A SOCIAL ACT: THE RISE OF SOCIAL RESEARCH AND THE CHALLENGES OF PARTICIPATORY DESIGN

SUSANNE COWAN AND AYDA MELIKA

In the 1960s, social upheaval and a crisis within the design professions led to a new approach in the design of the built environment: Social and Cultural Factors. A group of reform-minded designers had responded to design failures and urban protests by looking to social science fields for new disciplinary theories that could replace older modernist doctrines. While the 1960s was not the first time designers had reconsidered their role in society or had used social research, it was a period when these issues came to the forefront of design discourse and were applied more rigorously. For two decades the loose constellation of research, teaching, and practice known as Social and Cultural Factors grew as a subfield in design, promoting both evolutionary and revolutionary changes. By the 1980s, publications, degree programs, courses, and government policies demonstrated the institutionalization of this field and its influence on environmental design. Nevertheless, this approach has for the most part remained subordinate to other formal concerns in architecture. Socially-oriented designers and researchers have faced continued struggles to convince the profession of the importance of implementing their findings in design.

This chapter illuminates the reasons for the rise to prominence of Social and Cultural Factors in the 1960s and 1970s while also questioning the legacy of this research approach in both pedagogy and practice. The research for this chapter comes from surveying the published professional literature produced from the 1960s to the 1980s, as well as from oral history interviews with ten design professors who practiced and taught socially oriented design (Goodman 2011; Sommer 2011; Van der Ryn 2011; Marcus 2011; Sanoff 2011; Hester 2011; McNally 2011; Cranz 2011; Lifchez 2011; Comerio 2013). These interviews represent only a sampling of the experiences of that generation of designers and researchers. Nonetheless, their impressions, when interpreted through the publications of the time, start to highlight the successes and challenges of this movement in reshaping the direction of design in the post-modern period.

Historical context of the rise of social and cultural factors

While social research in architecture has its roots in the nineteenth century, the formation of the Social Factors field occurred later, in the post-war era. In both periods, the interest in social issues corresponded to an expansion of the role of designers in the public realm. In the Victorian era, industrialization, urbanization, and the modernization of infrastructure encouraged architects to take an increased interest in designing larger urban environments. This continued to be prevalent in the interwar period, as the modernists promoted a more universal approach to design considering multiple scales from the object, to the building, to the region as a whole, addressing both function and aesthetics. During that period a new generation embraced modernism as a socially emancipatory process, and many architects in Europe built socialist housing projects, which employed mass production to alleviate the poor living conditions for the working classes (Giedion 1929, Gropius 1929, May 1929). Under the leadership of Hannes Meyer, the architecture program at the Bauhaus incorporated sources in social science research to better prepare designers to address these types of economic and political issues in the built environment (Dutton and Mann, 1996). In the 1940s, the Royal Institute of British Architects (RIBA 1940, 1945, 1946, 1949) started to develop social science conferences in Britain to help to cultivate designers' skills in the growing fields of civic design and town planning. Under modernism, social research served as a means to understand the context for design. Through understanding demographic and survey data, designers and planners believed they could quantify urban problems and thus better develop rational solutions. However, this physical determinist attitude towards social issues remained positivistic, promoting designers' sense of certainty about their decisions, rather than encouraging debate or user participation. Although modernist architects looked for ways to address social issues in design, it was in the context of the early critiques of modernism that Social and Cultural Factors crystalized as a sub-discipline.

The social mission of architecture had become diluted and controversial as modernism solidified into the "International Style" during the complex political atmosphere of the 1930s. Although the early work of the Congrès International d'Architecture Moderne (CIAM) had focused on the socially emancipatory potential of science to address modern problems, the emphasis of the group became increasingly formalistic under the leadership of Le Corbusier (Dutton and Mann 1996). In the post-war period the application of the international style urbanism dramatically re-envisioned the built environments of Europe, the United States, and other modernizing cities around the world. Emboldened by the optimism of a new age and a booming economy, post-war urban designers oversaw the demolition of large sections of the old downtowns of cities in order to realize their modernist visions of urban renewal, public housing, and highway construction. These modernist utopian solutions, though still claiming to address the social problems of urban life, displayed a lack of sensitivity to the methods by which the designs would be applied and how they would affect people.

As a new generation of designers came of age in the 1960s, they began to question if some modernist planning projects had caused more harm than good. The vast roads and highways that had promised speed, growth, and connectivity had cut through the hearts of cities, leaving permanent scars that divided and devastated poor neighborhoods. The public housing projects, meant to eliminate poverty and allow the working classes equal access to quality housing, had become isolated ghettos of crime and discrimination. Many publications at this time were highly critical of modernism, questioning its social effects and proposing alternative approaches (Jacobs 1961; Gans 1968; Blake 1977; Jencks 1977).

This criticism of modern urbanism came not only from professionals but also from the public more broadly. Many citizen groups started to actively fight the imposition of design from above without attention to the needs and rights of citizens. In the context of the protests about Civil Rights, the Vietnam War, and Free Speech, revolutionary energy also manifested in demonstrations against the social injustices of redevelopment. In response, some members of the design professions were also galvanized by the realization that "something had gone very wrong" (Cranz 2011). Many designers and researchers remember how the events of the period were a "wake up call," raising their social consciousness (Sanoff 2011). For some, the concerns of citizens first led them to question the ideas and skills they learned in school (Goodman 2011). This group of concerned young designers began to question if architects had a deeper responsibility to the public, looking for "some other justification than serving wealthy clients" (Sommer 2011). Landscape architect Randy Hester (2011) recalled being particularly moved by the speech by John F. Kennedy that told the nation to "ask not what your country can do for you, ask what you can do for your country." He explained, "Kids like me took that seriously...whatever you were doing, as a profession, you were challenged to make it relevant...in my case relevant to social change." This recognition that citizens sought and deserved a voice in shaping society and the built environment motivated many young architects and social scientists to develop techniques for engaging the public in the design and planning process—to improve the built environment with and for the people who used it.

In this context, designers began to question the established doctrines of modern design and seek new methods that would be more receptive to social rather than aesthetic or technical considerations in designing the built environment. The rejection of modernist doctrines occurred not just among the Social and Cultural Factors group but across the spectrum of designers. Even within the CIAM, commitment to modernism began to unravel as some members began to question the organization's urban mission and its social methods. Fissures appeared during the CIAM conferences in the 1950s as Team X, a group of British and Dutch designers, began to challenge CAIM's functionalism and formalism as lacking adequate attention to the social and cultural character of the people they built for. Instead, members of Team X, who favored a more "humanistic" approach to "association," started to look to anthropological research and traditional housing types as inspiration for developing modernized forms that fit universal human needs (Bakema et al. 1954, Smithson et al. 1953, Smithson and Smithson 1956). These interests foreshadowed later interest among designers in social science and cultural forms under Social and Cultural Factors and Post-Modernism.

The International Style faced further critiques in the 1960s and 1970s in the light of a few infamous modernist urban design schemes, particularly public housing projects like Pruitt Igoe (Newman 1972; Jenks 1977). The field went through a stage of crisis in which a seemingly accepted and ubiquitous approach crumbled, leading designers to look for new methods and aesthetics to fill the void. Designers fragmented into contextualists and formalists, modernists and post-modernists, searching for a future direction for the field. Among these fragmentary counter-movements, Postmodernism asserted itself as the most prominent, calling for a revived emphasis on culture and history in design types and aesthetics. Publications and designs by Postmodernists responded to a variety of influences including anthropological studies of traditional architecture (Rapoport 1969), the perception of urban landscapes (Lynch 1960), historical high design (Venturi 2011) or commercial vernacular (Venturi, Scott Brown, and Izenour 1972). While these Post-Modern approaches usually did not align with the more scientifically rigorous Social and Cultural Factors research, both of these sub-field movements reflected concern in developing a more humanist approach to design.

In the 1960s and 1970s, interest in the social aspects of design flourished as the design field looked for new methods and aesthetics in the face of professional and societal upheaval. In particular, two branches of Social and Cultural Factors evolved as new counter movements in design theory and methods. The first focused on the application of social science research methods in architecture; this positivist approach used data and observation to ascertain knowledge about contextual conditions so that designers could better address these phenomena. Another parallel and sometimes interconnected approach, participatory design, focused on integrating citizens and users into the design process; this more relativistic approach highlighted the competing perceptions and values which shape the way people inhabit, produce and understand places. While many of the practitioners in Social and Cultural Factors operate to some extent in both modes, each approach has unique epistemological roots in relation to its development as a professional field. Analyzing the academic origins, research methods, and project applications of each sub-field highlights the strengths and challenges of applying these approaches to the design of the built environment.

Social science research methods in environmental design

The first of these sub-fields, social science research in design, came to prominence because many design researchers began to question how architects could better understand the way people have used and experienced the built environment and rethink the methods of design in order to improve the quality of the buildings and landscapes. Designers like Sim Van der Ryn (2005) argued, "architecture wasn't scientific enough"; architects needed to develop a means of "systematic evaluation of whether their buildings worked or not." This search for a more rigorous role for research in the design process led architects to look to the social sciences as a model for the techniques and theories with which to study, evaluate, and improve the built environment. In particular, designers looked to sociology, psychology, and anthropology in order to better understand the relationship between buildings and the people who inhabit them.

As those in the environmental design fields increasingly integrated social research into their work, social scientists also began to address the physical and spatial issues of the built environment. This was not a new trend in the 1960s, but rather a renewed interest, which had grown out of the turn of the century discourses. As industrialization and modernization had transformed human relationships and increased the size and density of settlements, social science researchers such as Tonnies (1957) and Simmel (1950) had studied the way these changes affected human experiences, relationships, and geographies. Fields such as social work and urban planning arose as discrete professions in order to address the growing problems of cities. Since the nineteenth century, surveys had been used as a way to illustrate the socio-spatial factors shaping urban issues like poverty, crowding, and crime. In the United Kingdom, early examples included the maps of poverty by Charles Booth (1888) and development of survey techniques by the London School of Economics. This tradition carried on through the war and post-war period in the U.S. and U.K. as a means of gathering social information for urban planning and design. Some schools of architecture, urban design, and town planning started to add social courses to their curriculum in the 1940s (Barry 1946; Sheppard 1946). Sociologists played a major role in developing and assessing post-war housing and planning projects in Britain. One of the most influential, Ruth Glass, conducted surveys both before and after urban redevelopment to question social conditions such as class relations and gentrification (Glass 1948, 1964; Westergaard and Glass 1954). These precedents provided a methodological base for the application and innovation of surveying techniques developed for use in the architectural fields in the 1960s.

The parallel development of social psychology in the turn of the twentieth century also studied the effect of urbanization, but focused less on demographics than on the experiences and social relationships of individuals and communities. In particular, Willy Hellpach (1924) developed some of the foundational ideas about how to study the psychological effects of built and natural environments. But this approach did not develop into a discrete field until the 1950s and 1960s, when researchers interested in environmental psychology began to gather together at conferences that served to build a new sub-discipline of shared theories and methods. Some researchers specifically addressed questions of architectural psychology, working closely with the design fields seeking answers to questions about social behavior in the built environment (Pol 2006; Pol 2007). By the 1970s this field had been formalized in academia in new educational degrees in environmental psychology as well as in the introduction of social science faculty and courses in the environmental design schools. Together these fields produced a plethora of projects and publications that applied social and physiological research methods to the study of the built environment.

As architects and social scientists increasingly found overlapping research interests in the post-war period, they began to share knowledge and methods to try to develop more scientific approaches to the study of the social conditions of the built environment. One of the most innovative techniques developed from this collaboration was Post-Occupancy Evaluation (POE) studies. While sociologists had conducted surveys before large projects, and psychologists and social workers had studied existing built environments, little research had been done after the construction of new buildings to compare the architect's original intentions with the social realities. Some of the early calls for these types of studies came from design methods researchers such as Rittel, Sanoff, and Fessenden (1966) who argued, "Very little is known about the actual performance of buildings in comparison to what the architect expects their performance to be." Thus designers started to conduct POE studies to try to understand how people used and experienced the buildings, and what design features worked or did not work. This information would be useful not only for assessing that specific project, but also for helping to understand the successes and failures of related building types. This research could then be summarized in best practice and design guides to be used by agencies or professionals in improving future designs.

Many of the early post-occupancy studies were done on public buildings and landscapes. As the national and local governments in the United States expanded their role in social welfare and urban development programs, the government supported a growing number of projects in public housing, schools, parks, hospitals, and prisons. In these public buildings, funded with tax revenue and open to the bureaucratic oversight of public agencies, there was growing pressure to demonstrate benefits and solve problems. Both social researchers and public agencies showed an increased interest in conducting surveys and POE studies of these projects, often funded by public grants.

In the 1960s, researchers focused in particular on building types like social housing. Some of the earliest POEs were studies of dorms on college campuses (Van der Ryn and Silverstein 1967). However, the most influential POEs assessed public housing projects. While housing authorities had always used census data and housing surveys to demonstrate the need for housing improvements and slum clearance before construction, POEs aimed to evaluate the success of these projects after completion. Interest in these surveys arose in response to the growing social problems in public housing in the 1960s. These studies linked the problems of alienation and crime in modernist high-rise housing to the lack of territoriality and poor design of public spaces (Cooper 1975; Newman 1972). Many of observations from these studies were translated into design guideline books, such as the manuals on "defensible space" by Oscar Newman (1976) and *Housing As If People Mattered* by Clare Cooper Marcus (1986), which illustrated the advantages of certain typological housing patterns. These publications aimed to make quantitative and qualitative research directly applicable to designers and policy makers.

Other institutional building types also received wide scale research attention, particularly those that sheltered large populations for long periods of time, such as hospitals, prisons, schools, and offices. In the post-war period, a hospital building boom and advances in medical care led to great attention on the effect of hospitals on patient care. Funding from the National Institutes of Health (NIH) was used to examine how changes in hospital organization, lighting, and interior design could improve recovery times, way finding, work flow efficiency, and overall quality of life for patients and health care providers (Wheeler 1964; Draper 1967; Levinson and Grossman 1972; Proshansky and O'Hanlon 1977; Sommer 1983). For example, one of the most famous studies by Roger Ulrich (1984) linked views of nature to improved recovery times. Similar techniques were applied in other institutional environments that had high impact on users such as prisons (Fairweather 1961; Peterson 1960; Flynn and Moyer 1971, Sommer 1983). Researchers also focused on parks and plazas in an attempt to improve the quality and use of public open spaces. In the most famous study, *The Social Life of Small Urban Spaces*, William Whyte (1980) observed various plazas in New York City in order to develop guidelines for improving their design for usability and liveliness. Other studies continued to gather user data as a means to improve information about what park amenities contributed to the most functional and beloved parks addressing issues such as gender and citizen participation (Kaplan 1980; Cranz 1983; Mozingo 1989; Marcus and Francis 1997).

As the scholars began to publish their studies, the field of socially-oriented design research grew, giving rise to the establishment of several research organizations. One of the first, the Design Methods Group, was started by Horst Rittel who tried to formalize the application of scientific research approaches such as operations analysis and systems theory to the study of the built environment. Another, the Environmental Design

Research Association (EDRA), grew out of an effort to establish a
rigorous application of research to the design process and cultivate "multi-
disciplinary collaboration." While EDRA's roots lay in the Design
Methods Group, which also aimed to make the design process transparent,
EDRA differed in its focus on the "development of social and behavioral
knowledge as to the man-environment relationship" (Sanoff and Cohn
1970). In 1969, architecture professor Henry Sanoff (2011) helped
organize the first EDRA conference in North Carolina with the intention to
"bring together social scientists and designers... who had similar interests."
Many of the researchers we interviewed noted how important the first
EDRA conference was in their professional development. Architecture
professor Galen Cranz (2011) remembers attending EDRA just after
graduating from the University of Chicago with a Ph.D. in Sociology and
realizing, "there are others around the country...that care about this place
between humanities and social sciences." Architecture and landscape
architecture professor Clare Cooper Marcus (2011) remembers what a
"wonderful boost" it was attending each year, a reminder that "You are not
alone. You are asking the right questions. Just keep going." As an
organization, EDRA played a major role in encouraging the development
and dissemination of research, serving as both a support system and a
resource for learning about new techniques.

Around the same time, design schools around the country started to
develop socially-oriented coursework, often taught by EDRA members. In
the late 1960s, the College of Environmental Design (CED) at University
of California became a nexus for research in the social aspects of the
design of the built environment. In 1966 Berkeley offered "Social and
Cultural Factors in Architecture and Urban Design," its first course in
social research in the Department of Architecture, formulated and taught
by Richard W. Seaton (1971), a lecturer in Behavioral Sciences in
Architecture. Architect Oscar Newman started teaching a similar course at
Washington University School of Architecture (1966) in St. Louis the
same year. Across the country, these types of courses proliferated in the
late 1960s and early 1970s. By the 1980s schools like Berkeley had several
faculty members teaching social coursework (Figure 2-1).

Despite these inroads in many architecture schools, not all design
faculty embraced Social and Cultural Factors methods as important to the
design process. Cooper Marcus (2011) remembers that the professors who
were interested in the social aspects of design typically remained isolated
from the other design faculty; she recalls that "it was kind of a lonely
situation to be in," noting that she "felt [a] little bit like a voice alone in the
wilderness." Many designers resisted the objectivity of the design pattern

books and other design guidelines developed from post-occupancy evaluation and design research, arguing that it limited their creativity.

Fig. 2-1. Professors from the Social Factors Group. College of Environmental Design, University of California, Berkeley. Source: Sue Rosoff. Courtesy of Environmental Design Archives, University of California, Berkeley.

Cranz (2011) recollects that many of the designers at Berkeley resented what they saw as "pseudo-science," and complained, "Nobody wants to be in a straight jacket." Although Cranz and Cooper Marcus tried to integrate social research methods into design courses at Berkeley, they both faced opposition from their colleagues. Cooper Marcus (2011) hoped the students could use their research in the studio, but some faculty blatantly told the students to "forget all that stuff you learned in social factors." She speculates that the design faculty felt that social research "was irrelevant, it was fuzzy, or possibly they felt it was threatening, because it was questioning...design as its form." Sanoff (2011) concurs that many "faculty don't want to do these kinds of things anymore, because they're very traditional, [they think] it's not architecture." This resistance meant that while most schools had one or two social science researchers with dedicated social courses, only rarely did other faculty members choose to apply these ideas in the larger curriculum. Thus despite an increasing institutionalization of "social factors" in design, the field remained on the sidelines of design theory and practice.

Nonetheless some social research was incorporated into design processes in schools and, to a lesser extent, into practice. Some architecture firms would conduct POEs on their own or other projects, using in-house design staff. Sommer (2011) notes that this was different from the model he had imagined, saying, "my notion was, like a chicken in every pot, every architecture firm would have would have their own behavioral scientist... but instead we ended up teaching those techniques so the designers could use them themselves." While many architects learned basic social research techniques in school, most used these skills only rarely in practice. Cranz (2011) argues that while a few firms have voluntarily conducted POEs of their old projects, "there is no money for evaluation" unless it is written into the contract. While she proposes that they could choose to "do it cheap internally" she speculates, "I don't think they want to do it. I think the impulse is to go onto the next building." Thus POEs are conducted by firms as an exception rather than as the rule. These exceptions are often when the government takes an active role in promoting evaluation of the built environment, especially following publically funded projects. Many agencies such as the NIH and the Department of Housing and Urban Development (HUD) have made grants available for POEs

By the 1980s there was a strong tradition of publically-funded research on social issues in the built environment. However, this institutionalization of research did not always lead to the application of policies or designs based on the findings. Social psychologist and architecture professor Robert Sommer (2011) notes that many people at the public agencies where he conducted surveys viewed him as "an outsider... a meddler." He remembered, "in most every setting which I worked, there were groups...wedded to the status quo, who would resist change." He recalls that he would often deliver a report on a building typology or policy, and "many times that is the end of the story. You never hear how it worked out...You do see some impacts and sometimes nothing." These challenges reveal the way in which government agencies, despite funding and encouraging research, did not necessarily have the impetus to directly apply the results to their own building projects and policies. The research conducted by social scientists often remained divorced from the process of policy-making and did not always get utilized or even communicated to the administrative leaders who could enact change. Nonetheless, it was the goal of promoting change to public projects which had first spurred much of the revolutionary fever in socially-oriented design research, not only among those conducting surveys and post-occupancy evaluations, but perhaps even more passionately among those involved in participatory and community design.

Participatory design and advocacy planning

The motivation to establish participatory design grew as a direct reaction to the anti-democratic planning that had been enacted in the slum clearance projects of the post-war era. In the 1960s and 1970s, participatory designers became advocates protecting the public from the unjust actions of public agencies. In particular, the aggressive relocation and demolition of working-class neighborhoods, under the auspices of construction for highways, housing projects, and private redevelopment, had mobilized some communities to try to halt future redevelopment and demand adequate representation.

One of the earliest surveys and participatory observation research studies of these communities was published by sociologist Herbert Gans (1962) in *Urban Villagers*, which both challenged the practice of destroying low-income neighborhoods and exposed the government's poor communication with residents during relocation. In his later book *People and Plans*, Gans (1968) called for reforms in government processes to allow communities more opportunities for participation in redevelopment plans and polices. In *The Death and Life of the American City*, Jane Jacobs (1961) also challenged urban redevelopment as an urban strategy. She encouraged urban planners to rethink their conception of cities as "disorganized complexity," which could be understood through statistics and analyzed through deductive theories, and instead work "inductively" by taking advantage of the knowledge of local people and places (Jacobs 1961, 435, 441). The type of local involvement Gans and Jacobs suggested started to undermine the top-down power structure that dominated urban planning. While modernist planners had developed and applied techniques for public consultation, such as surveys, exhibitions, and town hall meetings, these activities often had little effect on their planning proposals (Cowan 2010). In the essay "A Ladder of Citizen Participation," participation advocate Sherry Arnstein (1969) called this type of false consultation "manipulation," and entreated planners to adopt a true "delegation of power." Together these publications questioned the methods and ideas of urban planning and promoted more activist approaches to urban design.

Many of the earliest experiments in participatory design arose from
bottom-up community organizing that intentionally aimed to thwart
government-led projects such as slum clearance or freeway construction.
Planning Professor Robert Goodman (2011) remembers that as a graduate
student in the planning program at Massachusetts Institute of Technology
(MIT), a group of residents in Boston came to him for help to resist an
urban renewal project in their neighborhood. He remembers his naiveté,
"[a]t that time…those were the projects I was being trained to design…But
the more I got into it the more I realized that these kinds of urban renewal
projects…had a devastating impact on other people." In this project,
Robert Goodman and his colleagues, planner Chester Hartman and urban
anthropologist Lisa Peattie formed a non-profit group called Urban
Planning Aid to provide design services to the community to help them
fight official plans, particularly the Inner Belt highway.

This type of approach typified the combative nature of the early
participatory movement. Urban planner Marcia McNally (2011)
remembers feeling, "It was the good guys versus the bad guys. The good
guys were the righteous participatory designers, the bad guys were the
inflexible bureaucrats who didn't care about the citizens." In this
adversarial approach, designers served as organizers who helped
communities define their objectives and advocated for them to those in
power. As similar groups formed in other cities, these techniques became
known as "advocacy planning." The movement crystalized around the
publication of a seminal article by Paul Davidoff (1965) entitled,
"Advocacy and Pluralism in Planning." Goodman (1971) also went on to
publish his planning theories in his book, *After the Planners*, which used
comics and bold rhetoric to critique traditional modernists planning
methods, arguing for a more bottom-up approach to planning. This project
clearly broke with Goodman's planning education and his professors at
MIT thought his work was "too radical" to be accepted as a dissertation or
tenure-worthy publication (Goodman 2011). Having strayed from the
traditional practices, these young designers had to forge their own
professional paths.

This interest in engaging communities in planning eventually widened
beyond protesting government plans to include a broader field of
participatory design that aimed to find opportunities for user involvement
in many types of design projects. MacNally (2011), founder of the firm
Community by Design, defines participatory design as "design that is co-
authored." Participatory designers aim to design "with" rather than "for"
the people. Like POEs and survey-based research, this movement
attempted to improve the quality of design for large-scale government

projects. However, it rejected previous empirical forms of knowledge, challenging the efficacy of objective planning (Comerio 1987). Instead, participation advocates assumed that the values driving planning were relative. Landscape architect Randy Hester (2011) argues that in American society, "[w]e have very diverse goals, but at some points those goals have to come together. And the only real mechanism for doing that is deep democracy." Thus, these designers aimed to reinvigorate participatory democracy by activating "a volunteer society whereby citizens can work in partnership" (Sanoff 2011).

Some designers saw this bottom-up approach as impractical and idealistic for placing too much faith in users to understand their own needs and wants. However, architecture professor Mary Comerio (1984, 232) argued that this desire to incorporate user participation, was "not rooted in romanticism about human involvement but rather in the recognition that users have a particular expertise different than, but equally important to, that of the designer." Thus participatory designers did not abandon their technical expertise, but rather made it more available and responsive to the needs of the community.

Despite the early bottom-up approach of these movements in the 1960s, experiments in participatory design also became institutionalized by the 1970s as part of top-down federal programs. Starting under John F. Kennedy's "New Frontier" and realized under Lyndon Johnson's "Great Society" in 1965, the government launched a collection of policies intended to eliminate poverty and racial injustice. For instance, "The War on Poverty" led to the Office of Economic Opportunity (OEO) funding and overseeing community-based antipoverty programs, which included requirements for "community action" and participation. In urban areas, the "Model Cities" program fostered African American leaders and helped improve housing in low-income areas. These programs provided funding opportunities that facilitated the growth of community-based design groups. Grants were also available from the Department of Housing and Urban Development (HUD), the National Institute of Health (NIH), the Comprehensive Employment and Training Act (CETA), and Volunteers in Service to America (VISTA) of the American Peace Corps. By combining welfare-state funding with community service, these programs helped foster a new civic culture that both addressed urban problems and helped build local capacity in participatory democracy.

Universities also served as institutional anchors for many of the early experiments in participatory design. Many universities began to feel a responsibility to communities while also discovering the advantages of service learning as a productive educational opportunity for their students.

By the 1970s these types of student outreach opportunities and community oriented design practices became formalized in a series of Community Design Centers run in association with universities or as non-profit organizations. These centers organized faculty and students to provide gratis or low-fee services to community group (Figure 2-2).

Fig. 2-2. Mary Comerio with students at the Elmhurst Design Center in Berkeley. Source: Environmental Design Archives, University of California, Berkeley.

Henry Sanoff (1990, 6) noted that the purpose of the centers was to "offer design and planning services to enable the poor to define and implement their own planning goals" and allow communities "the right to participate in the planning of their own future." In 1968, Sanoff formed the Community Design Group at North Carolina State University, Raleigh (Figure 2-3). This non-profit design agency helped build projects by identifying communities in demand for architectural and planning services, and then recruiting students to develop projects that would also help them learn valuable design skills. While a few community design centers opened in the early 1960s, most started between 1968 and 1972 (Comerio 1984, 232). A survey conducted by the AIA in 1978 identified around sixty to eighty community design centers in the United States (Polzin 2008).

Despite the rapid proliferation of Community Design Centers in the 1970s, these organizations struggled to sustain themselves in the face of budgetary constraints and resistance from the traditional planning agencies.

Fig. 2-3. Henry Sanoff and his students from the Community Design Group at North Carolina State University. Source: Henry Sanoff.

In the 1970s many Centers had used a combination of grants from federal agencies like HUD and OEO and private and non-profit grants from the American Institute of Architects (AIA) and the National Endowment for the Arts. Mary Comerio (1987, 28) argues that while community-oriented practices thrived under the "War on Poverty" programs, many Community Design Centers faced challenges by the 1980s. The Nixon and Regan administrations cut federal poverty programs, and Comerio (2013) remembers, "As the political climate became more conservative" community designers were "forced to become less idealistic and more pragmatic." The number of centers dropped substantially from eighty in the 1970s, to around thirty in the 1980s, and only twelve of the original centers remained in 2002 (Comerio 1984, 232; Pearson and Robbins 2002, 11; Polzin 2008).

Besides finances, these participatory designers also faced power struggles with the official agencies in charge of redevelopment projects. In the post-war period, planning was primarily conducted by professionals working directly for government agencies such as the state highway-planning department and city urban-renewal agencies. Infamous for their unflinching focus on results over democratic process, many planners in these agencies strongly resisted any interventions in their projects. Robert Goodman (2011) recounts his attempt to share community concerns with the head of the Boston Redevelopment Agency, Edward Logue, who replied, "as long as there was any planning going on in Boston it was his agency that was going to do it." He remembers, "I realized then and there that the idea of negotiating this kind of planning…was just not going to work, that we were in a real long term struggle." While participatory planners sometimes successfully stopped or modified unpopular planning projects, they often could not fight the more powerful and entrenched political actors in shaping urban policies. Marcia McNally (2011) speculated, "A lot of bureaucrats thought the citizens were going to go away and they could go back to doing whatever they were doing." However, by the time she started practicing in the 1980s, she did not observe much of that antagonism. It took at least a decade for "official" planners to cede professional territory and begin to transition from empirical to participatory modes of planning.

The change in the culture of the planning profession reflected a gradual change as young activist planners came of age and began to work in the field. However, this process advanced also due to key policy changes as the public and community advocates put pressure on government agencies to democratize the process of decision making within urban planning. The 1966 Federal Freedom of Information Act and similar state "sunshine laws" aimed to rid government of backroom deals, opening the formerly oligarchic and technocratic planning agencies to greater transparency and accountability. Many states also issued requirements for planning agencies to conduct public consultation during the design process to allow people to comment on and possibly alter plans that would negatively impact their community. These laws greatly helped in normalizing and institutionalizing the process of participation.

Some advocacy planners have expressed optimism that participation has become normalized. Hester (2011) applauds the fact that the public consultation laws "produced far stronger participation and democracy than if we didn't have [them]." Goodman (2011) notes that participation has become "pretty standard in planning circles now" even if communities are sometimes disappointed by the results. McNally (2011) also expressed hope for the future of participatory planning, particularly as she witnessed the way in which her students had adopted and developed the processes she and her colleagues had taught; she assesses the development of participation as primarily positive, saying, "We have so many decades under our belt...sure there's a lot of bad participatory processes still, but there's a lot of good ones." Overall, the United States has achieved an institutionalized system for democratic engagement in urban planning.

Nonetheless, this institutionalization has not been uniformly positive and has been linked to a taming or bureaucratization of participation. Hester (1999, 2011) articulates this change as the maturation of community engagement over the past five decades, arguing that while practitioners of participatory democracy have become more sophisticated, they have also lost some of their revolutionary zeal; he asserts, "American participation since the civil rights movement has become much more technique driven. It is not nearly as raw as the protest movement. I would say, here in the United States we are in a period that is either really complacent or its getting close to dying." While public consultation has become ubiquitous in most major planning projects, this had not ensured that all communities have been equally empowered to protect their needs and rights. While participation has reformed the mainstream of planning practice, it has been less successful in sustaining its more bottom-up advocacy design approaches.

The state of the field of socially oriented design

In the field of architecture and urban design, interest in social issues has been cyclical, waxing and waning in design discourse. The 1970s and the early 1980s was the period in which the Social and Cultural Factors had its greatest influence in changing the focus of design theory, pedagogy, and practice. However, even during this high point, this movement was never the predominant approach in the design fields. Process-oriented design approaches grew side-by-side with other design theories like post-modernism and post-structuralism as potential alternatives to high modernism. As these more formal approaches took precedence in the 1980s, Social and Cultural Factors as a sub-field became increasingly marginalized in design theory and the broader field of architecture.

Since the 1980s many practitioners in the field have noticed increasing opposition to social research as a design approach. Cooper Marcus (2011) laments, "ironically it got less support in the college as more research and books were coming out." Her colleague Cranz (2011) agreed that at many schools, such as University of California, Berkeley, social research has been "on the decline." She admitted that she sometimes felt like the "last of the Mohicans," because she has been the only sociologist working in the College of Environmental Design and there are very few courses in social research methods. However, she also acknowledges that the designers' interest in social issues had not disappeared but transformed, pointing out that other specialists such as historians "have become more social and cultural in their interpretations of landscapes and buildings." While there may be fewer design students trained in post-occupancy evaluations or participatory design directly, there is more emphasis on social theory and social history as a means to analyze the historic and contemporary built environment.

Overall, the social agenda in design is still present in the design fields, but often applied in a more sporadic or less scientific way than in its 1960s and 1970s heyday. Hester (2011) speculates that the commitment to social coursework in schools is spotty, saying, "I think there are plenty of places where social factors or participation are non-existent in the curriculum [and] there are very few places that teach participatory design in a systematic way." The Collegiate Schools of Architecture and Planning has stated an objective for all architecture students to be prepared "to be active engaged citizens… to understand the ethical implications of their decisions…and to nurture a climate of civic engagement" (National Architectural Accrediting Board 2009). While these standards are a positive step in encouraging design schools to teach social issues in their coursework, the requirements are vague and open-ended. It leaves it up to the individual school to interpret this goal, not mandating a particular form of research methods or community engagement experience. While many schools address social issues in their design studios and seminars, they often do not use social research methodically, but rather address social issues within the framework of a still primarily formalistic design process. Thus it remains to be seen what role social conditions will have on the future development of design school curricula.

Another major question is to what extent designers have absorbed and assimilated the ideas, concerns, and methods into design practice. The most direct application of Social and Cultural Factors has been the rise of Evidence Based Design (EBD), an architectural design process based on available evidence from the literature, hypothesizing intended outcomes of design, measuring results, and reporting findings publicly (Hamilton 2003). This field has applied new technologies to increase the speed and sophistication of survey and data gathering methods to better measure user behavior, experiences, and opinions in situ. This field has become particularly influential in the design of complex influential environments like hospitals and office spaces to address issues such as efficiency and comfort. However, as with POEs, these highly specialized methods are not necessarily incorporated into less technical building types or to the broader practice of design.

By contrast, there has been a new burst of interest in socially-oriented architecture in the field as a whole. The rising interest in altruistic and volunteer design services has manifested in the appearance of new non-profit design organizations, like Architecture for Humanity in 1999 and Public Architecture in 2011, which encourage architects to provide pro-bono or low-fee design work to those who cannot afford to hire an architect. Socially-oriented design work has been featured in the popular media particularly due to post-disaster relief projects in New Orleans and Haiti. The profession has given increasing attention to socially-oriented designers such as Teddy Cruz, who works on informal architecture at the US-Mexican border, and institutions such as Samuel Mockbee's Rural Studio, started in 1993 at Auburn University in Alabama, which creates design-build architecture for low-income families out of reused materials. In recent years, these types of projects have taken center stage in well-publicized exhibitions such as "Small Scale, Big Change: New Architectures of Social Engagement" at the Museum of Modern Art (MOMA) in New York and "Design with the Other 90%" by the Cooper Hewitt Foundation. A plethora of publications address the social responsibilities of architecture (Feireiss 2011; Charlesworth 2006; Lepik 2010; Architecture for Humanity 2006, 2012). The Social Economic Environmental Design (SEED) Network formed in 2005 to help evaluate the social impacts of these types of design projects. While this trend seems to indicate a new era in which high-style design is tempered by the needs of less advantaged users, it does not necessarily correspond to a revived interest in the 1960s and 1970s' methods of social research and participatory design in their more rigorous forms. The approaches in these popular projects are more about social philanthropy than social research, about who to design for, not how to apply design methods.

Some of the early socially-oriented practitioners worry that the social aspects of contemporary projects are sometimes taken for granted, rather than thoroughly studied and understood. Cooper Marcus (2011) recounted a conversation with one of her colleagues on the faculty at Berkeley who stated, "Back in the 60s...when you were telling us about the importance of thinking about people and social factors, that was really important. But we have all absorbed that now. We all have a social conscience." She responded with concern, that having a social conscience is not enough, "that's a little bit like saying we don't really need design studios anymore because we have all got an aesthetic taste." The socially oriented designers of the 1960s and 1970s believed their design work was not only about having social objectives "for" the people, but also to create a rigorous process that could methodologically ensure social justice and better performance in design outcomes.

Looking back on the historical context of the 1960s and 1970s, it is clear that socially-oriented researchers and designers made major impacts on both design pedagogy and practice. Now, fifty years later, we can ask whether this change was reformative or revolutionary and what remains of the legacy of these changes. The 2011 conference *The Death and Life of Social Factors* at University of California, Berkeley, the inspiration for this book, challenged social and cultural factors practitioners to take stock and evaluate the state of the field. It questioned whether the movement is thriving, transforming, or disappearing as a fundamental influence on design education and practice. The historical research and oral history interviews conducted for this chapter raise concerns about how thoroughly the mainstream architects and urban planners have embraced the issues, methods, and objectives of the social science research and participatory design. While recent trends do offer hope for the revival for socially oriented design, there seems to be much room for improvement in the level of methodological rigor in contemporary "social" design. A positivistic use of social science research may never, and perhaps should never, be at the heart of design practice; however this type of research can serve to ground and substantiate the fervor of good intentions and desire for social reform that seem to remain a fundamental part of contemporary architectural discourse.

References

Architecture for Humanity. 2006. *Design Like You Give A Damn: Architectural Responses To Humanitarian Crises.* New York: Metropolis Books.

—. 2012. *Design Like You Give A Damn [2]: Architectural Responses To Humanitarian Crises.* New York: Harry N. Abrams.

Arnstein, Sherry R. 1969. "A Ladder of Citizen Participation." *Journal of the American Institute of Planners* 35 (4): 216–24.

Bakema, Jacob, Aldo Van Eyck, H.P. Daniel Van Ginkel, Peter Smithson, and Alison Smithson. 1954. "Statement on Habitat: Doorn Manifesto." In *Architectural Theory Volume II: An Anthology from 1871 to 2005*, ed. Henry Francis Mallgrave and Christina Constandriopoulos, 323-324. Oxford, UK: Blackwell Publishing.

Barry, Gerald. 1946. "The Place of the Architect in the Post War World." *Journal of the Royal Institute of British Architects* 53 (9): 272-376.

Bauer, Catherine. 1934. *Modern Housing*. Boston: Houghton Mifflin.

Blake, Peter. 1974 *Form Follows Fiasco: Why Modern Architecture Hasn't Worked.* Boston: Atlantic Monthly Press.

—. 1977. *Form Follows Fiasco: Why Modern Architecture Hasn't Worked*. Boston: Little, Brown.

Booth, Charles. 1888. "Condition and Occupations of the People of East London and Hackney, 1887." *Journal of the Royal Statistical Society* 51 (2): 276–339.

Brill, Michael. 1975. "Bosti: A Working Model of Education Through Research." *Responding to Social Change*, 242.

Charlesworth, Esther. 2006. Architects without Frontiers: War, Reconstruction and Design Responsibility. Amsterdam: Elsevier.

Comerio, Mary C. 1984. "Community Design: Idealism and Entrepreneurship." *Journal of Architecture and Planning Research* 1 (4): 227-243.

—. 1987. "Design and Empowerment: 20 Years of Community Architecture." *Built Environment* 13 (1) 15–28.

—. 2013. "Design as a Social Act." Interview by Susanne Cowan and Ayda Melika. Video.

Cooper Marcus, Clare, and Carolyn Francis. 1997. *People Places: Design Guidelines for Urban Open Space*. New York, NY: John Wiley & Sons.

Cooper Marcus, Clare. 1986. *Housing as If People Mattered: Site Design Guidelines for Medium-Density Family Housing*. Vol. 4. Berkeley, CA: University of California Press.

Cooper, Clare C. 1975. *Easter Hill Village: Some Social Implications of Design*. New York: Free Press.

Cowan, Susanne. 2010. *Democracy, Technocracy and Publicity: Public Consultation and British Planning, 1939-1951*. Ph.D. diss., University of California, Berkeley. ProQuest, UMI Dissertations Publishing, 3444627.

Cranz, Galen. 1983. *Women and Urban Parks: Their Roles as Users and Suppliers of Park Services*. Berkeley, CA: Institute of Urban & Regional Development, University of California.

—. 2011. "Design as a Social Act." Interview by Susanne Cowan and
    Ayda Melika. Video.
Davidoff, Paul. 1965. "Advocacy and Pluralism in Planning." *Journal of
    the American Institute of Planners* 31 (4): 331–38.
Draper, Peter. 1967. "Community-Care Units and Inpatient Units as
    Alternatives to the District General Hospital." *The Lancet* 290 (7531):
    1406–9.
Dutton, Thomas A. and Lian Hurst Mann. 1996. Eds. *Reconstructing
    Architecture: Critical Discourses and Social Practices*. Minneapolis:
    University of Minnesota Press.
Fairweather, Leslie. 1961. "The International Study Group on Prison
    Architecture." *Brit. J. Criminology* 2: 185.
Feireiss, Lukas. 2011. Testify! The Consequences of Architecture.
    Rotterdam: NAi Publishers, Netherlands Architectural Institute.
Flynn, Edith E., and Frederic D. Moyer. 1971. "Corrections and
    Architecture: A Synthesis." *The Prison Journal* 51 (1): 43–53.
Gans, Herbert. 1962. Urban Villagers: Group and Class in the Life of
    Italian-Americans. New York: The Free Press.
—. 1968. People and Plans. New York: Basic Books.
Giedion, Sigfried. 1929. Liberated Living. In *Architectural Theory Volume
    II: An Anthology from 1871 to 2005*, ed. Henry Francis Mallgrave and
    Christina Constandriopoulos, 228. Oxford, UK: Blackwell Publishing.
Glass, Ruth Ed.1948. *The Social Background of a Plan: A Study of
    Middlesbrough*. London: Routledge and Kegan Paul Limited.
—. 1964. *London: Aspects of Change. Edited by the Centre of Urban
    Studies*. London: McKibben and Kee.
Goodman, Robert. 1971. *After the Planners.* New York: Simon and
    Schuster.
—. 2011. "Design as a Social Act." Interview by Susanne Cowan and
    Ayda Melika. Video.
Gropius, Walter. 1929. "The Sociological Foundations of the Minimum
    Dwelling." In *Architectural Theory Volume II: An Anthology from
    1871 to 2005*, ed. Henry Francis Mallgrave and Christina
    Constandriopoulos, 226-227. Oxford, UK: Blackwell Publishing.
Hamilton, D. Kirk. 2003. "The Four Levels of Evidence-Based Practice."
    Healthcare Design 3 (4): 18–26.
Hellpach, Willy, and Emil Abderhalden. 1924. *Psychologie Der Umwelt*.
    Urban & Schwarzenberg.
Hester Jr, Randolph T. 1999. "The Place of Participatory Design: An
    American View. In R. Hester and C. Kweskin (Eds.) Democratic

Design in the Pacific Rim: Japan, Taiwan, and the United States. Mendocino, CA: Ridge Times Press.

—. 2011. "Design as a Social Act." Interview by Susanne Cowan and Ayda Melika. Video.

Jacobs, Jane. 1961. *The Death and Life of the American City.* New York: Random House.

Jenks, Charles. 1977. *The Language of Post-Modern Architecture.* New York: Rizzoli.

Kaplan, Rachel. 1980. "Citizen Participation in the Design and Evaluation of a Park." *Environment and Behavior* 12 (4): 494–507.

Lepik, Andres. 2010. Small Scale, Big Change: New Architectures of Social Engagement. New York: Museum of Modern Art.

Levinson, Robert B., and Larry Grossman. 1972. "What's Going On: More Effective Correction the Goal of Behavioral Research Center." *Hospital Topics* 50 (7): 20–20.

Lifchez, Raymond. 2011. "Design as a Social Act." Interview by Susanne Cowan and Ayda Melika. Video.

Lynch, Kevin. 1960. *The Image of the City.* Cambridge, Mass.: The MIT Press.

Mallgrave, Harry Francis, and Christina Contandriopoulos. 2008. *Architectural Theory. Vol. 2.* Malden, MA; Oxford: Blackwell.

Mallgrave, Harry Francis, and David Goodman. 2011. *An Introduction to Architectural Theory: 1968 to the Present.* John Wiley & Sons.

Mallgrave, Henry Francis. 2005. *Modern Architectural Theory: A Historical Survey, 1673-1968.* Cambridge, U.K.: Cambridge University Press.

Marcus, Clare. 2011. "Design as a Social Act." Interview by Susanne Cowan and Ayda Melika. Video.

May, Ernst. 1929. "Housing Policy of Frankfort on the Main." In *Architectural Theory Volume II: An Anthology from 1871 to 2005*, ed. Henry Francis Mallgrave and Christina Constandriopoulos, 224-225. Oxford, UK: Blackwell Publishing.

McNally, Marcia. 2011. "Design as a Social Act." Interview by Susanne Cowan and Ayda Melika. Video.

Miller, William C. 1971. "Architectural Research Centers." Council of Planning Librarians. Exchange Bibliography. 199.

Moore, Charles, Donlyn Lyndon, and Sim van der Ryn. 1962. "Toward Making Places." *Landscape*, 31–41.

Mozingo, Louise. 1989. "Women and Downtown Open Spaces." *Places* 6 (1).

Mumford, Eric. 2009. *Defining Urban Design: CIAM Architects and the Formation of a Discipline*, 1937-69. New Haven, Conn.: Yale University Press.

Mumford, Lewis. 1934. *Technics and Civilization*. New York: Harcourt, Brace and Company.

—. 1938. *The Culture of Cities*. New York: Harcourt Brace.

National Architectural Accrediting Board (NAAB), 2009 Conditions for Accreditation. Washington, DC: National Architectural Accrediting Board.

Newman, Oscar. 1972. *Defensible Space*. New York: Macmillan.

—. 1976. *Design Guidelines for Creating Defensible Space*. National Institute of Law Enforcement and Criminal Justice, Law Enforcement Assistance Administration, US Department of Justice.

Pearson, Jason and Mark Robbins. 2002. University Community Design Partnerships: Innovations in practice. New York: Princeton Architectural Press.

Peterson, A. W. 1960. "The Prison Building Programme: A Postscript." *British Journal of Criminology* 1: 372.

Pol, Enric. 2006. "Blueprints for a History of Environmental Psychology (I): From First Birth to American Transition." *Medio Ambiente Y Comportamiento Humano* 7 (2): 95–113.

—. 2007. "Blueprints for a History of Environmental Psychology (II): From Architectural Psychology to the Challenge of Sustainability." *Medio Ambiente Y Comportamiento Humano* 8 (1/2): 1–28.

Polzin, Jodi. 2008. "Executive Summary of Case Study Research," *Community Design Centers and Civic Engagement Initiatives in the Academic Design Disciplines.* St. Louis: Sam Fox School of Design and Visual Arts, Washington University. (Unpublished)

Proshansky, Harold M., and Timothy O'Hanlon. 1977. "Environmental Psychology: Origins and Development." In *Perspectives on Environment and Behavior*, 101–29. Springer.

Rapoport, Amos. 1969. *House Form and Culture.* Englewood Cliffs, N.J.: Prentice-Hall.

RIBA, 1940. "Conference on Problems of Social Environment," *Journal of the Royal Institute of British Architects* 47 (4): 62-63.

—. 1945. "Human Needs in Planning: The Contribution of Social Sciences to Architecture and Planning," *Journal of the Royal Institute of British Architects* 52 (12): 345-346.

—. 1946. "Human Needs in Planning-Conference at the RIBA," *Journal of the Royal Institute of British Architects* 53 (4): 126.

—. 1949. "Ministry of Education National Short Course for Teachers of Architecture," *Journal of the Royal Institute of British Architects* 56 (7): 332.

Rittel, Horst W.J., Henry Sanoff, and Robert Fessenden. 1966. *Evaluative Methods to Measure the Performance of Buildings.* Department of Architecture, College of Environmental Design, University of California.

Rowe, Colin and Fred Koetter. 1984. *Collage City.* Cambridge, MA: The MIT Press.

Sanoff, 1990. *Participatory Design: Theory & Techniques.* Raleigh, N.C.: H. Sanoff

Sanoff, Henry and Sidney Cohn. 1970. *EDRA 1: Proceedings from the 1st Annual Environmental Design Research Association Conference.*

Sanoff, Henry. 1978. *Designing with Community Participation. Stroudsburg, Pennsylvania: Dowden, Hutchinson & Ross.*

—. 2011. "Design as a Social Act." Interview by Susanne Cowan and Ayda Melika. Video.

Seaton, Richard W. 1971. Social Factors in Architectural and Urban Design. Monticello, Ill.: Council of Planning Librarians.

Sheppard, Richard. "Sociology and Architecture." *Journal of the Royal Institute of British Architects* 53 (9): 386-394.

Simmel, Georg. 1950. "The Metropolis and Mental Life." *In The Sociology of Georg Simmel*, 409-424. Ed. Kurt Wolff (Trans.) New York: Free Press.

Smithson, Peter and Alison Smithson. 1956. "Open Letter to Sert and Team 10." In *Architectural Theory Volume II: An Anthology from 1871 to 2005*, ed. Henry Francis Mallgrave and Christina Constandriopoulos, 325. Oxford, UK: Blackwell Publishing.

Smithson, Peter, Alison Smithson, Gillian Howeel, William Howell and John Voeker. 1953. "Urban Reidentification: Grid, CIAM, Aix-en-Provence." In *Architectural Theory Volume II: An Anthology from 1871 to 2005*, ed. Henry Francis Mallgrave and Christina Constandriopoulos, 322-323. Oxford, UK: Blackwell Publishing.

Sommer, 2011. "Design as a Social Act." Interview by Susanne Cowan and Ayda Melika. Video.

Sommer, Robert. 1983. *Social Design: Creating Buildings with People in Mind.* Englewood Cliffs, NJ: Prentice-Hall.

Tonnies, Ferdinand. 1957. *Community and Society.* London: Courier Dover Publications.

Ulrich, Roger. 1984. "View through a Window May Influence Recovery." *Science* 224 (4647): 224–25.

Van der Ryn, Sim, and Murray Silverstein. 1967. *Dorms at Berkeley: An Environmental Analysis*. Berkeley, CA: Center for Planning and Development Research, University of California.

Van der Ryn, Sim. 2005. *Design for Life: The Architecture of Sim Van Der Ryn*. Gibbs Smith.

—. 2011. "Design as a Social Act." Interview by Susanne Cowan and Ayda Melika. Video.

Venturi, Robert, Denise Scott Brown, and Steven Izenour. 1972. *Learning from Las Vegas: The Forgotten Symbolism of Architectural Form*. Cambridge, Mass.: MIT Press. Venturi, Robert. 1966. *Complexity and Contradiction in Architecture*. New York: The Museum of Modern Art Press.

Washington University School of Architecture (1966) "Bulletin 1966-1967." Washington University Archives: Publications - College of Architecture. Box 3 Folder 8.

Westergaard, John and Ruth Glass. 1954. "A Profile of Lansbury." *Town Planning Review*. 25(1).

Wheeler, Edward Todd. 1964. *Hospital Design and Function*. New York: McGraw-Hill.

Whyte, William Hollingsworth. 1980. *The Social Life of Small Urban Spaces*. Washington, D.C.: Conservation Foundation.

Wolfe, Tom. 1981. From Bauhaus to Our house. New York: *Farrar, Straus & Giroux*.

CHAPTER THREE

REASSESSING SMALL URBAN SPACES

DOMINIC L. FISCHER

Two pocket parks in Manhattan, two stories

Film footage of a Harlem street, replete with what would become the principles for successful small urban space in Manhattan, opens William H. Whyte's acclaimed film, *The Social Life of Small Urban Spaces*. Whyte then quickly panned to the Seagram building plaza and other privately owned public spaces (POPS) of Midtown Manhattan where his team collected astute observational data through behavioral mapping, time-lapse video, and nuanced surveillance.

"Do people in New York City still use small urban spaces in the same way?" An undergraduate landscape architecture student asked me this while watching *The Social Life of Small Urban Spaces* for the first time. Unsure of an updated answer, I directed the student to the comprehensive and democratic work of Jerold Kayden's book *Privately Owned Public Space: The New York City Experience*. This was a panoptic view, but inconclusive in terms of applicable design lessons. Thus began my preliminary research to re-assess the small urban spaces from the film to determine whether indeed Whyte was still right. The study began by mapping each of the spaces Whyte and his team had examined in the video, using layers of geographic information system (GIS) data. The map showed that the spaces were surprisingly limited by a very tight proximity, largely within blocks of one another in Midtown Manhattan and a few near Wall Street. Similar spaces had been created all over the country, but our guiding design principles were based on a small section of spaces from perhaps our most anomalous American city. How then did this very small sample area influence designers working in quite different environs? A literature review of other early parks in the era lead me back to Harlem, revealed a series of relatively unknown spaces on 128th Street that shared designers and advocates, but preceded the celebrated Paley Park. These

unstudied spaces had been absent from relevant literature since their
ribbon cutting in the early 1960s. The heavily used Midtown spaces are
still highly utilized, but what about the first pocket parks in New York
City? Why were they forgotten?

My study question changed. Rather than asking whether people still
use these room-size parks and privately owned public plazas (Gus the
hotdog guy at Seagram's Plaza now has been succeeded by five to seven
food trucks/vendors on any given weekday), I ask, "What can be learned
from the history of parks that shared design principles, yet did not
succeed?" The full study paired six seemingly similar small spaces in
socio-economically divergent areas of Manhattan. In this chapter I focus
on the story of two: Paley Park and its predecessor, Collyer Brothers Park.
This allows for a closer analysis of small urban space utilizing new
geographic information system (GIS) data, new time-lapse and observation
studies, and rapid ethnographic research to discuss the limitations of this
park type and provide generalizable lessons for future small urban space
development. I chronicle the inception of pocket parks and other small
urban spaces, the theories that led to their rise in the 1960s, and the
divergent futures of both studied and unstudied spaces, evaluated by
(re)assessing them.

The historic case study of Collyer Brothers Park presented here in
relation to Paley Park illuminates the limitations of these park typologies
by evaluating their differences. I have used archival research to explain the
story and context of each as individual cases, and revisited Paley Park and
evaluated Collyer Brothers Park with the same criteria. An analysis of the
social and geographic context of each park indicates that pocket
park success and design differs with both ethnography and geography.

Ethnographic research of each space was conducted; I interviewed
managers, security and maintenance workers, volunteer groups, and users.
When available I also interviewed the landscape architect, project
manager, or designer of the space. The interviews for individual users
were open ended, but the group interview for Collyer Brothers was
focused on day-to-day park issues. User observation, field notes and
physical traces were also used as empirical evidence of patterns of use.

My model for physical and geographic analysis closely follows Mark
Francis's (1999) case study methods for landscape architecture. This
included over ten visits to each site at different times of day and different
seasons for observational site analysis and time-lapse recording when
relevant and possible. Documentation of the role of the designer, program
elements, maintenance and management, peer reviews and criticism,
concludes with generalizable lessons. The combination of the two methods

covers a historical research gap in the study of small urban spaces for public space use.

The assessment analysis measured, as Whyte did, the average number of users, gender, singles, pairs, groups and behaviors. Field notes identified empirical evidence of neighborhood and context changes and summarized them for themes that reoccurred during research and interviews. Digital reproductions of each park were modelled (see Fig. 3-1) to study sun patterns that have changed since park openings and correlations in park use and sun/shade patterns. Further geographic information was procured for viewing active business lists and demographic data of each park.

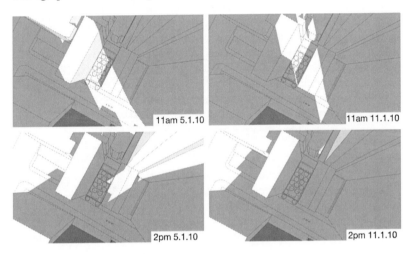

Fig. 3-1. Paley Park sun studies and use correlation. Source: Author.

History of the pocket park

The concept of "vest-pocket parks" was first introduced in 1897 by Jacob Riis, a social reformer and journalist, when he was the secretary of a city Committee on Small Parks. Riis is well known for stating, "Any unused corner, triangle, or vacant lot kept off the market by litigation or otherwise, may serve this purpose well" (Seymour 1969). However, the implementation of such parks was not realized until much later when American park typologies shifted from the Recreational Facilities of the 1960s to an Open Space System with irregular parks in residual spaces as part of a citywide network. The rectilinear and single-use park was no longer adequate to address the shift in urban park users. Galen Cranz (1982) documents the social context of these changes in park types in *The Politics of Park Design*. The Open Space System began with the unstated goal of public participation; this shift was not without contention and is reported in two *New York Times* articles, the first, "Tiny Parks Draw Attack by Moses," (Bennet 1966) and the second, "Mayor and Moses Clash in Park; Argue Over Permanency of Site," where "Mayor Lindsay and Robert Moses stage a tempest in a vest-pocket park." In these articles Moses, the former Parks Commissioner of twenty-six years, derided the idea of citizen participation stating, "if this means encouraging them to form committees to influence design and the sort…it's a poor idea and can only end in disappointment and recriminations" (Ingraham 1967). City revitalization, and the quelling of riots were also key social problems addressed by these new parks. Trends in park use were free-form play, and public participation was encouraged. The size also changed to include small irregular sites within the broader matrix of the Open Space System. Politicians, environmentalists, artists, and designers promoted the new system with intentions of benefitting residents, workers, poor urban youth, and middle class members often excluded from the large reform parks of the 19th century. In Cranz's summary of the social context of parks and their planners, she cites the generational swing in park definitions that changes approximately every 30-50 years.

The vision and design of the pocket parks for Midtown were first introduced at a 1963 exhibit "New Parks for New York" sponsored by the Park Association of New York, and created by the landscape architecture firm of Robert Zion and Harold Breen. Text from the exhibit urged for "a pool of space removed from the flow of traffic—even pedestrian traffic; an outdoor room, human in scale, enclosed and protected, and sheltered from noise" (Seymour 1969).

In 1965 New York, the regime change of both the mayor and parks commissioner, to Mayor John Lindsay and Parks Commissioner Thomas P.F. Hoving, played a strong role in bringing "vest-pocket parks and other small urban spaces to neighborhoods across the city. Before that, thinking regarding park planning—particularly by Robert Moses, the "master builder"—was that three acres minimum were needed to justify the maintenance and management of park space. During the late 1960s and early 1970s many vacant lots were converted into vest-pocket parks for neighborhoods that lacked open space. New York Parks Commissioner Hoving famously said in a 1966 *New York Times* article, "Utopia would mean a park—some large, some small—every four or five blocks" (Hoving 1966).

Since the conclusion of William Whyte's research, film production and subsequent print publication of *The Social Life of Small Urban Spaces* in 1980, many new studies have taken place in the vein of environmental and behavioral research to inform public space planning, design, and management. (The idea of using observations, surveys, interviews, and workshops first originated in the sociology discipline as a way of better designing interior office space.) Interviews I conducted for this study with practicing landscape architect, Thomas Balsley, Ethan Kent of Project for Public Spaces, and Amy Gavaris of the New York Restoration Project (NYRP) all yielded abundant references to Whyte's landmark work. The non-profit organization Project for Public Spaces (PPS) was founded on the research and mentorship of William Whyte and has evolved into the practice of "placemaking." The term "placemaking," which has seen a significant use among designers in the public realm, is defined by the Project for Public Spaces website as "both an overarching idea and a hands-on tool for improving a neighborhood, city or region. Rooted in community-based participation...placemaking involves the planning, design, management and programming of public spaces."

Vice President of PPS, Ethan Kent recounted in a 2011 conversation that he was unfamiliar with Collyer Brothers Park, but he was interested in the resurgence of pocket parks as viable public space. He recently had fielded a phone call from *Time* magazine on the topic of pocket parks' increase in popularity and their effect on public space. A *New York Times* keyword search found the term "pocket park" or "vest-pocket park" used more than 45 times in the 1960s. The term's use slowly decreased to less than five in the 1990s; however, it has seen a recent surge with more than 20 mentions in the last two years.

Paley Park, the keystone to this research, has cast a shadow over the unstudied and relatively unknown Collyer Brothers Park. Heralded from its opening in 1967, Paley Park was praised alongside Collyer Brothers Park by Whitney North Seymour, Jr., in his 1969 book *Small Urban Spaces*. Seymour was a champion of civil rights, and he struggled to "bring about a shift in official attitudes toward the small city park" by advocating for small urban spaces and publishing associated research in his book, which included work by Jane Jacobs, Lewis Mumford, and the designer of both Paley Park and Collyer Brothers Park. William Whyte's work followed Seymour by approximately ten years, but the findings were focused solely on privately owned public spaces in Manhattan, of which there are now more than 500. These privately owned public spaces are the products, or in many cases bi-products, of the 1961 zoning resolution, which offered bonus provisions (increased building floor ratios) to developers who created such publicly-accessible open spaces. Although public sentiment about parks had shifted, the definition in typologies came later with Paley Park cited as the "epitome" of this change to "the open-space mentality" (Cranz 1982).

Recently public space has been studied for the acceleration in its privatization, the policing of public parks (Low 2000), and the accessibility of what are ostensibly public spaces but which exclude many users to different degrees (Miller 2007). In New York City the privately owned public spaces have still garnered the most attention, particularly in Jerold Kayden's *Privately Owned Public Space* (2000). This work brings to light the neglect of many of these marginal spaces in a comprehensive and systematic way, but there are many spaces outside this list that remain largely unstudied, including Collyer Brothers Park presented here.

A pocket park is born in Harlem: Collyer Brothers Park

Collyer Brothers Park was created as the first vest-pocket park in New York City, and there is as much to be gleaned from its devolution as from the celebrity of its sister park, Paley Park.

Designed and constructed in 1963 as a "sitting park" or pocket park, Collyer Brothers Park occupies the former site of the infamous Collyer Brothers residence, known for their hoarding which included a total of fourteen grand pianos and a car engine. The park was built on the corner of 128th Street and 5th Avenue in Manhattan as part of a series of three vest-pocket parks. The total construction cost for the 2,000 square-foot park was $7,003. It was in keeping with the ordered nature of modernist landscape architecture and used minimal but sturdy materials like the ubiquitous New York City octagonal paver set under London Plane trees with a Paris-inspired perimeter of asphalt dusted with cement.

When constructed, the park received extensive media attention along with political attention from Secretary Stewart L. Udall and then Senators Robert F. Kennedy and Joseph Clark who had supported Harlem Youth Opportunities Unlimited (HARYOU). Thanks to national publicity and new government programs such as HARYOU, the West 128th Street vest-pocket parks and their descendants in New York City encouraged pocket park implementation in other cities including the Land Utilization (later the Neighborhood Park Program) in Philadelphia (Seymour 1969) and the Neighborhood Improvement and Beautification (NIB) Program in Chicago (Cranz 1982), among others.

Robert Zion, whose nationally-renowned landscape architecture firm, Zion & Breen Associates, would later design Paley Park, designed the adult sitting park as a "labor of love," choosing the International Style based on European parks. Zion was instrumental in bringing the concept of pocket parks to fruition in New York City, with Collyer Brothers Park being the first to be completed. He was active in seeing that sturdy material palette be used, and a canopy of trees was created. Zion was also available to oversee that the construction work was done properly by the contractor.

The financial crisis of the 1970s that followed the park's ribbon cutting impacted the parks department decision to shift responsibility of opening and closing parks to volunteers. GreenThumb was created at the same time to provide support to these volunteer park groups via the New York City parks department. Between 1970 and 1980, Collyer Brothers Park was completely enclosed by an eight-foot steel fence with a small gate on the 5th Avenue (east) sidewalk; formerly the park was focused towards the 128th Street (south) sidewalk.

During the recession of 1973 to 1975 and the ensuing decade, the Parks Department work force was cut in half and did not recover until the early 1980s. As the work force was slowly restored, vacant lots were turned into public gardens, and the public was largely allowed to improve them without outright ownership. GreenThumb, the largest community gardening program in the nation, was created to provide programming, advice, and material support for community gardens. Collyer Brothers Park is one of these parks, and it shared maintenance and administration with the Harlem 5th Avenue Association and Rev. Linnette C. Williamson Memorial Park Association.

The Christ Community Church provided part-time maintenance and ownership, but the park fell into neglect by the 1990s. In 1998, ownership was transferred to the Parks Department. Today, Collyer Brothers Park is maintained with help from Operation GreenThumb and volunteers from the Harlem 5th Avenue Association and Rev. Linnette C. Williamson Memorial Park Association. The neighborhood has seen a resurgence of redevelopment in the past 10 years. Geographic information data available shows the neighborhood income is increasing, but still lags significantly behind national and city averages. The density of buildings and pedestrian traffic is also much lower than its Midtown counterpart (see figure 3-2). Churches and few retail businesses with limited daily operating hours dominate a survey of businesses within three blocks of the park. The area is predominantly residential, and the site itself is a former brownstone in the neo-Grec-style of 1870s Harlem.

Fig. 3-2. Figure Ground Maps of Collyer Brothers Park neighborhood (left) and Paley Park neighborhood (right). 2008 U.S. Census Data. Source: Author.

A neighborhood park member meeting for the association on March 28, 2011, drew thirty volunteers and members ranging in age from children to grandparents, and spanned a broad mix of ethnicities. The meeting in the pink-hued basement of the Christ Community Church of Harlem was led by Francois Malichier, the exuberant volunteer caretaker for the park and community gardens on the block who lives nearby, houses the master keys, keeps the parks clean, and organizes meetings for volunteers who use the gardens and parks. Concerns from volunteers revolved around maintenance and specifically on the difficulty of keeping the park open during the day. Malichier was adamant that all parks be locked before the schools let out. The shared maintenance agreement between the volunteers and GreenThumb requires that the park be open from at least 8am until 3pm each day. Janine, a young volunteer expressed concern about parties that gathered on the sidewalk near the gates of the parks to barbeque and smoke. Physical evidence of both litter and ashes were traced to areas near the park boundary, and posted signs prohibit public areas in the neighborhood from such use.

Today the Collyer Brothers Park gate is locked unless a member of the Harlem 5th Avenue Association opens it. The group shares this responsibility between members in attempts to keep the park open on a daily basis.

Fig. 3-3. Collyer Brothers Park observation photo Sept. 3rd, 2010. Source: Author.

Observational site visits to the park on ten occasions in 2010, 2011, and 2013 yielded no activity in the park (see fig. 3-3). Posted physical documents and web postings have shown signs of clean-up days, a bulb-planting day for the park, and the Harlem 5th Avenue Association's active meetings. Interviews with local residents reiterated the perceived closure of the park.

A Collyer Brothers Park user comment posted to the blog site *Bespoke + Harlem* on May 7, 2009, stated,

> "My biggest problem with these little parks that are managed by neighborhood groups is that they're rarely open. A park should be open to the public with regular daily hours, not just for a group of connected long-time residents who hold the keys and decide to throw events there from time to time."

If Collyer Brothers is a public space, it is perceived as selectively privatized.

My first field observations undertaken for this study indicated that the park was nearly defunct and unused, a complete upending of intended use when comparing archival photographs (Ross photos 1963) of the site. These black and white photographs show New York City Mayor Wagner, Senator Kennedy, Senator Javits, and Secretary of Interior Udall touring and praising the park. The photographs show a community engaged and gathered in a clean plaza with an open connection to the sidewalk. Handsome row houses remain unchanged in the background. Udall, after completing a tour of the park, commented, "More people would get pleasure out of these small neighborhood parks than do out of some of our huge National Parks" (Kaplan 1965).

Today the park is unrecognizable from the historic photographs. The only surviving evidence of the original park are twelve of the twenty London Plane trees that can be seen in historic photos as new trees in a modern plaza of hexagonal pavers and concrete-dusted asphalt. The hexagonal pavers have been removed: a fence surrounds the entire property, and grass and shrubs occupy the site along with a few wooden benches. After further investigation and interviews with local community groups, the park still seems to be a beloved place for local residents, but the volunteer maintenance and management are too understaffed to make the park a full-time public space. Collyer Brothers Park is today used for gardening activities, children's reading programs, and an annual Christmas tree displays, but is unavailable for its original use as an adult sitting park. Along with staffing issues there are also physical limitations to the park's viability. The steel fence, which was constructed when the park became property of the NYC parks department, is the main factor limiting public use. It surrounds the park and has changed the park into more of a private garden, thus limiting the use of the space even more (see figure 3-3). The shift in use from a passive, highly-used sitting park to a gated garden with a patch of grass in place of durable pavers reminds one of a quote by Jane Jacobs from 1962:

> I can remember the people in East Harlem hating a patch of green grass. I couldn't understand why until one of them told me that their tobacco store had been torn down, the corner newsstand was gone, but someone had decided the people needed a patch of green grass and put it there (Alexiou 2006).

Mature London Plane trees have outgrown the small space, but according to a *New York Times* article, it was suggested by the association that the park be renamed "The Reading Tree Garden," a distinct departure from its original use and vision (Gray 2002). The proposal for changing the park's name was made to Community Board 10, but it failed the full board vote by one.

The need for active supervision and community sponsorship is crucial to the success of a park in this predominantly residential context. This can be formal or informal, though in a residential setting it is even more important that an organization be active to maintain and supervise the park. An active funding source or volunteer group for cleaning and maintenance, and a physical change to open site lines and re-introduce durable materials and seating is vital.

Replacing the entrance gate with a larger retractable gate and opening up the full connection to 128th Street could open up the park once again to the sidewalk for better visibility and legibility as public space. Even with these changes, the greatest limitations are the surrounding uses and lack of activity. Collyer Brothers Park land-use and business inventory within three blocks (the effective market radius for small parks established by Whyte) of the park reveals predominantly residential properties with several churches scattered throughout; no retail or consistent daily-operated business are within the park's vicinity. In comparison, Paley Park has a built-in food kiosk and a multitude of retail businesses that have seen resurgence in the last 20 years. The most successful small urban spaces are often extensions of an already active street and are strongly a part of their "place." This small but valuable point was first made by Whyte's observation of the material change into the sidewalk of successful small urban spaces. Collyer Brothers Park has evolved to become a residential garden with very little use, but its first life would have been better suited just a few blocks to the south along the 125th Street corridor in the heart of Harlem where it could be publicly accessed and surveilled by the critical flow of pedestrians and retail store activity.

A pocket park with a legacy foundation: Paley Park

Paley Park, erroneously considered the first pocket park, is located on 53rd Street between Madison and 5th Avenue in Midtown Manhattan. It is a premier example of a vest-pocket park as described by the 1963 "New Parks for New York" exhibit for the Park Association of New York. Built in 1967 (four years after Collyer Brothers Park) and considered a model for pocket parks, it is listed as one of the top parks in the world by the Project for Public Spaces. With a 20-foot "water wall" and 17 honey locust trees raised slightly above the street, its many users often reference it as an urban refuge.

Paley Park is 4,200 square feet and occupies the former site of the Stork Club. It is described by Jerold Kayden (2000) as "a modernist landscape" with "ordered nature." It is enclosed on three sides by its own ivy-covered, brown brick walls. The rock-clad 20-foot water wall sets the stage, and beckons passers-by. The waterfall is inactive during January, but for the other months 1,800 gallons per minute recirculates through its system, heated by steam turbine when needed.

Fig. 3-4. Paley Park observation photo from Sept. 3rd, 2010. Source: Author.

The Paley Park material palette is durable, and rugged square stone pavers form the ground plane with the exception of the small tree grates for the seventeen honey locust trees, planted 12-feet on center forming an overhead plane during the summer months and a mottled canopy of winding tree architecture in its dormant season. Two gatehouses frame the stepped entrance, which is gated when the park is closed, though the waterwall is lighted and can be seen even after the park has closed (see figure 3-4). Each gatehouse serves a separate function: in the southeast corner a small refreshments kiosk is housed, and in the southwest the mechanical equipment and park supervisor's tools are stored. The park connects directly to the sidewalk with the transition of large granite pavers at its entrance and outstretched canopies of two adroitly-placed honey locust trees visible from the corners of 5th and Madison Avenue. Comparisons in archival photographs find even annual plantings relatively unchanged. Also unchanged are the sixty movable Bertoia chairs and 20 movable tables, both white and of wire-mesh construction (Maurice 1967). Appropriately-dimensioned ivy planters that run the entire length of each brick wall, framing the water wall, also provide additional seating. Completing the park furniture in matching white are six wire wastebaskets, five granite-veneered ashtrays, and a drinking fountain, also housed in granite.

Paley Park was created as the second privately-financed public vest-pocket park, the first of several in midtown. The total cost of land and construction was $1 million. Built by William S. Paley, then the chairman of the board of the Columbia Broadcasting System, the park is a memorial to Mr. Paley's father, Samuel.

The design process for Paley Park was unique for the fact it was privately funded. Opening concurrently with the 29th Street Playground designed by landscape architect M. Paul Friedberg, it showcased ideas championed by Commissioner Thomas P. F. Hoving. Mr. Paley in a *New York Times* article described the project as "an ideal place to try a new experiment for the enjoyment of the out-of-doors in the heart of the city" (Huxtable 1966).

Parks such as Paley, he says, "stimulate impulse use," as many pedestrians will "do a double take as they pass by, pause, move a few steps, then, with a slight acceleration, go on up the steps" and into the vestibule of the park (Whyte 1980). More recent observations by Kayden in his catalogue of *Privately Owned Public Spaces* (2000) reports, "on any given day, the roster might include random visitors from New Jersey or Japan as well as landscape architects and designers making the educational journey" to Paley Park. Several observations included for this study show similar results, with many of the same social theories at work. Groups will often accelerate up the stairs and directly to the stage that is the step and platform in front of the waterwall. Lovers still seat themselves in the front, in the direct path of most viewers' focal point. Single park users occupy the edges and the turnover rate is high, so prospect refuge theory seems to mix comfortably within the sublime symmetry of the park (Kayden 2000).

Concerns about using Paley Park as a vest-pocket park design template include limitations in social, ecological, and economic issues—in a way circumnavigating them all with its privileged mid-town location and privately funded Greenpark foundation. Reviews of Paley Park are predominantly positive, as a gem of an oasis, but other reviewers have commented on what may make some users feel excluded: "Beware of the disgruntled custodian who will yell at you across the park if you pull out a chair onto 'the walkway.' Beware of the angry clerk who runs the

refreshment stand," commented Rich W. from Brooklyn of his experience
in the park. These comments, while uncommon, point to issues of a
selected privatization. The ten sessions of what Whyte coined "sighting
maps" done for this study showed a slightly lower overall use of the park
from the original study. Whyte's team counted an average of 125 people
using the park during peak periods of the day, while counts for this study
ranged between 20 and 40 (see fig. 3-5).

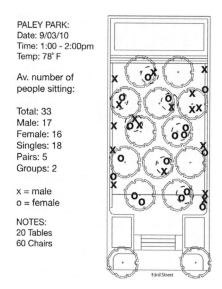

Fig. 3-5. Paley Park sighting map, Sept. 3rd, 2010. Source: Author.

The midtown setting limits and filters the social status of many of the
park's users. The presence of a full-time security guard directing use can
be a limiting factor in its "publicness." As defined by Benn and Gaus, in
the 1983 publication of *The public and the private: concepts and actions
from Public and Private in Social Life*, "a place is public; therefore, if it is
controlled by public authorities, concerns people as a whole, is open or
available to them, and is used or shared by all the members of a society."
Though often seen as a benefit, it reveals why similar parks can be seen as
discriminatory.

Paley Park is also a privately owned public park, but with limited
functions for everyday use. Its location is removed from any sizable
amount of residential units and fits the criteria of a corporate meeting
room. The park supports an active user group, but it is mostly balanced

between midtown site seers and corporate office workers who visit the park as a destination. A study of sighting maps and interviews with users revealed a much higher use of the park by women, many with lunch bags in tow. There seems to be an equitable distribution of where men and women choose seating locations, contrary to Whyte's documentation that suggests men tend to sit near the front. This could also be in a shift of employee makeup of midtown and an increased ratio of female to male office workers.

Paley Park also benefits from a relatively homogenous user group and singular vision; it is that vision that accompanies its transcendent design and has allowed it to succeed while so many others have faded. Paley Park is like a palm tree; it thrives in a very specific part of urban ecology that few other neighborhoods or cities can support. The seemingly subtle design features set it apart from hundreds of other similar spaces that have been marginalized by lack of design features, poor maintenance, or in some cases parked cars. The simple choice by landscape architects Zion & Breen to bring granite material of the park foyer into the sidewalk was noted by Whyte and can be seen as glimpse into the future as public plazas have moved from vest-pockets to the public right of way into the streets themselves.

Conclusions

Paley Park vs. Collyer Brothers Park is a destination space solidified in the history of our Open Space System as a premier pocket park. These two studies illustrate how profoundly similar spaces can yield disparate results when applied in different contexts. Collyer Brothers Park, although designed and constructed first, was never able to live up to its expectations as uptown's Paley Park.

Utilizing data to show business and land-use locations quickly gives a clear picture of the difference in density, use, socio-economics and pedestrian experience between these two spaces.

A staple element of the plaza is the presence of food vendors, which have increased from William Whyte's "Gus" (the Seagram's Plaza stalwart) to a half dozen of his progeny, many now with gas-powered full service vans with menus accessible on the Internet. Since the time of Whyte's study, the number of food vending permits has increased from 3,400 in 1978 to nearly 25,000 today. This increase is another indicator of the necessity of the presence of food in successful public space.

As Low (2005) has shown, access to parks is also linked to the economic and "cultural patterns" of park users. The answer of how to sustain park use and access is difficult and on the minds of both the designers and the volunteers who ostensibly operate the parks. They strive to keep the parks open, but have few answers of how to address the concerns of park vandalism, loitering teenagers, and "illegal" smoking and barbeques that often leave behind large amounts of litter that then have to be cleaned by the volunteers. The conflicts in social interaction in small urban spaces are often amplified, and it can be difficult to accommodate "spatially adequate territories" for multiple user groups—residents, office workers, and tourists in Paley Park, and different generational needs in Collyer Brothers Park where barbequing competes with reading, and fenced-in community gardens have replaced passive sitting spaces for adults. This also leads to the conclusion that parks are better defined as public and identified for uses in neighborhoods that are missing or unequally serviced. Residents of Harlem and 128th Street, when asked about Collyer Brothers Park, were unsure when it was open, had rarely if ever seen the park in use, and had felt that the park was limited to use by those neighborhood groups who retained the keys.

When a park can be identified as a community asset it may be easier to police, as it becomes a semi-private extension of the community. When it is gated, it can be assumed that it will be managed by a private entity and the responsibility no longer lies within the community.

William Whyte's high praise of small urban spaces as "multipliers" should come with a stronger disclaimer about the drawbacks of pocket parks in places where a midtown mix of density and use cannot be duplicated. Is Whyte still right? Whyte's exegesis is still invaluable, but cannot be applied verbatim to seemingly similar spaces in communities underserved by healthy streets and opportunities. Continued studies of these missing performance dimensions, evidenced in the exemplary place-making work by Whyte's predecessors and environmental researchers and designers, will reveal the social network inherently connected to these and other unstudied small urban spaces.

One of the meta-dimensions for assessing the success of small urban spaces is its relationship to the street. Whyte himself would have recognized the immediate limitations of the placement and use of Collyer Brothers Park. While the park has embedded itself into the history of its neighborhood, it would not be considered successful by the metrics set forth by Whyte's team. Design cannot solve social problems, but it can perpetuate or alleviate open space issues by accommodating multiple user groups, maintenance, and regular hours of operation. The New York City Department of Transportation—no longer captive to developers' bonus provisions and considering the performance dimension of access to the street—has taken the lead in creating neighborhood plazas by transforming residual pieces of the public right of way into new social public spaces.

The strongest conclusion when analyzing Paley Park and its uptown counterpart Collyer Brothers Park is that although they are of the same typology, their success is dependent on very specific factors of their urban ecologies. This is a history lesson that needs to be retold for design professionals to understand the importance of place and cultural use before a successful model of space, open or otherwise, is replicated.

The lack of sidewalk traffic and neighborhood retail businesses coupled with volunteer maintenance and an unclear identity of use for residents limits the intended use of Collyer Brothers Park, an historic site in its own right, but one waiting an improved urban context.

It is often fine to build nothing; in most urban cases a building is often the best replacement for a building, not an assumptive pocket park. If small urban spaces are the living room of a neighborhood they must be placed appropriately, that is, inside the "house," connected to the street with access to the hearth of community activity via the observed criteria begun by Whyte, but expanded to include activities and events for all users with cultural public input before design and construction.

References

Alexiou, Alice Sparberg. 2006. *Jane Jacobs: Urban Visionary*. New Brunswick, NJ: Rutgers UP.

Benn, S.I. and Gaus, G.F. 1983. *The Public and the Private: Concepts and Actions from Public and Private in Social Life*. New York: St. Martin's Press.

Bennet, Charles G. 1966. "Tiny Parks Draw Attack By Moses." *The New York Times*. May 11.

Carmona, Matthew. 2000. "Contemporary Public Space: Critique and Classification, Part One: Critique." *Journal of Urban Design* 148 123-148.

Francis, Mark. 2003. *Urban Open Space: Designing for User Needs*. Washington: Island.

Gray, Christopher. 2002. "Wondering Whether a Park Should Keep Its Name." *The New York Times*. June 23.

Huxtable, Ada Louise. 1966. "Experiment in Parks: Vest-Pocket Concept to Get First Test on Prime Land." *The New York Times*. February 2.

Hoving, Thomas P. 1966. "Think Big About Small Parks." *The New York Times*. April 10.

Ingraham, Joseph C. 1967. "Mayor and Moses Clash in Park; Argue Over
    Permanency of Site." *The New York Times*. June 22.
Jacobs, Jane. 1961. *The Death and Life of Great American Cities*. Vintage
    Books, NY.
Kaplan, Samuel. 1965. "U.S. Will Promote Little Urban Parks, Udall Says
    Here" *New York Times*. June 8.
Kayden, Jerold S. 2000. The Department of City Planning of the City of
    New York, and the Municipal Art Society of New York. *Privately
    Owned Public Space: The New York City Experience*. New York, NY:
    John Wiley & Sons, Inc.
Low, Setha. 2000. *On the Plaza: The Politics of Public Space and Culture*.
    Austin: University of Texas Press.
Low, Setha, Taplin, Dana, and Scheld, Suzanne. 2005. *Rethinking Urban
    Parks: Public Space and Cultural Diversity*. Austin: University of
    Texas Press.
Miller, Kristine F. 2007. *Design on the Public: The Private Lives of New
    York's Public Spaces*. Minneapolis and London: University of
    Minnesota Press.
Seymour, Whitney North. 1969. *An Introduction to Small Urban Spaces.
    Small Urban Spaces: The Philosophy, Design, Sociology and Politics
    of Vest-Pocket Parks and Other Small Urban Open Spaces*. New York:
    New York University Press.
Whyte, William H. 1980. *The Social Life of Small Urban Spaces*.
    Washington D.C: The Conservation Foundation.

PART 2:

PERSPECTIVES ON USER

CHAPTER FOUR

ENACTING THE SOCIO-MATERIAL: MATTER AND MEANING RECONFIGURED THROUGH DISABILITY EXPERIENCE

ANN HEYLIGHEN

Introduction

About ten years ago, I spent six months as a visiting researcher at the University of California, Berkeley, together with a colleague researcher from my home university. It was the second time I had visited the campus, and the first for my colleague. At home, he belongs to a group of people commonly considered as disabled—both legally, as evidenced by his disabled parking permits and the officially determined impairment percentages for his upper and lower limbs, and practically, as evidenced by the arrangements he has to make on a daily basis to navigate the built environment. Yet, once on the Berkeley campus, his disability seemed to disappear to some extent. Simple features of the environment like abundant disabled-parking spaces close to the entrance of each university building, or clear signage indicating the shortest route to the elevator, eliminated the need for making practical arrangements. When my colleague had a meeting or lecture in a building he had not visited before, he did not have to worry whether or not he would be able to get there, or inspect the route a day in advance, as he tends to do at home. On the Berkeley campus, my colleague, although still legally disabled, became much less practically disabled. The disabled parking spaces, elevators, and signage connected him in a new way with able-bodied researchers, students, etc. Somehow, this campus thus grouped people differently than the campus of our home university did. And yet, in my previous visit, I had not noticed anything special about it. This made me realize that my understanding of the built environment was very limited, even though I had been studying and conducting research about architecture for several years.

In this chapter I consider the experience of being or becoming disabled—henceforth referred to as disability experience—a resource for expanding our understanding of space in general, and for addressing the idea of the social in space in particular. Conceptions of disability have shifted considerably over the past decades, and the explorations are still ongoing, both within and beyond the field of disability studies. Nonetheless in this chapter I hope to build on this shift to explore not so much what architecture can bring to disability studies, but rather how disability experience can inform or challenge prevailing ways of understanding and designing architecture. After outlining the shift that has taken place in thinking about disability, I will, unravel how the material and social together configure everyday experiences and practices of disabled people. In doing so, I will attempt, in line with the work of Ingunn Moser (2005, 689), to "articulate and make visible and present the actually existing alternatives." As I will demonstrate, the alternative socio-material configurations following disability experience are not *outside of* the social, they just differently reassemble the social. Therefore, I argue in this chapter that the social is not apart from or external to either person or built environment, but enacted in the relation between both.

Becoming disabled

Traditional conceptions of disability tend to consider it as an individual, physiological, disorder. The disorder is situated in a person's body and the solution to the problem caused by it lies in a treatment or cure to restore the body's function. These individual and medical models of disability "perceive and classify disability in terms of a meta-narrative of deviance, lack and tragedy, and assume it to be logically separate from and inferior to 'normalcy'" (Corker and Shakespeare 2002, 2). Moreover, in these models, disability is defined by means of measurable criteria and arbitrary thresholds. For instance, in the *International statistical classification of diseases, injuries and causes of death*, the World Health Organization (WHO 1993) defines disability based on measurable aspects of the human body. Once measured, a threshold can be chosen regarding this specific aspect's contribution to the person being disabled.[1]

During the past decades, however, these traditional conceptions of disability have been challenged. Critiques of the individual and medical models place the body in its socio-material context and stress the role of environmental determinants in performing day-to-day activities and fulfilling social roles (Fougeyrollas 1995). The social model of disability therefore makes a conceptual distinction between disability and impairment. It considers disability as socially constructed on top of impairment (Corker and Shakespeare 2002), and explains its changing character through the organisation of the society in which it is found (Butler and Bowlby 1997),[2] including the spaces and technologies in which this organization takes shape.

This move to embrace disability as a social issue can be traced to the *UN Convention on the Rights of Persons with Disabilities* (2006) and the WHO's (2001) *International Classification of Functioning, Disability and Health* (ICF). The latter recognizes disability as a complex phenomenon reflecting the interplay between features of a person's body and features of the environment and society in which that person lives. It makes a distinction between an "impairment" (a problem in a body function or structure), an "activity limitation" (a difficulty encountered in executing a task), and a "participation restriction" (a problem experienced in involvement in life situations). In the words of the WHO (2002),

> [disability] is not something that only happens to a minority of humanity. The ICF thus 'mainstreams' the experience of disability and recognizes it as a universal human experience (3).

While the social model of disability is recognized as a major step forward in our understanding of disability, several authors have questioned the comprehensive nature of a model that fails to recognize the importance of individuals' embodied experiences and multiple identities, including those of impairment, in their lives (Butler and Bowlby 1997, 413). Some authors believe that, even though society creates the greater obstacles to disabled-people's independence, limitations placed on the functioning of the body by impairment have an undeniable role to play in the problems they face (Shakespeare 1996). Others criticize that little attention is paid to the differences of both impairments and the social, economic, and political factors such as gender, race, class, and sexuality (Butler and Bowlby 1997, 413). Ingunn Moser (2005) points out that, in the social model of disability, an image is created of a very powerful, normalizing discourse, and that the problematic inference is drawn that this discourse works to order society in a *unified* and *coherent* way. This unified ordering is assumed to apply also to the built environment, *i.e.* the spaces in which social life occurs.

Without ignoring these critiques, in this chapter I acknowledge and build on the shift the social model has initiated in our understanding of disability by recognizing the two-way relationship between a disabled person and his or her socio-material environment (Butler and Bowlby 1997, Gray, Gould and Bickenbach 2003), while at the same time recognizing the role played by the embodied experience of impairment in disabled-people's lives. Conceiving disability not as an attribute—either of a person or environment—but as an *effect* implies a shift from static to dynamic understanding: "disabled is not something one *is*, but something one *becomes*" (Moser 2005, 669). If we are to address the social in the built environment, the experience of becoming disabled may offer us particularly interesting insights.

Designing space

Besides contributing to the discussion about the social in the built environment, the experience of becoming disabled is also relevant to design practice. The recognition of the two-way relationship between a disabled person and his or her environment has led to the development of design approaches like Universal Design (Mace 1985), Design for All, and Inclusive Design (Clarkson *et al.* 2003). The latter, for instance, denotes "a general approach to designing in which designers ensure that their products and services address the needs of the widest possible audience, irrespective of age or ability" (Design Council 2009).

These design approaches focus on issues of social inclusion in that they aim at "designing environments that facilitate people's emancipation from artefacts that restrict or prevent their ease of mobility and access" (Imrie 2012, 876). Despite their appearance, however, they also have

vestiges of a medical model underpinning its value-based, and clinical and physiological rather than cultural (social) criteria appear to be defining and shaping its design mentalities and approaches (874).

In line with Newton D'Souza (2004) and Jim Tobias (2003), Rob Imrie (2012) points at the positivist predisposal of these approaches towards the propagation of universal principles, their normative prescription of rules defining what good design is or ought to be, and their instrumental and pragmatic character in seeking to influence the usefulness or utility of designed artifacts. As such, they seem to fit into a "problem-solving paradigm", whereby "the design problem is posited as an objective entity that, through the development of applications and standards, will result in the correct outcomes" (876).

In reality, design outcomes are interpreted and experienced by people in ways that may considerably differ from the designers' intentions (Crilly, Maier and Clarkson 2008). This holds true in particular for the experience of disabled people (Heylighen 2008): through their bodily interaction with the designed environment, I will demonstrate, they can detect obstacles or appreciate qualities that designers may not be attuned to. In this respect, designers may have much to learn from disabled people about differences between design intentions and people's experiences, and in particular about how the way space is designed relates to the way the social is enacted.

In what follows, I therefore explore how people living with various impairments experience and relate to the built environment, in order to make visible alternatives for prevailing ways of understanding the material and the social. In doing so, my attention goes, in particular, to boundaries within and between the socio-material. In this way, I reconsider how the social—such as able-bodied normativity inscribed in the built environment—is not some sphere *behind* or *underlying* the material (*i.e.,* the built environment), but is enacted *within* and *through* a person's experience of and interaction with it (Ingold 2000; Latour 2005).

Methods and material

In reconsidering the social in the built environment, I draw on a range of empirical data collected in studying the spatial experience of people living with particular impairments or conditions. This study was conducted within the context of a project entitled "Architectural design In Dialogue with disAbility" (AIDA) and related projects for which AIDA formed the framework.[3] These projects took place under my supervision at the Department of Architecture at the University of Leuven, Belgium. Researchers involved in collecting the data drawn on in this chapter are Stijn Baumers, Jasmien Herssens, Greg Nijs, Megan Strickfaden, Iris Van Steenwinkel, and Peter-Willem Vermeersch. While the data collected in the context of these projects have already been analyzed separately in response to the respective aim of each project, I analyze them collectively here in order to reconsider the relationship between the social and the material in the built environment.

The research studies the spatial experiences of people born blind or those who had lost their sight, people with difficulty walking or using a wheelchair, people diagnosed on the autism spectrum, and those living with dementia. The spatial experience of these people was studied in different ways, resulting in a variety of written, interview, and observational data. The data include autobiographies and other writings by people who lost their sight (Hull 1992, 2001), were diagnosed on the autism spectrum (Baumers and Heylighen 2010), or are living with dementia (Van Steenwinkel et al. 2012, Van Steenwinkel et al. 2014).

These were selected based on the dual condition of having been written (1) by people themselves and (2) about experiences of their own lives. The written reflections on these experiences are used as a source to analyze how they interpret and deal with the built environment. A second data set covers semi-structured interviews with, and videos of guided tours by, twenty-two blind adults (seven women, fifteen men) in their home environment (Herssens and Heylighen 2010), recruited through a forum for blind people, the regional association for the blind, the bimonthly journal of the Association of People with a Visual Impairment, and schools for the blind. A third data set includes interviews with, and documents of projects designed by, an architect who lost his sight (Vermeersch and Heylighen 2012; Vermeersch 2013). And finally I draw upon notes and photos made during participation in visits to university buildings by students and staff living with various impairments in collaboration with architecture students (Heylighen 2012). During these visits, each disabled student or staff member was accompanied by two architecture students who attended an elective course on inclusive design.

Out of these data, the examples referred to in this chapter have been selected because they are indicative of how disabled people's experience may expand our understanding of space and the role of the social therein, and not because they are typical of the participants or representative of a so-called special population.

Matter and meaning reconfigured through disability experience

The shift in understanding disability has triggered studies of the ways in which people become disabled, from different backgrounds and with various degrees of attention of the role of the built environment therein. Drawing on interview data with visually impaired people, Ruth Butler and Sophia Bowlby (1997) investigate how social attitudes towards disabled people affect their ability to move freely within public spaces. Butler and Bowlby point out that there may be a link between the limitations imposed by the material/physical environment and those imposed by the social environment. For instance,

a physical environment which enables the presence of disabled people in space may stimulate positive social attitudes towards people with bodily impairments and more positive attitudes should encourage more positive physical planning (412).

Nevertheless, their study focuses on social attitudes towards disabled people in public space, such as overprotective attitudes or the assumption that physical impairment implies a lack of intelligence. David Gray et al. (2003) interviewed focus groups of people with mobility impairments, their significant others, and healthcare and built-environment professionals to explore views on barriers and facilitators to disabled people's full participation in major life activities. All groups agreed that social institutions and attitudes can be important barriers to participation, yet they differed in their assessment of the role of the built environment. While the built environment professionals ranked it more frequently as a facilitator than a barrier, the other groups found it to be a very significant barrier to participation. Gray et al. conclude that designers and other people involved in construction may learn from disabled people.

In this chapter I hope to contribute to this learning by collectively analyzing the data outlined above. These data provide a nuanced insight in the perspective of disabled people. However, as I will demonstrate, they also reveal alternatives for prevailing ways of understanding the material and the social, particularly with regard to boundaries within and between them—boundaries within the material, boundaries between the material and the body, and boundaries within groups of people. Socio-material configurations that tend to be taken for granted are questioned from the perspective of disabled people; the boundaries within them are reshuffled, become blurred or are entirely disregarded. On the other hand, their perspective reveals boundaries within socio-material configurations that are not generally considered as such.

Boundaries within the material environment

In architecture, space is typically understood as defined by the sensory qualities of the objects making up its boundaries (Heynen 2004). The perspective of disabled people contributes to a much more nuanced understanding of these boundaries, and of the space they define.

In his book *Architecture: Form, Space and Order*, Francis Ching (1979) clearly distinguishes between horizontal elements and vertical elements defining space. The former include base planes and overhead planes, the latter both linear elements and vertical planes. In architectural design, the building elements that define space (floors, ceilings, walls, etc.) indeed are typically considered and conceived as separate elements; they are often made of different materials and at times even constructed by different contractors.

Some people who are blind, however, seem to experience these different building elements as a whole. Blind people who showed a researcher around in their house, tended to refer to ceilings as walls, which could suggest that they experience spatial boundaries more as a whole (Herssens and Heylighen 2010). Moreover, they seemed to consider furniture as part of that whole, suggesting that they do not distinguish between fixed building elements (*e.g.*, a wall) and movable objects (*e.g.*, a table or chair).

Blind people's perspective also reveals boundaries that sighted people may not generally consider as such. For instance, John Hull (1992), who writes about when he became blind, contends that he loves thunder. Because it puts a ceiling on his world, it prevents him from wandering in infinity that is frightening and disorientating. Hull (2001) compares the role of sound with "turning on the light" for sighted people. Sounds can make the environment *audible*:

> the first thing I do is get out my little portable radio set, which I carry with me almost always. And the first object I come to, [...] I lay my little radio down and I turn it on. That is my way of turning on the light (2001).

This also relates to Hull's great liking for rain, which allows him to perceive different silent objects from a distance. He hears the rain against the windows, but also in the driveway, on the bushes, on the street. The rain elicits slightly different sounds when it his different things in the environment (Hull 1992).

Besides sound, a difference in temperature can reveal spatial boundaries. Carlos Mourão Pereira—a Portuguese architect who lost his sight—points out that, in the absence of sight, the part of a room that is lit by sunlight is an entirely different space than the part in the shadow (Fig. 4-1) because the warmth of the sun provides a completely different experience to the sense of touch (Vermeersch and Heylighen 2012). The difference in temperature introduces a boundary that partitions the visually coherent room into two different spaces.

That spatial boundaries are not always as discrete as the space/object boundary, as Pereira teaches us, has important implications for how space is understood. Rather than the void between or containing objects, space in itself is also a filled entity with its own sensory qualities that can be designed deliberately (Vermeersch 2013). In fact, multiple sensory spaces can be said to interact in this entity.

Fig. 4-1. In the absence of sight, the part of the room lit by sunlight is a different space than the part in the shadow because of temperature differences. Source: Rob Stevens.

Striking in this respect is that Pereira, after becoming blind, extended the range of materials used in designing built environments by including water and air. He designed a series of bathing facilities that offer the exceptional multi-sensory experience of swimming in the sea to swimmers and waders of all ages and abilities. One of these facilities is a sea bathing facility which converts the concrete structure of redundant fisheries into basins for swimming and engaging with sea life (Fig. 4-2). Receptacles for various marine species offer a collage of colours, textures and concavities within reach. In this project, the water that fills up the basins is as much part of the architecture and the experience as the concrete used to shape the basins (Vermeersch and Heylighen 2012). For Pereira, the experience of the space would change considerably if water was omitted; by consequence it becomes as much a building material as, say, concrete. Similarly, he describes how the placement of a wall on the beach can shape the wind, and change a person's experience of it: different orientations of the wall relative to the direction of the wind can change its effect from almost unnoticeable when aligned to very disruptive when transversed.

Fig. 4-2. Sea bathing facility, Lourinhã (Portugal), proposal and section. Source: Carlos Mourão Pereira.

Pereira points out that both water and air are very special building materials in that they allow a person to be "involved in the material" (Vermeersch and Heylighen 2012, 399). Water and wind encompass the body and transmit their motion and temperature to the skin (Vermeersch 2013). During high tide, for instance, one can feel the motion of the waves throughout the main basin. During low tide, by contrast, the whole basin is cut off from the sea and provides a calm experience. As such, Pereira's extension of building materials with water and air brings us to a next set of boundaries: those between the material and the body.

Boundaries between the material environment and the body

Butler and Bowlby (1997, 419) observed that disabled people's self-conception cannot be isolated from social discourses as it is formed in social interactions. The data collected on the spatial experience of people with autism and people with dementia suggest that this observation could be extended so as to include the role of the material. Because, on the one hand, for some people, material objects and spaces seem to play an important role in forming or holding on to their self-conception; on the other hand, in some circumstances, other people's bodies are considered—and thus likely interacted with—as inanimate objects.

Most of us rarely seem to bother about the boundary between the material environment and our body; convinced that this boundary is clear, we hardly give it a moment's thought. Some people diagnosed on the autism spectrum, however, do linger over and question the boundary between the material environment and their bodies. One person with autism, for instance, describes his fear of remaining seated on a chair for too long, because it ends up blurring the difference between the chair and his body (Baumers and Heylighen 2010):

> At a certain moment, the interface of the chair is as warm as my body temperature, and at that moment I have lost the boundary between me and that chair (Landschip and Modderman 2004).

The testimony of this *auti*-biographer illustrates how his self-conception changes through his bodily interaction with a chair, and so cannot be isolated from the material environment.

However, boundaries between the material environment and the body are challenged not only from the perspective of people with autism. A similar experience is described by woman with early on-set dementia who writes poems about her life with the disease (Van Steenwinkel et al. 2014). In these poems and in interviews with a researcher, she talks about mist, almost literally, to indicate that it tends to lead her to lose contact with her environment. Sometimes the mist seems to come so close that she nearly loses the notion of her own body and feels like a dust particle that can fly away any moment. Interestingly, her way of trying to keep contact with her environment, and thus with herself, is by claiming certain places and objects in the house as her own: she has *her* cupboard in the kitchen, *her* seat at the dining table, and *her* armchair in the living room. Moreover, these places are arranged such that she has her belongings "ready to hand"—in her cupboard her corn flakes, her water glass, her wine glass, and her jar are always put in the same place, as are her blanks, her basket, her coffee table, her books, her drinks, and her candy next to the armchair. By regrouping places and objects, and strengthening her connection with them, it is as if she tries to hold on to herself, to maintain her self-conception.

In the examples described above, the boundary between the material environment and the body, between object and subject is being questioned and reshuffled. At times, however, the boundary between objects and subjects may be entirely *disregarded*. Several stories written by people with autism suggest that, for them, there is no essential difference between material objects and other people's bodies. One *auti*-biographer describes that human bodies or faces can be seen as physical entities in space (Baumers and Heylighen 2010): "Those faces were as lacking in content as furniture, and I thought that, just like furniture, they belonged in the rooms I saw them in." Consequently, "sitting on the lap of a stranger, on the lap of an empty face, hadn't been any more difficult than sitting on an armchair" (Gerland 1996). Other *auti*-biographers note the same essential similarity between people and objects: "When I'm not concentrating on people, they just look like shapes, like furniture and trees are shapes" (Rand 1997). It seems as if in the experience of these authors, inanimate objects and other people's bodies are regrouped to constitute a single category.

Boundaries between groups of people

Last but certainly not least, disabled people's perspective on the built environment highlights boundaries between groups of people, boundaries that able-bodied people may not always be aware of. I started this chapter by illustrating how features of a university campus may connect and group people in particular ways. Similar examples can be found in the empirical data analysed here.

A first example came to the fore during visits to buildings on the KU Leuven campus in collaboration with disabled students and staff. During these visits, a staff member using a wheelchair pointed at a social boundary that arises when in an auditorium: the first row of seats starts on a step. This one element in the spatial configuration implies that people using a wheelchair always have to sit alone in front of all other people, literally raising a boundary between both groups. This boundary could be easily avoided in this case, by starting the first row of seats on the ground level, and foreseeing a few empty spots or removable seats, so that wheelchair users can easily fit in. When an auditorium is not completely filled, however, the first rows often remain empty. As a consequence, often people using a wheelchair still end up sitting all alone in the front, even when seats are available on the ground level. In a familiar context, chances are that at least someone will move to the front. Yet, in new situations, say the first day at university, this may be more problematic. Even better would therefore be to make an entrance in the middle of the auditorium and foresee a number of places for wheelchair users.

This simple example about the spatial configuration of seats in an auditorium suggests that, in the experience of this wheelchair user, the social is not some sphere behind or underlying the material environment, but is enacted in and through it: just because of the spatial configuration of the seats, he may quickly end up in a situation of social isolation. The spatial configuration of the seats enacts the social in the sense that it regroups people according to their place in the auditorium: it disconnects wheelchair users from the other people in the audience, and makes them feel part of a separate group, or not part of a group at all.

What holds for spatial configuration also seems to hold for sensory aspects of the built environment, such as sound. The latter was brought to our attention by Carlos Pereira, in explaining his design of a river-bathing facility in Switzerland. Originally, he had imagined locating the bathing facility very near to the falls present on site. Yet, eventually, he decided to change the location. Listening to tapes recorded near to, and far from, the waterfalls, he realized that in his first proposal, people would be unable to talk and listen: the sound of the falls would become too noisy for talking. For people who are blind, this would raise a boundary between them and other people as they risk losing their only way of communicating. In the context of swimming in a river, this is not only unpleasant, but may even become dangerous. Hence, Pereira decided to locate the bathing facility a little farther from the water falls, so that all swimmers and waders can communicate and not risk ending up in isolation.

Besides raising boundaries between people, the built environment may also obscure them. Striking in this respect is the remark of a student with autism who participated in a visit to the building accommodating the KU Leuven student services. During this visit, he uncovered, in a very direct way, problems that all of us all somehow feel, but never can point to so well: he opened every door with some hesitation, as its opaque surface did not show him whether or not the room behind was open to the public. For this student, the door obscured the boundary between himself and those in the room behind it. It was a mental threshold to overcome, without any hold that he was really allowed to take the next step. As an architecture student who accompanied him formulates it: "Before this visit, we [the architecture students who accompanied the student with autism] would never have spent so much attention to mental thresholds."

The quote of this architecture student draws our attention to another boundary between groups of people. It illustrates how visiting a building together with disabled people becomes a learning situation for architecture students, in which they learn to perceive the built environment in novel ways, thus blurring the boundary between (future) architects and non-architects, between experts and laypeople. This has important implications for design practice and education.

Implications for design practice and education

In his book *Design Meets Disability*, Graham Pullin (2009) points out:

Many designers [...] perceive disability in terms of approaching legislation that threatens to compromise their creativity, rather than as a source of fresh perspectives that could catalyze new directions and enrich the whole of their work.

This holds true especially for designers in architecture, where disability experience still is rarely considered a valuable resource for design. Building legislation considers accessibility of buildings as something taken care of by professional experts, instead of something to which people are attached or exposed. As a result, disabled people are left as seemingly incapable of joining the dialogue because they are supposedly no experts in the field. Their experiential knowledge often stays unaccounted for.

The examples presented in this chapter, however, make it clear that disabled people's experiential knowledge can be articulated and shared with others, and that their knowledge may considerably change the design of places. Here, the work of Carlos Pereira may initially come to mind, yet other examples, such as the spatial configuration of seats in an auditorium, are also relevant in this respect. In general, disabled people's perspective may make designers more aware of the various types of boundaries they are not aware of, and invite them to perceive socio-material configurations in novel ways. By reshuffling these boundaries, the alternative socio-material configurations brought out in this chapter reveal the relativity of prevailing frames of reference in design. These configurations invite designers to perceive the socio-material environment—and the role of their own expertise therein—in novel ways, and to reconsider their methods of designing accordingly. As such, the analysis reported in this chapter tells us at least as much about design practice as about disability experience.

With regard to design education, the situation is somewhat more nuanced. In the late 1980s, disability was acknowledged as a valuable resource for education by University of California, Berkeley Professor Raymond Lifchez (1987), who developed a curricular experiment by inviting physically-disabled consultants to participate in the education of fledgling architecture students. Only by devising curricula that encourage students to view buildings through the eyes of their clients, he argued, will the next generation of designers gain the necessary understanding of human variability and complexity. The building visits with disabled people drawn upon in this chapter demonstrate that Lifchez's ideas are still relevant today—even though their being part of an elective course means that only a relatively small number of architecture students are confronted by with them.

Conclusion

Drawing on a range of empirical data, I have shown in this chapter how, in disabled people's experience of, and interaction with, space, boundaries are being reshuffled, revealed or disregarded: boundaries within the material environment, between the material environment and the body, and between groups of people. People who are blind, for instance, remind us that, because we focus on the visual, we forget to pay attention to non-visual qualities of the built environment (temperature, sound, air, etc.) and to their potential to subdivide spaces. The perspective of people with autism or dementia highlights the role of the material in forming and maintaining one's self-conception. And building visits with wheelchair users or people with autism uncover how features of the material environment may connect, disconnect and regroup people in various ways. In addressing the question of the social, the examples presented in this chapter thus suggest that the social is not apart from, or external to, either person or built environment, but enacted in the relation between both.

In addition, these examples illustrate that acknowledging the role of the embodied experience of impairment in disabled people's lives does not necessarily mean the need to return to the view that disability is caused by individual impairment (Butler and Bowlby 1997, 413). On the contrary, in unravelling disabled people's experiences, I have illustrated not only *that* one becomes disabled as a result of the interplay between features of one's body and features of the environment, but also *how* the material figures in this becoming. At the same time, however, I hope to have demonstrated that the boundary between disabled and able-bodied people is but one of several boundaries about which designers can learn from disability experience.

Acknowledgements

This research has received funding from the European Research Council under the European Community's Seventh Framework Programme (FP7/2007-2013)/ERC grant agreements n° 201673 and n° 335002; Research Foundation-Flanders (FWO); Agency for Innovation by Science & Technology (IWT-Vlaanderen) and Research Fund KU Leuven.

Thanks to all who contributed to this paper: Stijn Baumers, Jasmien Herssens, Greg Nijs, Megan Strickfaden, Iris Van Steenwinkel, Peter-Willem Vermeersch. Special thanks to everyone who participated in the video ethnography, interviews, and/or building visits for sharing their time and insights, and to the editors for their comments on earlier versions of this chapter.

References

Baumers, Stijn, and Ann Heylighen. 2010. "Harnessing Different Dimensions of Space. The Built Environment in Auti-Biographies." In *Designing Inclusive Interactions*, edited by Patrick Langdon, P. John Clarkson, and Peter Robinson, 13–23. London: Springer-Verlag.

Butler, Ruth, and Sophia Bowlby. 1997. "Bodies and spaces: an exploration of disabled people's experiences of public space." *Environmental and planning D: Society and Space* 15:441–433.

Ching, Francis D.K. 1979. *Architecture: Form, Space & Order*. New York: Van Nostrand Reinold.

Clarkson, P. John, Coleman, Roger, Keates, Simeon, and Cherie Lebbon, ed. 2003. *Inclusive Design: design for the whole population*. London: Springer-Verlag.

Corker, Mairian, and Tom Shakespeare. 2002. "Mapping the terrain." In *Disability/Postmodernity: Embodying Disability Theory*, edited by Mairian Corker and Tom Shakespeare, 1–17. London: Bloomsbury Academic.

Crilly, Nathan, Anja M. Maier, and P. John Clarkson. 2008. "Representing Artefacts as Media." *International Journal of Design* 2(3):15–27.

Design Council. 2009. Inclusive design education resource. Accessed August 13, 2014.
http://www.designcouncil.info/inclusivedesignresource/

D'Souza, Newton. 2004. "Is universal design a critical theory?" In *Designing a more inclusive world*, edited by Simeon Keates, P. John Clarkson, Patrick Langdon, and Peter Robinson, 3–10. London: Springer-Verlag.

Fougeyrollas, Patrick. 1995. "Documenting environmental factors for preventing the handicap creation process: Quebec contributions relating to ICIDH and social participation of people with functional differences." *Disability and Rehabilitation* 17(3–4):145–153.

Gerland, Gunilla. 1996. *A Real Person. Life on the outside*. London: Souvenir Press.

Gray, David B., Mary Gould, and Jerome E. Bickenbach. 2003. "Environmental barriers and disability." *Journal of Architectural and Planning Research* 20(1):29–37.

Herssens, Jasmien, and Ann Heylighen. 2010. "Blind Body Language." In *Proceedings of the 5th Cambridge Workshop on Universal Access and Assistive Technology*, edited by P. John Clarkson, Patrick Langdon, and Peter Robinson, 109–118. Cambridge: University of Cambridge.

Heylighen, Ann. 2008. "Sustainable and inclusive design: a matter of knowledge?" *Local Environment* 13(6):531–540.

Heylighen, Ann. 2012. "Inclusive Built Heritage as a Matter of Concern: A Field Experiment." In *Designing Inclusive Systems*, edited by Patrick Langdon, P. John Clarkson, Peter Robinson, Jonathan Lazar, and Ann Heylighen, 207–216. London: Springer-Verlag.

Heynen, Hilde. 2004. De ontdekking van de ruimte. [The discovery of the space.] In *Dat is architectuur, sleutelteksten uit de twintigste eeuw* [That is architecture, key texts of the twentieth century], edited by Hilde Heynen, André Loeckx, Lieven De Cauter, en Karina Van Herck, 782–789. Rotterdam: nai010 uitgevers.

Hull, John. 1992. *Touching the rock: An Experience of Blindness*. New York: Vintage Books.

—. 2001. "Sound: An Enrichment or State, *Soundscape*." *The Journal of Acoustic Ecology* 2(1):10–15.

Ingold, Tim. 2000. *The perception of the environment: Essays on livelihood, dwelling and skill*. London: Routledge.

Imrie, Rob. 2012. "Universalism, universal design and equitable access to the built environment." *Disability & Rehabilitation* 34(10):873–82.

Landschip, and Loes Modderman. 2004. *Dubbelklik: autisme bevraagd en beschreven*. Berchem: EPO.

Latour, Bruno. 2005. *Reassembling the social. An introduction to Actor-Network Theory*. Oxford: Oxford University Press.

Lifchez, Raymond. 1987. *Rethinking Architecture: Design Students and Physically Disabled People*. Berkeley: University of California press.

Mace, Ron. 1985. "Universal Design, Barrier free environments for everyone." *Designers West*. Los Angeles.

Moser, Ingunn. 2005. "On Becoming Disabled and Articulating Alternatives." *Cultural Studies* 19(6):667–700.

Pullin, Graham. 2009. *Design meets disability*. Cambridge: The MIT Press.

Rand, Brad. 1997. "How to Understand People who are Different." Accessed August 11, 2014. http://www.autism-pdd.net/brad.htm.

Shakespeare, Tom. 1996. "Disability, identity, and difference." In *Exploring the Divide: Illness and Disability*, edited by Colin Barnes, and Geof Mercer, 94–113. Leeds: The Disability Press.

Tobias, Jim. 2003. "Universal design: is it really about design?" *Information Technology and Disabilities* 9(2).

UN. 2006. *Convention on the rights of persons with disabilities*. United Nations.

Van Steenwinkel, Iris, Chantal Van Audenhove, and Ann Heylighen. 2012. "Spatial clues for orientation: Architectural design meets people with dementia." In *Designing inclusive systems*, edited by Patrick Langdon, P. John Clarkson, Peter Robinson, Jonathan Lazar, and Ann Heylighen, 227–36. London: Springer-Verlag.

Van Steenwinkel, Iris, Chantal Van Audenhove, and Ann Heylighen. 2014. "Mary's little worlds. Changing person-space relationships when living with dementia." *Qualitative health research* 24(8):1023–32.

Vermeersch, Peter-Willem, and Ann Heylighen. 2012. "Blindness and multi-sensoriality in architecture. The case of Carlos Mourão Pereira." In *The place of research, the research of place*, edited by Richard L. Hayes, and Virginia Ebbert, 393–400. Architectural Research Centers Consortium (ARCC).

Vermeersch, Peter-Willem. 2013. "Less vision, more senses. Towards a more multisensory design approach in architecture." PhD diss. University of Leuven (KU Leuven), 256 p.

WHO. 1993. *International statistical classification of diseases, injuries and causes of death, tenth revision*. Geneva: World Health Organization.

—. 2001. *International Classification of Functioning, Disability and Health: ICF*. Geneva: World Health Organization.

—. 2002. *Towards a Common Language for Functioning, Disability and Health: ICF*. Geneva: World Health Organization.

Notes

[1] In the case of visual impairment, for instance, this is done by measuring the visual acuity and the field of vision (WHO, 1993). Visual acuity indicates how well a person can distinguish an object and is measured in terms of distance ratio. Having a visual acuity of 1/20 means that you have to stand at 1 meter to recognize an object a 'normal' person can see at a distance of 20 meters. The field of vision is measured in terms of angles. When reaching forward with your arms and gradually opening them up until they become invisible, the field of vision is the resulting angle between your arms. A 'normal' monocular visual field typically spans 160°.

Using these two measurable aspects, the WHO defines visual impairment as having a visual acuity of less than 3/10, and blindness as having a visual acuity of less than 1/20 and/or a field of vision of less than 10°.

[2] Butler and Bowlby (1997, p. 415) point out that the impairment-disability dichotomy has similarities with the sex-gender dichotomy, in that both posit a clear distinction between biological capabilities and socially produced characteristics and inequalities. Both disability campaigners and feminists "have to concern themselves with the tension between the recognition that much of our experience of the body is socially constructed and our individual experiences of the physicality of our bodies and their strengths and limitations."

[3] The AIDA project was supported by a Starting Grant of the European Research Council (ERC grant agreement n° 201673). The related projects received support from the Research Foundation Flanders (FWO), the Agency for Innovation by Science and Technology (IWT), and KU Leuven Research Fund.

CHAPTER FIVE

THE ALGORITHMIC VS. THE MESSY: USER RESEARCH IN ARCHITECTURAL PRACTICE

EMILY GOLEMBIEWSKI

At its core, the architectural program is a quantification of spatial requirements. It is created in the early stage of an architectural project and it provisionally defines the type, size and quantity of spaces within the building. The program can be for a new building or for a remodel of an existing building, and it is typically calculated in usable square meters or usable square footage, with flexibility to plan for contingencies. Historically, programming was often done by the architect, as part of the pre-design or programming stage. It was focused on outlining requirements for the project, but also on mitigating risk for the architect. The dominant method for this traditional model of programming was an exercise in questionnaires and spreadsheets—balancing columns of usable square footage and core in order to meet a gross square footage target which is predetermined by space, budget, or form. This is what we might call the traditional approach to programming, and it is still the dominant mode in architectural practice.

But the limits of traditional programming have been the topic of debate in a small body of work reaching back nearly fifty years. The discourse complicates and empowers the notion of the program, as seen in John Summerson's 1966 lecture "The Case for a Theory of Modern Architecture," where Summerson describes the architectural program as "the description of the spatial dimensions, spatial relationships, and other physical conditions required for the convenient performance of specific functions."

Summerson's short description does two important things. First, it places the emphasis not just on the spaces themselves but on the functions performed within the space—the work, the activity, the entertainment, and the interaction. This inverts the balance of power between spaces and the functions within them to the point where spaces might begin to be seen as developed in the service of, or as a container for, functions and activities. Secondly, Summerson's description mentions spatial relationships. The inclusion of spatial relationships opens the door to a greater degree of complexity in planning a building, and it also expands the importance of the program by giving the program a greater role of authorship, and by expanding its reach into later phases of design. If a program describes spatial relationships, the conceptual design or schematic design phases will likely be more tied to the program than if the program simply listed those spaces, and left it to the architect to place those spaces. These two points are intricately related, because spatial relationships are often derived in part from functional drivers.

While Summerson's work begins to untangle the way in which program negotiates functional components and spatial expression, the work of Bernard Tschumi and Rem Koolhaas has created a forum around these issues. In the introduction to the 2010 issue of Praxis, which was devoted to the concept of Programming (Praxis 8), Amanda Reeser Lawrence and Ashley Shafer contextualize the early projects of Rem Koolhaas and Bernard Tschumi and their specific focus on programming as an approach "liberated from functionalism." In this case, functionalism refers to a quotidian or utilitarian approach to design. This is distinct from Summerson's outline of function as the human activity within spaces.

According to the Praxis article, Koolhaas and Tschumi "recast program's parameters to include multiple configurations of spaces, and reciprocally, proposed the possibility that a given form or space could house any number of programs." The authors go on to say that it is through these projects that program is transformed "from a spatially....determinant instrument to an indeterminate one, reintroducing program as a generative tool." This idea of program as a generative tool is key to understanding Koolhaas and Tschumi's work—and to understanding how new methods of programming have grown within architectural practice.

Rem Koolhaas's Delirious New York (1997) and Bernard Tschumi's Manhattan Transcripts (1994) outline a model for creating layers of program informed by a matrix of potential user variables. Bernard Tschumi's work can also be seen in practice. His projects such as Parc de la Villette and Le Fresnoy Art Center layer programs to create a series of possible user options. Tschumi describes the Le Fresnoy Art Center layers as a method to "accelerate the probability of chance-events by combining diverse elements... juxtaposing great roof, school /research laboratory and the old Fresnoy (into a) place of spectacle." Koolhaas's Seattle Public

Library also utilizes programmatic strips described in his earlier conceptual work.

The exciting idea of multiple programs—and of program as a generative tool—extends the influence of program even further than Summerson's work suggests, but it also complicates the practice of programming: the collection of data and the documentation of multiple programs in a format which traditionally has been driven by linear spreadsheets.

If programming as it is most traditionally practiced is a documentation of spatial requirements and allocations, then an alternate school of thinking positions programming, in contrast, as a nuanced negotiation which strategically outlines the vision and ambition for the overall project. It employs user research methods to identify needs and project drivers, which may be organizational, financial, functional, or cultural in nature. It weighs scenarios and options against these drivers, and unifies the client around the shared vision for the project.

While Summerson, Koolhaas, and Tschumi make a compelling case for a more nuanced and thoughtful approach to programming, the practice of this new breed of programming is largely located in big architectural firms. Most large architectural firms have small strategy groups (as it is called in practice) that practice a more rigorous and involved approach to programming, although the approach varies widely. One of the first big architectural firms to take this on was Hellmuth, Obata + Kassabaum's Advance Strategies consulting group, which includes leadership acquired from famous Texas firm Caudill Rowlett Scott (CRS). HOK relies heavily on a process-driven approach to programming, including a five-step structure and a number of analytical frameworks. The approach has become second-nature to many professionals. It is taught in many architecture schools and is heavily used in architectural offices. It was described in 'Problem Seeking: An Architectural Programming Primer' written in 1977 by HOK leaders Willy Pena and Steve Parshall, currently in its fourth printing.

In contrast to this process-driven approached, Duffy, Eley, Giffone and Worthington established DEGW in 1973, which was a consultancy company focused on office planning and the people inhabiting those spaces. The founders came from the world of academia—Duffy holds a PhD from Princeton and has written several books—and applied research methods to the programming process. DEGW was similarly acquired by a large firm interested in this kind of practice, by Davis Langdon, whose firm was in turn acquired by AECOM.

While strategic programming may be a more recent development in programming, it is worth noting that it is not necessarily on the path to replace more traditional programming, mainly because strategic programming is a more complicated and involved process. Whether process-driven, research-driven or by some other approach, it typically takes more time and therefore is more expensive. It requires specialist practitioners, and those specialists are most often embedded in very large organizations. It also requires greater participation from the client organization including engaging major project stakeholders to do some difficult thinking about future aspirations and scenarios.

This chapter outlines a framework for strategic programming, particularly strategic programming which relies heavily on user research. In order to better define the benefits, challenges, and limits of this mode of programming, the author proposes three models for strategic programming: the algorithmic, the messy, and the hybrid. These three terms are specific to this article, and are intended to be useful for sorting out the various ways that programming can be leveraged in architectural projects. In order to clarify these three models, this chapter describes research methods employed, including standard practice tools like utilization studies and surveys, as well as original tools developed by the author, including a rapid prototyping tool and a roundtable workshop design. The client examples are drawn from the author's work experience and include large technology corporations, non-profits and museums.

The algorithmic

The algorithmic mode of programming is predictable, reliable and repeatable. This mode of programming relies on a large amount of quantitative data, which—as its name implies—is mathematically manipulated to guide the development of a set of recommendations. It also makes the trade-offs between the different sets of recommendations understandable by representing the implications numerically.

The Algorithmic Approach often begins with utilization studies and user surveys, and builds upon logical assumptions and mathematical formulas to produce programming recommendations from a pre-defined vocabulary of spaces. This approach is the closest to the traditional mode of programming in that it has a relatively linear process whereby a pre-defined set of inputs feed into a series of formulas to produce a pre-defined set of spaces. The Algorithmic Approach typically benefits large corporate clients in that it is scalable, replicable, and all their information can be benchmarked against other corporate clients who have undertaken similar efforts. The input data set is large and statistically relevant, so the results are defensible to internal and external audiences.

The following example illustrates the appeal and the limits of the algorithmic method. It is drawn from a large corporate client who was interested in creating and piloting a flexible work program. The client was a mature software company with 10,000 employees around the world. They were also in the process of reshaping their company's focus, and simultaneously making strategic lay-offs and acquisitions, which made headcount highly volatile. The flexible work program would allow employees to work "where they want, when they want" by decoupling individuals from assigned spaces. There were a variety of reasons for undertaking the program, which were identified in meetings with leadership; those included employee retention and productivity, but also sustainability and space savings, and managing the challenges of rolling out real estate in an environment with constant change.

The initial research phase was a massive effort that spanned multiple offices in three countries and on three continents. It included a time-utilization study (TUS), which rigorously measured the usage of spaces over the course of a number of weeks. The TUS is a standard tool, and it is accomplished by walking the floor regularly and taking occupancy information on offices, workstations, meeting rooms and other common spaces. The observer records whether the space is in use or not, and if it is in use, how many people are occupying it and what they are doing. All these data points are fields in a handheld computer and are pre-defined. In this case, the research effort was so involved that there were over 100,000 data points from the utilization study alone.

This observation data was balanced with a workplace performance survey (WPS), another standard tool which asks employees to describe their typical day, collaboration patterns, and other aspects of their work and workspace. This self-reported data provides information on perceived usage (how people think they use the space) and on preferences (how they think they would like to use the space). While surveys quickly gather a lot of information from the stakeholders and are very popular with clients as decision-making tools, most corporate populations are over-surveyed at this point. Moreover, the results are self-reported, and for a host of reasons are therefore not nearly as reliable as objectively-observed behaviors such as TUS.

But surveys are helpful for clearly outlining the perception of employees, and the gap between that perception and the observed reality. For example, in the case of this client, our observers recorded spaces as occupied only 37% of the time. This was an average across time, location, and type of space. So whether it was a private office in San Francisco at 10am, or a meeting room in Sydney at 3pm, on average we found that the space types were occupied only 37% of the time. By contrast, when we asked in the survey where people were spending time during the workday, we found that most people estimated their occupancy at close to 80%— double the observed average. This means that people's perception is that spaces are occupied twice as much as they actually are. This gap is not at all unusual: we find that when people are asked to estimate the amount of time they spend in spaces, their estimate is typically double that of actual use. This is true across clients, sectors, and geographies. So while the survey results may not be an accurate portrait of usage, they are helpful in indicating a significant perception gap on the part of users of spaces. And, because the new spatial recommendations will be built primarily on usage rather than preference, particularly with the algorithmic method, it is our job to expose that gap in order to work through the reason for the change to a mobility program.

While TUS and WPS are broad quantitative tools, we also used some qualitative research tactics, including leadership interviews and focus groups. Leadership interviews are one-on-one conversations about a leader's goals, challenges, team culture, and core work processes. Focus groups are interactive workshop sessions with twelve to twenty employees, which provide an opportunity for a high level of input from a representative sample of employees. Both efforts are high-touch efforts, meaning that the amount of face-to-face time is significant, but in return, these qualitative activities yield deep information about the team's work, culture, and preferences.

The combined research effort produced a series of findings that informed our recommendations. One of the key findings was that managers really wanted their employees to be on-site, and that most employees were coming to the office most days—they just were not at their desks very much. This led us to the conclusion that we needed to design an internal mobility program rather than an external mobility program. An internal mobility program is designed and marketed as something to help employees who may be working in a variety of places with a variety of people, but mostly within the building site. This is in contrast to external mobility, which would support working from cafes, airports, or homes. While the technology for the two programs may be similar, the intent of the program is radically different to users and managers. There was a significant concern internally about "sending people home" and a "loss of connection" among team members. Fortunately, the observation data supported the fact that their employees were coming to the office every day, although when they were in the office, they were at their desks only 37% of the time. When they were not at their desks, they were at colleagues' desks, in meeting rooms, the cafeteria, in transit, or to a smaller extent, off-site or working from home.

Once the internal mobility program was defined, we needed an implementation strategy. One of the key strategies of implementation was the introduction of an assessment survey, which was designed to help bridge the perception gap of perceived vs. actual space utilization.

The assessment survey was designed to categorize employees into one of three categories, resident, mobile, or super-mobile. The categorization method needed to go beyond simple space utilization, since there was such a strong perception gap among employees that allocation based on utilization statistics would likely be very poorly received. In other words, even though we had observation data about the occupancy levels of different groups, we could not assign spaces based on that information, since most groups thought their occupancy was double the observed number. It would be too disruptive to base assignment on usage alone, and it would be based on historical patterns, which is problematic.

Furthermore, the categories of resident, mobile, and super-mobile each described a work style, but also had spatial implications in terms of assigned or unassigned desks, which employees were aware of to a variety of levels. When designing the survey, we were aware that if given the choice, many employees would likely choose to be a resident, based either on personal preference or on their perception of how much time was spent at the desk.

But we also knew that while employees might not choose to be in the mobile or super-mobile category (for a variety of reasons), the majority of people were very well suited to working in that fashion, based on observed patterns of actual usage. And the mobile and super-mobile category better suited the organization. Mobility would achieve the business goals of collaboration, cross-fertilization of ideas and Best Place to Work status[1]. And in the long term, it would support real estate goals of using spaces more wisely and being able to more easily accommodate rapid growth, re-organizations, and acquisitions.

So we had a perception gap, but we also had an element of persuasion at play. And we had the challenge of differentiating between the initial survey, which gathered data, and the assessment survey, which yielded to categorizing employees.

The resulting assessment survey asked a series of questions that indirectly inquired about preference (what would one prefer?), behavior (how is one currently working?), and job function (what does one's job require?). We understood that each of these three aspects was equally important in forming a categorization which would enable the success of the program. So certain questions were specifically directed at preference, others at job function, and behavior was supplemented by observation data. The questions were not explicitly labelled as such, but the survey was engineered such that different questions fed into the categorization. Additionally, the back-end had a lot of math for calculating the thresholds of the mobile, super-mobile, and resident categories. We had to come up with formulas that weighed the different types of questions. Does preference count more, or less, than actual behavior? How much more or less? Does it count how difficult it is it to get into the resident category? How difficult is too difficult? Or how difficult is so difficult that participants might distrust or manipulate the survey results?

After carefully engineering the questions and the categorization logic, we were also very conscious when designing the survey to play back the results to the people who took the assessment survey. The "results" page not only lists the recommended categorization of mobile, super-mobile or resident, but it gives two distinct categorizations—one for "preference" and one for "capability." For example, while an administrative assistant may have a preference to be mobile and enjoy the freedom, her capability might recommend resident, given the nature of her work and the demands of keeping physical files and supporting a team. This separation explicitly communicates the perception gap back to participants and the transparency makes for a more trustworthy tool, which is increasingly important with an over-surveyed and data-savvy population.

Finally, this double categorization was followed by a detailed assessment in five related subject categories, including ability to work independently, and work-life balance. The assessment survey again makes the logic explicit by showing relative strengths and weaknesses in the different areas and by recommending training where applicable.

A true Algorithmic Approach takes all the quantitative data gathered in research and not only plays it back to participants, but also uses it to produce solutions. In the case of the above assessment, the quantitative data was used to categorize staff to build a demand projection of how many spaces would be needed over time. The data not only provided a picture of how the organization was currently working but also how critical areas of usage were underperforming. In another project for a large Federal agency, a front-end questionnaire and spreadsheet led users to a range of sample layouts. These layouts were not meant to be immediately implemented—they would need to be translated for building type at the very least—but designers streamlined and rationalized much of the design process in order to quickly produce sample layouts which in turn serve as a very fast way to discuss relative trade-offs and implications with clients.

These projects represent the Algorithmic Approach to programming, in that they rely heavily on proven methods and large sets of quantitative data in order to make recommendations. This approach is often appropriate for large corporate clients with a significant amount of real estate, who need a consistent process for rolling out space and a defensible method for making real estate decisions. It also can be helpful in quickly turning around space by automating the production of a program.

The challenge with the algorithmic method is that there is little opportunity for creating an exciting new idea, or for significant end-user input. Methodologically, both the survey and observation tools limit the range of possibilities by asking specific questions with a pre-defined set of answers. There is very little opportunity to answer outside of the known range, or for a breakaway idea to float to the surface. This is partly due to schedule demands, and it is also because the scale is so large. A two-week observation yielded over 100,000 data points. There is simply not enough manpower to handle that size data set if the questions were open-ended, since the resulting responses would be so disparate. There are some automated versions for handling disparate sets, but to date these tools are either unreliable or cost-prohibitive. Related to this is the challenge that the design which results from the Algorithmic Approach tends to necessarily address the average. All voices count the same as equal data points in the TUS or WPS, with the exception of the leaders who make the ultimate decision. This does not allow for the fact that some voices are more visionary or helpful than others. For this reason and others, many clients are better suited to what we are calling the Messy Approach.

The messy

The Messy Approach operates based on a high degree of face-to-face work with the client and end users. It is complicated, involved, and sometimes circuitous. It deploys participatory models of engagement which muster the resources of various constituencies to collectively solve the design problems at hand, often through workshops or charrettes. Unlike the algorithmic mode of programming, it is not necessarily linear, and it does not presuppose the outcomes or the parameters of the possible solution. This openness often requires more time and resources, but it also opens itself to the potential of a breakaway idea, a novel solution, or a surprising idea. It is more likely to produce a result that is really right for the audience. By digging deep in the research phase, there is a very close connection between the built solutions and the people who will be inhabiting them. For these reasons, the Messy Approach works well for clients who have the time and appetite for an extended process, and who understand and value the potential gains of this approach.

To best understand the Messy Approach, we use the following example from a major American museum that was planning a significant building expansion and viewed the expansion as an opportunity to redefine its spaces, operations, and role in the community.

Our first step was a series of workshops over the course of several days. These workshops were intensive sessions where group thinking was applied to solve specific problems. We held collaborative themed workshops on a variety of topics including the office space, the gallery space, and whether to close during construction or remain open. We also held a vision session, which was designed to define the overall direction. These sessions provided direction on the development of the program and of the design. They produced the tagline for the new museum, which was to be "magnetic, generous and transformative." They also identified three areas that needed greater attention: visitor experience, audience-information interface, and audience development. These three areas were places where the institution felt it had an opportunity to innovate beyond what most museums were doing, and to rethink the current offering.

Because the museum was explicitly interested in innovating in these areas, we proposed looking outside the museum world for novel strategies and inspiration. We designed a series of expert roundtables, which featured guest speakers and an activity component which applied the lessons to the specific museum context. The outside voices were from a variety of industries that had faced and successfully navigated similar challenges, though not in the art world. For the visitor-experience roundtable, which was dedicated to the experience of the visitor when on-site, we featured four speakers, including the head concierge of St. Regis Hotels, who talked about the challenge of providing hospitality and service which is at once consistent to the brand and specific to individual preferences. We also had a speaker from Disney talk about training programs and how to create a culture that is visitor-focused. The presentations by the speakers were followed by a workshop session, which directly applied the lessons learned. For example, after listening to St. Regis and Disney, we would then break into small groups and work to redesign the hospitality experience at the museum through a structured exercise which directly applied the lessons. At the end of the all-day session, we reported back as a group and discussed the ideas that came out of the session.

This approach to user engagement falls firmly in the "messy" category in terms of time commitment, negotiating differences of opinion, and considering the implications of the ideas generated. The roundtable sessions for the museum were attended by staff and board members, two groups that had not typically worked together. They were very successful in thinking through these specific subject areas, and also in stretching the creativity of the group. Selecting and recruiting the speakers took many rounds of research and discussion, and a significant networking effort from many people involved in the project. The conversations that resulted were tricky—they unearthed big questions about balancing education with entertainment and about the future of the institution.

These debates lasted beyond the roundtables, and overflowed into other activities. In some instances, they complicated the program and potentially the project schedule. For example, the visitor-experience roundtable resulted in a shared vision for a museum, which would be very highly visitor-focused. This is a principle which was driven by multiple stakeholders, but the expression of that value was hotly contested. Would it mean having ticketing agents come to visitors with a handheld device for purchasing and printing tickets? Or would that be alienating to older visitors, a key demographic of the museum? Or would demographics shift by the time the museum was constructed?

In addition to the round-tables, the research phase included an all-staff survey and departmental interviews. All the data from the research phase was documented and distilled in the creation of four different scenarios, each of which had an organizing principle. For example, the "Museum as warehouse" scenario would expand on-site art storage and back of house transparency whereas the "Museum as marketplace" scenario would move art storage off-site in order to keep staff on-site, and feature enhanced public spaces with art in "free" areas. The four scenarios negotiated a number of variables, most specifically the amount of back-of-house functions that would be on-site, and whether the experience was focused mainly on the gallery spaces, or if it was a continuous experience that included before, during and after the gallery spaces. The scenarios were presented to leadership in a work session, which negotiated the trade-offs for each one of these scenarios. The scenarios were presented as a narrative summary description of the scenario, a concept diagram, and a draft program. Because the museum had been so heavily involved in all stages of the project, the scenario session was also highly interactive. We filled an excel spreadsheet and developed programs as the conversation evolved, so that the client could understand the implications of certain decisions.

Ultimately the challenge of the session was to translate the vision of a "magnetic, generous and transformative" institution into an actual plan. Does generous mean that there is art in the free areas? Or does transformative mean that the public areas are free of art, in order that the galleries make a bigger impact? How are competing values negotiated, and how do they find spatial expression?

Another messy technique we often use for scenario or design development is rapid prototyping. Rapid prototyping is a method of engaging potential end users of spaces, objects, and processes in an immersive design workshop. As a process, it functions as a quick, highly iterative, three-dimensional brainstorming session that allows end users to collaborate on speculative designs. While more elaborate frameworks for rapid prototyping might use digital technology such as three-dimensional modelling programs and fabrication equipment, our rapid prototyping sessions are most often conducted using cheap and readily available everyday materials like clay, construction paper, foam core, and pipe cleaners. The familiarity and the material qualities of these supplies embolden even beginners to work quickly and easily, so that prototypes can be created in a few hours in the session. A rapid prototyping session should allow potential end users to easily manipulate materials and collaborate without any prior training or skill with the material or process.

Rapid prototyping workshops assign participants a problem to solve in small groups—for example, to build an office environment for six people, or design the visitor experience and entry sequence for a museum. Constraints are defined prior to the workshop (the constraints of a room, floor plate or building envelope, modelled to scale), so that participants are able to scale their concepts against pre-defined and properly scaled boundaries. By establishing these "ground rules" of limited materials and other constraints based on context, workshop participants can quickly collaborate and compare the end results of their efforts. Materials most frequently used in rapid prototyping sessions might include chipboard, cardboard, pipe cleaners, origami paper, Legos, and hot-glue guns for rapid assembly.

The interesting thing about rapid prototyping is that while it is highly pragmatic and material, our experience is that it often results in very abstract or conceptual conversations about culture and organization. A participant might be explaining a sliding whiteboard mechanism and segue into explaining teaming and privacy norms. Therefore, rapid prototyping is instrumental from multiple points of view: it musters additional resources in solving complex problems, it makes end users aware of the trade-offs and challenges, and it opens a dialogue about other less-tangible aspects like culture.

This overview of a Messy Approach includes visioning workshops, scenario building, roundtables, and rapid prototyping, but there are a host of other tools we have employed on these types of projects. Because the Messy Approach is so highly specific to the client and requires an intimacy with the organization, many tools or methods are customized or invented for the particular project. The Messy Approach can be very rewarding; the roundtables for the museum project were wonderful events and they resulted in ideas that likely would not have surfaced in a more traditional process. But this approach is messy. The scenarios unearthed difficult questions and longstanding debates within the institution. The work was labor-intensive and more time-consuming for the client and the consultant than a traditional approach to programming. Finally, the Messy Approach often involves a much larger group in the process than the Algorithmic Approach does. Leadership must be comfortable with engaging more voices, and with empowering those voices to influence the outcome. For all these reasons, the Messy Approach is most often employed when an organization is making a major change, either in building a new building, planning a significant expansion, or when a behavioral shift requires more hands-on time.

Because the Messy Approach has such compelling engagement and results, but sometimes includes an off-putting commitment and messiness, many organizations choose to borrow some methodologies from the Messy Approach, yet streamline it in a more algorithmic fashion. We are calling this approach the Hybrid.

The hybrid

The Hybrid Approach uses some of the tools of the Messy Approach in order to more accurately understand client needs and desires. But rather than follow the Messy Approach all the way through to design, which can sometimes result in a baroque or protracted design phase, the Hybrid Approach attempts to rationalize the design process by creating modules or the programmatic equivalent of mass customization. Like the Messy Approach, the Hybrid Approach has the benefit of involving more people in the initial phase, getting more input, and allowing space for the breakaway idea. But unlike the Messy Approach, the Hybrid tends to more tightly manage user input into the design process by firmly locating user input in the research phase, but not the design or approvals phase. The challenge with the Hybrid Approach is in understanding this balance between research and design output. What are some of the implications for using research to create rules of thumb for organizational planning and growth? How can these rules be revised so that organizations can learn and improve upon them so that their space can adapt and change?

The following example illustrates the Hybrid Approach in practice. It is drawn from the headquarters' redesign of a large professional member organization. While the organization had historically been located in Houston, a central premise of the project was that all locations would be considered when developing the location and function of a new headquarters space. While the majority of members were traditionally in North America, the organization had been experiencing exponential membership growth in other parts of the world, specifically China, India, and Europe. This put the organization in a challenging situation. How could they maintain the knowledge and skills of the current workforce and maintain operational continuity while creating new venues for interaction with a rapidly growing global membership base? How does a not-for-profit service organization extend its ability to connect with membership while considering cost and the need for a phased approach to global expansion?

After the project kick-off, we conducted a series of quantitative and qualitative studies to define the work patterns of the current staff. These included surveys of both staff and membership, a time utilization study of the current facility, along with interviews with key leadership and workshops with staff. The results of this study were compiled into an initial strategic brief for the future headquarters. While this answered questions about space usage and collaboration patterns, as well as presenting a new vision of how teams might better work and learn from one another, critical questions of how this might impact the greater global vision remained unanswered. How could the organization maintain global growth but also be adaptable to local issues?

It was from this perspective that we co-created with the organization a global kit of parts. Based on research conducted with various component departments, we were able to create a series of scalable modules that could be adapted and used as a basis for selecting future bases of operation. Using this global kit of parts, the concept of a central headquarters for a member service organization became less relevant. Instead, the headquarters began to evolve into a series of global hubs each with different functionalities and specialties. Since the leadership frequently travels, these global hubs would accommodate their movement as well as be tailored to the specific local needs of the organization.

The basic premise of the module organization was a customer-oriented front of house and a staff-oriented back of house. The front of house area was scalable to accommodate the needs of local groups and how they engaged their member base. For example, local centers that conducted substantial amounts of training and held member events would have a large front of house space with a multi-purpose room, breakout spaces, and other meeting venues. Centers that focused more on the production of educational content or member relations and less on member engagement would minimize this front of house space. In a similar fashion, back of house modules were customized to provide work space and complementary support space to programmatic modules, such as educational-content production and member relations.

When creating a Hybrid Approach to spatial programming, large organizational research efforts are undertaken and condensed in a way that creates general principles for thinking about and planning space. The Hybrid attempts to leverage some of the benefits of the Messy with the efficiencies of the Algorithmic. This method does sacrifice some of the benefits of each method, but for organizations that want to closely understand their constituency and their future direction, but need a strategy for rolling out spaces across geographies, it can be a very useful approach.

While these three approaches provide an overview of the different types of user research currently employed in design practice, and the reasons clients might be drawn to user research, there is much that happens after the program is completed and the building is built. While the Messy, the Algorithmic, or the Hybrid Approaches may accurately define the organization as it is at a moment in time, and how it expects to grow or evolve, concepts of adaptation and feedback are essential in thinking about how environments can adapt and change to the constantly evolving organizational landscape.

In The Fifth Discipline, Peter Senge (1994) talks about the importance of creating a language of "interrelationship…a language made of circles" within organizations. Senge is referring to the interconnectedness of the different aspects of an organization and in advocating this view, he begins a discussion of how organizations can leverage feedback and systems thinking to become more adaptable and agile while also promoting collective problem solving. While this concept of feedback could apply to almost any area of organizational design, it has a specific application here in underlining the agility and adaptability of programming in an organizational system where space is not viewed as distinct from organizational, financial and cultural matters, but rather as part of a composite whole.

Post-occupancy evaluation is critical to assessing the effectiveness of new environments and the evolving link between spatial environments and organizational objectives. It is best to wait six to twelve months after move-in to evaluate the success of the project, in order to give occupants time to live in the space. At that point, there is an opportunity to re-engage users to understand how a new space addresses goals and ideas initially articulated through the research process. The success of the new environment should be assessed not only against the original goals of the project, but also against the ongoing evolution of the organization.

Future directions

The introduction to this chapter poses "traditional programming" against other types of programming—Summerson's relational or function-based programming, Koolhaas or Tschumi's matrix of program, and strategic programming processes used by a number of large architectural and strategic planning firms.

While "traditional programming" is still the dominant mode in architectural practice, the programming methods outlined in this chapter would benefit most projects, in particular larger projects and those most affected by complexity and uncertainty. The three methods introduced in this chapter allow organizations to quickly link business and organizational goals to spatial implications in order to be more responsive to changes in the business climate and the resulting implications of how people work together.

So if the programming methods outlined in this chapter would benefit most projects, yet "traditional programming" is still the dominant mode in architectural practice, how can we advance the discipline of programming? Perhaps the answer lies in part in making strategic programming more central to architecture. For that to happen, research methods, processes, and tools need to adapt to meet current business cycles. If research processes are to stay a step ahead of organizational design and its spatial implications, tools that combine aspects of qualitative and quantitative research need to be rigorously evaluated and updated.

Beyond the development of research methods, it is our job as programmers to compete in the marketplace by making ourselves more accessible and more agile—being flexible enough to facilitate a vision session and quickly plan a 30-person office, or to find a way to do utilization studies faster and cheaper.

But if this mode of programming is truly to advance, we must look to architectural education to get architects excited about research and data visualization. Architectural education should explore the (sometimes tense) relationship between programming and design. Most of all, it should teach a healthy respect for programming as a discipline distinct from design.

Programming—when done well—is a very specialized skill set, one that in many ways is different from design. It requires advanced skills in research and facilitation and it requires thinking in plan, section, 3D, spreadsheets, and organizational charts. Most of all, it requires seeing patterns through mountains of data and disparate information.

Design requires some of these skills, but many are sublimated to the current demands of design, particularly given the current software requirements and the accelerated pace of design. Building Information Modelling (BIM) software has a significant learning curve, and it creates the impression of instant renderings. The economy has driven design firms to push out more versions faster. These two factors alone have conspired to greatly increase the demands on design professionals, which makes it all the more critical that programming remain a distinct discipline in support of the design effort. There is also a benefit in a creative tension between programmers advocating for the requirements of the users, and designers advocating for the requirements of the space. It is only through a discourse between these two disciplines that a design can emerge that is better than if either discipline were solely responsible for the outcome.

References

Lawrence, Amanda Reeser and Ashley Shafer. 2010. *Praxis. Re: Programming.* 8.

Koolhaas, Rem. 1997. *Delirious New York: A retroactive manifesto for manhattan.* New York: Monacelli.

Pena, Willy and Steve Parshall. 1977. *Problem seeking: An architectural programming primer.* CBI Publishing Co, Inc.

Tschumi, Bernard. 1994. *Manhattan transcripts.* New York: John Wiley & Sons.

Tschumi, Bernard. "Le Fresnoy National Studio for Contemporary Arts." http://www.archined.nl/oem/reportages/fresnoy/fresnoy4.html

Vidler, Anthony. 2003. "Toward a theory of an architectural program." *October* 106 (Fall): 59-74.

Senge, Peter. 1994. *The fifth discipline: The art & practice of the learning organization.* New York: Doubleday Business.

Notes

[1] Placement on Fortune Magazine's Best Place to Work list is highly coveted mainly by large companies for the recruiting value it brings. The inclusion of a mobile work or remote work program is one of the factors in placement on the list.

CHAPTER SIX

THE HEALTH-PROMOTING POTENTIAL OF PRESCHOOL OUTDOOR ENVIRONMENTS: LINKING RESEARCH TO POLICY

CECILIA BOLDEMANN, MARGARETA SÖDERSTRÖM, FREDRIKA MÅRTENSSON, ROBIN MOORE, NILDA COSCO, BRAD BIEBER, PETER PAGELS, ANDERS RAUSTORP AND ULF WESTER

Children´s active lives have, until recently, mostly been spent outdoors in the streets and open spaces of the local community but are nowadays often restricted by modern society. Changes in children's environments, including increased road traffic, inflexible use of time, parental apprehensions, and the attraction of "screen time," have increased sedentary behavior and reduced children´s independent mobility in ways that can put their health and development at risk (Karsten 2005, Björklid and Nordström 2012). Another change in western societies is the growing proportion of young children who attend preschools during the major part of their weekdays. Preschools have increased gender equality and made it possible for both parents to pursue careers, but also have engaged children in a radically different pattern of child rearing. Consequently, preschools have an obligation to provide rich environments to replace home surroundings that may have previously supported their healthy physical, mental, and cognitive development (Janz et al. 2010). In particular, for children to acquire sufficient levels of physical activity, preschools need to accommodate boisterous outdoor play that in previous generations more likely happened in neighborhood spaces close to home.

Bilateral, interdisciplinary collaboration

Because childhood lifestyle and its health consequences are common issues across many countries, they are ripe for collaborative study by international groups willing to pool expertise, work within the same methodological framework, and share measurement tools and training for their application. This chapter bears the fruit of such collaboration, in this case between Swedish and United States (US) researchers in a common quest to assess the built environment quality of preschool outdoor environments and their health-promotion potential. We will focus on evidence showing how the outdoor environment of preschools can provide stimulating, diverse, and developmentally appropriate settings to support children's healthy physical development by motivating both children and teachers to spend active time outdoors. We will also address the related issue of sun exposure and skin cancer risk, which could be considered a hazard unless shade is provided as an essential component of outdoor settings.

As far as we know, the first interdisciplinary study *combining* the impact of the preschool outdoor environment on physical activity, sun exposure and other health outcomes, was conducted in 2004 in the northern, urban landscape of Stockholm County, Sweden, Latitude 59 °N (Boldemann et al. 2006). The research team included scholars in public health sciences, medicine, environmental psychology, education, and landscape architecture. The combined impact of physical activity and solar ultraviolet (UV) exposure was explored. Eleven preschool sites (199 children) participated. Individual health variables were based on anthropometric measurement (height, weight, and waist girth) and data obtained through a survey of parents about their children's health. Additional studies were conducted in 2009 by a similar interdisciplinary team at two preschool sites (33 children) in the Research Triangle Park, North Carolina, USA, Latitude 36°N, with a southern subtropical landscape, and at nine preschool sites (169 children) in Malmö, South Sweden, Latitude 55 °N, with a northern agricultural landscape. The purpose of this further, bi-cultural study was to explore the generalizability of the Stockholm results to other climates and landscapes. Findings from these three locations are presented here with a particular focus on understanding relationships between attributes of the physical environment and relevant health factors.

Physical activity

Below a certain threshold, lack of physical activity (PA) is hazardous, especially for young children. Blood vessels may stiffen and sugar metabolism can be disturbed (Sääkslathi et al. 2004, Weiss et al. 2004). Hampering PA can jeopardize a child's cardiovascular health from an early age (Tanha et al. 2011). Conversely, a certain level of PA is essential for keeping the cardiovascular system in good health. Vigorous physical activity, which typically occurs in spurts during free play, is also required for healthy bone growth (Janz et al. 2010). Consequently, children should never be continuously motionless for more than sixty minutes except when asleep (National Association for Sport and Physical Education 2002; Janssen and Leblanc 2010, Karolinska Institutet and Center for Epidemiology and Public Health, Stockholm County Council 2013). Children tend to be more physically active outdoors than indoors (Raustorp et al. 2013). Preschool outdoor environments that promote physical activity of children may positively affect cardiovascular systems and bone health (Harvey et al. 2012) but must be attractive enough to compete with TV or computer games.

Homo sapiens, especially the young, require certain habitat conditions for healthy development through play, which can be seen as nature's way of satisfying an inborn urge for survival by interacting with surroundings and thereby discovering inherent risks and opportunities through playful interaction (Heft, 1997). Young children engaging in "risky play" take on physical and social challenges and develop environmental competence (Sandseter 2009). Through experiences such as grasping stinging nettles, discovering heavy stones that can be turned over, and finding bushes that have edible berries, children learn to discriminate the potentials and limitations of the physical world. At the same time, children are vulnerable and need protection from potentially harmful situations.

Sun exposure

If the health benefits of sustained outdoor physical activity are to be promoted, then the importance of shade and access to shady outdoor settings must be stressed. Because regulation of body temperature is less stable in children than in adults, children need to be free to seek the cooling, protective attributes of the outdoors. If they are confined to unshaded outdoor environments, the risk of overexposure to ultraviolet radiation (UVR) increases the risk for skin malignancy later in life; sunburn at an early age increases the risk of skin cancer (Armstrong 2004).

The prevalence of sunburn in preschool children is high (Bränström et al. 2006). Exposure to more than five to thirty minutes of midday summer sun depending on skin type and latitude can be hazardous to a child[1]. Shorter exposure is normally sufficient for every child to form necessary amounts of vitamin D through solar exposure of unprotected skin. Sun exposure varies by season and latitude (Wester & Josefsson 1997). At latitudes higher than 40°N, solar UV radiation from September to late March does not constitute a risk of sunburn according to the scale of solar UV strength (the UV-index) established by the World Health Organization (Figures 6-1 and 6-2).

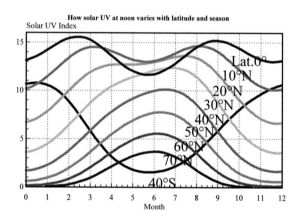

Fig. 6-1. Latitudinal and seasonal variation of the solar UV-index at noon calculated for cloud-free sky and climatically normal stratospheric ozone layer. Source: Wester & Josefsson, 1997.

EXPOSURE CATEGORY	UVI RANGE
LOW	< 2
MODERATE	3 TO 5
HIGH	6 TO 7
VERY HIGH	8 TO 10
EXTREME	11+

Fig. 6-2. UV-index exposure categories, ranges and protection requirements, as established by the World Health Organization Source: WHO, 2002.

The UV-index at such latitudes is then "low" (<3) or "moderate" (3-5) (WHO 2002). Also at mid latitudes 30-40°N, the risk is low provided there is shade that reduces solar exposure by more than half (Parsons et al. 1998). Furthermore, the improvement of outdoor environment is increasingly discussed in order to have sunshine during fall and early spring to provide Vitamin D from suberythemal (below the threshold value for reddened skin) sun exposure.

Limiting sun exposure is recognized not only by scientists but also by policy makers (U.S. Department of Health and Human Services, 2014:47). In Sweden, new policies are being implemented that attract children's play to the shade and thereby trigger sun-protective play "underneath and between" (Karolinska Institutet and Center for Epidemiology and Public Health, Stockholm County Council 2013). As a contribution towards establishing a baseline of childcare center outdoor quality in North Carolina (NC), a survey of environmental conditions in outdoor play areas was conducted by the Natural Learning Initiative (NLI) and reported by Cosco and Moore (2003). Results relevant to this chapter show that NC childcare centers use several types of sun protection strategies, most of which are aligned with U.S. National Cancer Institute recommendations (sunscreen, protective clothing, and shade on sunny days). Of the centers in this survey (n=326), 48% considered trees as adequate protection of their children from the sun; 26% used other types of devices (canvas, tents, etc.), 22% installed awnings, and 5% used arbors (Figure 6-3). A requirement of the NC childcare licensing rules (.1402) is "The outdoor play area must provide an area that is shaded, [and] out of direct sunlight" (page 3.19, North Carolina Division of Child Development, 2009).

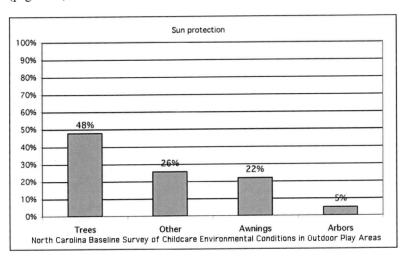

Fig. 6-3. Baseline Survey of Environmental Conditions in Child Care Centers. Source: Cosco and Moore, 2003.

Measuring policy-relevant childcare outdoor quality

The role of physical surroundings in *early childhood* play have been empirically explored since the 1990s in attempts to discover significant relationships between built-environment attributes and children´s play, physical activity, UV exposure (Boldemann et al. 2004), and attention (Grahn et al. 1997; Faber Taylor et al. 2001; Kuo and Faber Taylor 2004; Mårtensson 2004; Cosco 2006). U.S. co-authors Cosco and Moore, were part of the team that developed the *Preschool Outdoor Environments Measurement Scale* (POEMS, DeBord et al. 2005), to provide a valid, reliable and dichotomous scale to measure the overall outdoor quality of preschool play areas, including shade and other items related to active outdoor settings. Early Swedish studies explored generalized categories of "green" play settings (Grahn et al. 1997; Söderström et al. 2004). Later qualitative investigations produced the Outdoor Play Environment Categories (OPEC) (Mårtensson 2004). OPEC was developed to measure environmental attributes promoting play sequences deemed both vigorous and restorative, as children switch between rapid bursts of physical activity and moments of calm behavior (Mårtensson 2009, 2013). UV protection was investigated by Boldemann et al. (2004) and was found to be associated with the protective qualities of a lush outdoor environment, which not only attracted play but also enabled prolonged time outdoors without risk of sunburn. Strategies for long-term preschool sun protection by natural means therefore look promising, especially since sunblock is expensive and requires frequent reapplication which requires staff time.

Increasingly, research evidence suggests that preschool outdoor environments need to be designed as places where children spend longer time engaged in free play and learning activities and take safe risks in sunny spaces during fall and early spring (for formation of vitamin D), protected from suberythemal sun exposure during late spring and summer, and with diverse settings and features that trigger recommended levels of PA year round. To achieve these ends requires careful design of vegetation relative to sun angles, type (deciduous or evergreen), and size (trees and shrubs). On-going management of plant material is critical for maintaining appropriate, year-round shade quality (deep, partial, dappled, etc.), which in turn can affect thermal comfort (though thermal comfort was not the subject of our studies). A primary driver for the research described here was to produce findings with potential to influence the policies of local agencies charged with regulating preschool quality so that preschool outdoor environments may be recognized, designed, and managed as critically important health-promoting spaces for young children. Examples describe how findings so far have been implemented in local, state, and national policies.

Sweden-USA Bi-lateral Research

Site selection

Swedish sites were selected according to the quality of their outdoor environment as assessed using the OPEC protocol (Mårtensson 2004, Mårtensson et al. 2013), and by socioeconomic factors (Stockholm county: 11 sites, n=199, Malmö: 9 sites, n=169). North Carolina sites were a convenience sample of two preschools attended by children of middle class families (n=33). All twenty-two selected preschools and individual parents and children agreed to participate (Boldemann et al. 2006, 2011).

Measurement of independent variables

OPEC: Codes included size of the outdoor area, the amount of trees, shrubbery or hilly terrain, and the overall integration of vegetation, open areas and play areas (Table 6-1).

Dimension	Score of 1 (low score)	Score of 2 (midrange score)	Score of 3 (high score)
Size of the outdoor area (m^2) A*	$<1200m^2$	$1200-3000m^2$	$>3000m^2$
Size of the outdoor area (m^2) B*	$<2000\ m^2$	$2000-6000m^2$	$>6000m^2$
Proportion of surfaces with trees, shrubbery or hilly terrain	Little/non-existent	< half of area	≥ half of area
Integration between vegetation, open areas and play areas	No integration. Open spaces, vegetation and play areas in separate parts of the environment.	a) Trees or shrubbery adjacent to play areas OR b) Open spaces are located in between the play areas.	a) Trees or shrubbery adjacent to play areas AND b) Open spaces are located in between the play areas.

The sum of the scores for each outdoor setting is divided by 3. In dichotomous analysis the cut-off for high-scoring, "good" environment and low-scoring, "poor environment" is set at >2.0/≤2.0

*Evaluation of the size of the area was adjusted to the variation of environmental quality in the region of study (A: North Carolina and Malmö, B: Stockholm County).

Table 6-1. Outdoor Play Environment Categories (OPEC) tool, including three dimensions and dichotomized, three-level cut-off limits for high-score and low-score preschool outdoor environment.

Sky view: Sky view was measured using a camera with a fisheye lens to take photos from play locations defined by the staff and by direct observation by the research team (Figures 6-4 and 6-5).

Fig. 6-4. Images show ground locations and matching sky views from each of the preschools located in the Research Triangle Park, North Carolina (March-April 2009). In the top left image, one of several vine-covered pergolas (just coming into leaf), provide large patches of shade on the primary pathway (the most popular and active setting). A forest line on the south side (bottom left) provided sun protection, even though children did not have access to the forest. Nonetheless, they were observed playing along its edges with only the fence separating them from the wild landscape beyond. Source: Cecilia Boldemann, Fredrika Mårtensson, and Brad Bieber.

Fig. 6-5. The upper left image shows an inner-city site in Malmö with a sky view from a favorite setting under two trees (May 1, 2009). Here, physical activity was high combined with optimal UVR exposure. In the bottom row, a site in Malmö with flat, unstimulating sun-exposed surfaces. Here, physical activity was low in combination with relatively high UVR exposure. Source: Ulf Wester, Cecilia Boldemann, and Fredrika Mårtensson.

In Stockholm County, the outdoor environment scoring was combined with sky-view photography from the positions most frequently used for play by the children (defined as behavior settings). The proportion of free sky above a behavior setting was thereafter computed in order to capture a proxy for solar UV radiation to compare with the empirically collected UV data.

In North Carolina and Malmö the pattern of children's play was measured more precisely using behavior mapping (Cosco et al. 2010), which enabled the simultaneous collection of data for location, environmental attributes, intensity of physical activity and behavioral attributes such as social interaction and type of play (Pagels et al. 2013). Sky-view photography was linked to behavior setting, which made possible more precise calibration of types of play setting and sun exposure.

Measurement and analysis of dependent variables

The primary dependent variables were physical activity and sun exposure. Anthropometric data (height, weight, waist girth) were collected for all children. Waist girth and body mass index assessed body composition. Data for parent-rated potential confounder variables regarding the children's health were obtained via parental survey that included items on socioeconomic status, mother's education, and being outdoors on ordinary Sundays, and diaries asking for the child's bedtime and waking-up time, symptoms of infection, and illnesses requiring medication.

Physical activity: Physical activity was measured by pedometry (Yamax Digiwalker SW-200 pedometers) applied during one week (5 days) to record step counts. Accelerometry (Actigraph GT1M accelerometer) was used to measure time and intensity of physical activity (Tudor-Locke et al. 2004).

UV exposure: UV exposure was measured with polysulphone (PS) dosimeters. For diurnal variation measurements of the global UV intensity, a UV monitor for a "farm weather station" (Davis sensor 6490) was located on a nearby roof with uninterrupted sky view. PS dosimeters placed near the UV monitor recorded ambient daily global UV exposure (Boldemann et al. 2011). PS dosimeters worn by the children recorded individual UV exposure for the study period. Children's time outdoors was clocked and recorded. Global UV exposure during children's time outdoors was calculated from the roof dosimeter using the intensity variability records of the UV-monitor. The fraction of individual to global UV exposure (relative UV exposure) during the periods of time outdoors was calculated from the individual and the global measurements.

Impact of OPEC and sky view on PA and UV exposure: OPEC scores and sky view were dichotomized for analysis (OPEC score $\leq 2/>2$, sky views $\leq 50/>50\%$). The combined impact of the outdoor environment upon physical activity and UV exposure was jointly analyzed by multilevel modelling (Boldemann et al. 2006, 2011).

Findings

Positive landscape effect on physical activity and sun exposure

For all sites, OPEC scores and sky views were significantly and negatively correlated, i.e. the higher the OPEC score the lower the sky view and vice versa. Combined positive health outcomes for physical activity and sun exposure were identified, related to high quality preschool outdoor environments (OPEC score >2.0, i.e. spacious and diverse outdoor environment with trees and shrubs attractive for play). In Stockholm County and Malmö the children were more physically active and took 1500–2000 additional steps/day during a 7-hr preschool day (Boldemann et al. 2006, 2011) in high-scored environments. Children stayed outdoors all day in late spring and summer without risk of sunburn (>40 lat N) (Boldemann et al. 2006, 2011). In North Carolina, UV exposure was low and a lush outdoor environment would have enabled longer outdoor stay in spring than the scheduled outdoor time in spite of the low latitude. In both North Carolina and Malmö the children were more physically active outdoors than indoors, as well as being engaged in more vigorous physical activity outdoors (Raustorp et al. 2012).

The combined impact of outdoor environment upon physical activity and sun exposure was almost identical in Stockholm County and in Malmö. In both locations high-scoring OPEC sites increased physical activity by 21% and reduced relative UV exposure by 35-40%. Furthermore, prolonged time outdoors was found to be more common in high-scoring sites (Table 6-2).

Table 6-2 demonstrates the links between physical activity, UV exposure, and time outdoors depending on environment scores in terms of space, amount of vegetation, and integration in children's play. Depending on the degree to which these criteria are met, physical activity increases and relative UV exposure is moderated. Environments scoring high OPEC (>2) enable much "time outdoors" with little risk of sunburn in Sweden year round and in North Carolina from September to April with UV exposures less than 200 Jm^{-2} and low relative UV exposure. During these months even longer time outdoors would have been possible in North Carolina in spite of its low latitude, due to the abundance of vegetation. Time outdoors was considerably higher in high-scored OPEC environments. We know that—at least in Sweden—high quality outdoor environments encouraged time outdoors (Söderström et al. 2004). Free sky and relative UV exposure were highly correlated.

	Stockholm County, 2004	North Carolina, 2009	Malmö, 2009
Climate, latitude and landscape	Temperate/hemi boreal Lat 59°N rocky, pine forests	Subtropical Lat 36°N lush, deciduous forests	Temperate /maritime Lat 55°N Agricultural
Fieldwork and dominant weather	May –June 2004 sunny	March-April 2009 sunny	May 2009 rainy and windy
Temperature range during fieldwork	8.6 – 25.6C 47.5 – 77.5F	18.3 – 25.6C 64.9 – 78.1F	13.0 – 18.0C 55.4 – 64.4F
Physical activity, (steps/ minute) OPEC >2 OPEC ≤2	21.5 (5 sites) 17.7 (6 sites)	- 12.3 (2 sites)	21.2 (3 sites) 17.6 (6 sites)
Sun exposure (Jm^{-2}) OPEC >2 OPEC ≤2	202 192	- 70	145 98
Relative UV exposure (%)* OPEC >2 OPEC ≤2	15 24	- 27	26 43
Time spent outdoors (%) OPEC >2 OPEC ≤2	66 48	- 17	72 33
Free sky (%) OPEC >2 OPEC ≤2	38 65	- 46	40 58

Relative sun exposure is the fraction of individual to global exposure. (Global UV is a measure of the UV-radiation reaching a horizontal surface at a spot with free unobstructed horizon. It includes both direct radiation from the sun and diffuse radiation from the sky.)

Table 6-2. Geographic characteristics of the investigation sites, and dominant weather conditions during fieldwork, vs. physical activity (steps per minute), sun exposure (Jm^{-2} and relative exposure), and time outdoors.

Further positive landscape effects from Swedish case studies

Additional developmental and health-related variables that were only investigated at each one of the Swedish locations indicated that further synergies may be gained by the high-score environments that promote children's physical activity and optimizes their UV exposure.

Attention behavior was studied in Stockholm county in 2004 on the same occasion when physical activity and UV exposure was investigated, (using the observation protocol, ad modum, McCarney 1997), and recorded by the preschool teachers. Assessment was based on standard scores for inattention and impulsivity—(1) behavior within normal range, (2) behavior indicating concern, (3) behavior of serious concern—following the protocol by McCarney (1997). After controlling for confounders, and as assessed by OPEC, children attending preschools with high-scoring outdoor environments showed inattentive behavior significantly less often (Stockholm County, 2004). High-scoring outdoor environments also correlated with low levels of impulsivity/hyperactivity behavior, although the correlation was not significant. Also, fewer inattention and impulsivity/hyperactivity behaviors were observed in outdoor environments with lower sky views, i.e. with more trees cutting the view (Mårtensson et al. 2009).

Another developmental variable relevant to children's everyday functioning and wellbeing is night sleep. The time that a child sleeps at night has implications for general health, as sleep supports several aspects of health such as immunity, growth, and alertness (Besedovsky et al. 2011). Night sleep was thus studied in Malmö on the same occasion that physical activity and UV exposure were investigated. Even in a population of healthy children, outdoor environment was identified as influential (Söderström et al 2013). Children attending preschools with high-scoring outdoor environments slept significantly longer on weekdays at night than peers attending preschools with low scores (658 versus 642 minutes), and had significantly leaner bodies which refers both to a higher proportion of normal body mass index in the children and a narrower waist girth (48.2 versus 53.9 cm) at the age of five years (Söderström et al. 2013).

Summary of findings

In Stockholm County and Malmö, children´s access to spacious, outdoor play settings with vegetation and/or hilly terrain were associated with decreased sunburn risk, in spite of long periods outdoors, and increased physical activity during free play in springtime and summer. Step counts per minute during free play in high-scoring environments were associated with more than 20% of physical activity compared to that generated in low-scoring environments. Children were attracted to trees and bushes for play and thus spontaneously engaged in "unintentional" sun-protective behavior that decreased relative UV exposure by 35-40% with decreased sunburn risk during the Swedish spring and summer. These health-promoting behaviors were mainly associated with the physical environment in terms of the effect it had on children's free play. Children attending preschools with low-scoring outdoor environments (cramped, flat, with scant vegetation along the edges) were more frequently either at risk of sunburn or were kept indoors, and their level of physical activity was significantly lower. The results were controlled for socioeconomic status, mother's education, and being outdoors on ordinary Sundays. None of these potential confounders impacted the results, meaning that they were not related to physical activity. At all sites in both Sweden and North Carolina the children were more active outdoors, and due to the abundance of vegetation the children were at no risk of sunburn in North Carolina in spite of its low latitude.

Policy implications

In Sweden, preschools (all supervised by the Swedish National Agency for Education) are mostly run by local governments who own much of the land occupied by the properties. In the United States, childcare location may be influenced by local land use regulations; however, regulation of childcare programs typically occurs at the state level, except for the federally administered Head Start and Early Head Start programs for disadvantaged children.

Time outdoors

Swedish preschool children were observed spending more time outdoors than North Carolina children who were also observed to be cumulatively less physically active compared to their Swedish peers. Besides the overall organization of the day, there may be more specific differences between Sweden and North Carolina in how children´s behavior is regulated by adults, which may in turn affect the quality and quantity of play. For instance, at the Swedish sites children went outside on their own accord at a given signal, whereas at the North Carolina sites, going outside involved a lining-up routine with several minutes of low-level physical activity. North Carolina childcare rules mandate a morning and an afternoon minimum time outdoors of 30 minutes at full-day centers. Possibly, such a rule-directed routine has become informally institutionalized; first, with the concept of a defined "time outdoors" twice a day, no more, no less; and second, for a fixed duration (even though individual centers and teachers may adopt a voluntary standard of more than 30 minutes). That said, the step counts of the children attending the two NC preschools were more than twice as high in comparison to data reported from other U.S. preschools with flat, unstimulating environments in deprived areas, where step counts per minute averaged around six (Robinson et al. 2010; Reznik et al. 2013). The higher step counts of the NC study sites may be explained by the higher quality outdoor environments compared to the sites in deprived areas. Even though the OPEC scores for the NC outdoor environments were not as high as the Swedish sample, the influence of the outdoor environment on children in terms of physical activity and protection from UV exposure may be similar in both cases. Even if the center has a high-quality environment and children want to go outdoors, time outdoors may be governed by a routine schedule.

Staffing and site management

No preschool was understaffed during data collection (fully staffed means one fulltime staff per six children), except for two days at a high-scoring site in Stockholm County when the remaining workforce reported that they had to tend to the toddlers in the sandbox and tell the older children to stay within eyesight, meaning that in practice the children were constrained to a radius of ten meters (approximately thirty feet). During these two days, physical activity plummeted by nearly half. The sandbox was shaded but a sun-exposed scene would have increased the risk of overexposure to UV and kept all children indoors to protect them from sunburn, thereby reducing physical activity even more. The study by Cosco (2006) identified how different types of teacher interaction and daily "zoning" of the outdoor space could influence children's behavior. In other words, there is a likely teacher effect on how an outdoor environment is used and levels of physical activity generated. In particular, understaffing may have negative consequences even in high-quality outdoor environments.

Land management

Swedish legislation facilitates individual use of private and public land for play, recreation, and education. This societal system enables incorporation of woodland, including rerouting of lanes adjacent to preschool grounds to extend the usable space for children's play. In contrast, the majority of US preschools are privately run, many for profit, so the childcare site is usually privately owned with limited access to neighboring land. The location is usually regulated at a local level as part of the land-use codes. In Sweden, municipalities have started incorporating and applying new guidelines for high-quality preschool environment in land use policies (Altin et al. 2013). Administrative routines are gradually being adapted to follow up and monitor the quality of preschool outdoor environments. Upgrade actions for preschool outdoor environments include expanding functional areas by incorporating adjacent land. In the planning of future preschools, new criteria are considered so that outdoor environments will meet new standards, harmonize with municipal land use guidelines, and become integrated into routine health and environment impact assessments. When adjacent woodland is available, innovative centers manage it as a shared resource usable by all age groups as a "field trip destination" with parental permission.

Site subdivision

During implementation of the recommendations, resulting from quantitative and qualitative data yielded by the Swedish research, an observation was made that fences sometimes subdividing preschool outdoor space could curb children's drive to be physically active in free play and put them at risk of "physical activity deficiency"—and also stop them from seeking shade when the sun was strong. Access passages around buildings and sheds or through sheds with openings in both gables, and spaces between buildings and fences were observed to offer the potential to link different spaces together and increase physical activity by creating connectivity. These observations were later corroborated in a Danish study (Olesen et al. 2013). The removal of hampering fences has thus been initiated as a Swedish policy aim (Altin et al. 2013).

In North Carolina, licensed centers are required to install an external boundary fence enclosing the whole outdoor space, which for security reasons is typically tied into each end of the center building to create a continuous security cordon. Only centers with large outdoor spaces are not obligated to subdivide the whole space by age group. In contrast to

Sweden, in North Carolina, as in the majority of US states, infants, toddlers, and preschool-aged children cannot occupy the same outdoor space at the same time. Also, installed equipment must be "developmentally appropriate." In practice this means that to meet regulations, the large majority of childcare centers subdivide age groups with interior low fences or some form of permanent barrier. If the play and learning space is not large enough to be subdivided by age group (75sqf/child or roughly 7m^2), the outdoors can be shared if a prescribed schedule is followed to ensure age groups do not overlap. The resulting lack of connectivity often limits opportunities for the *sustained* physical activity that children who are strongly motivated to explore their surroundings enjoy (Cosco et al. 2010). Periodic review of regulations may avoid such unforeseen consequences such as slowing down or discouraging free play or limiting access to green areas where children can receive sun protection and find thermal comfort (Boldemann et al. 2004, Mårtensson 2004, Mårtensson et al. 2013).

Safety

An important issue involving children in preschools concerns safety. In Sweden, local government safety inspections increasingly include UV exposure and physical activity in monitoring the quality of preschool outdoor environments, which are conducted according to applicable legislation[2]. The aim is to integrate environmental quality into health inspection protocols so they are handled similarly to issues such as pollutants and noise. Injunctions that are imposed on a preschool by the local government may involve additional planting or planting in combination with manufactured shade structures. The North Carolina Child Care Rules, defined in General Statutes, are contained in the *Child Care Center Handbook*, Chapter 3: Outdoor Learning Environment (North Carolina Division of Child Development, 2009), which provides a comprehensive set of mandated requirements and recommended best practice standards of care administered by the (now) Department of Child Development and Early Education (DCDEE). Recommendations for active play and shade requirements are covered but possibly not to the level of precision of standards that are being developed in Sweden, and e.g. deliberately aim at triggering active play under and between vegetation, thereby promoting physical activity and sun-protective behavior in play.

Increasing natural diversity

Resulting from studies reported here, the Swedish Radiation Safety Authority, a government agency for control of radiation hazards, and the regional administrative councils recommend including in children's preschool outdoor environment sun-protective factors which also promote physical activity, e.g. more trees, grass, and stones; increased space by removal of unnecessary fences; natural materials, and ropes in trees for lianas. By working with these recommendations, the authorities expect UV exposure to be reduced sufficiently in a way that longer times outdoors are possible during the major part of the day, but with little or no risk of sunburn regardless of skin type. This policy is also in line with recommendations for fixed play equipment to be integrated with natural features (trees, shrubbery and hilly terrain) and shaded by leafy trees between 11 am and 3 pm. This gives sufficient sun protection, as the sky view is generally below 50%.

Manicured vegetation or flowerbeds close to buildings were observed by Swedish preschool staff to reduce physical activity and generally were not expected to become part of children's more vigorous physical activity environment (Altin et al. 2013). Because it is usually close to the ground, such vegetation is also not a first option for sun protection. However, it may constitute a valuable outdoor education resource. The North Carolina *Child Care Center Handbook* recommends including in the Outdoor Learning Environment "natural elements such as plants, trees, grass, gardens, and hills to provide opportunities for children to experience and interact with natural materials and learn about nature" (p.3.16). In the North Carolina study sites, native plants were successfully integrated into the Outdoor Learning Environment (OLE), including species to attract butterflies and other pollinating insects that fascinate children, keep them moving, improve ecosystem health[3] and add educational value and aesthetic enhancement for all users (Cosco et al. 2014).

Expanding recommendations by the Swedish authorities, in the name of human health, to increase natural components provides an example of advances in best practice in the design of outdoor environments that may empower landscape designers to improve environmental quality and therefore health—a win-win for all parties.

Informing best practice policy

In 2007, after years of lobbying by NC childcare professionals, "playground" was officially changed in North Carolina licensing rules to

Outdoor Learning Environment, now viewed as an educational resource that should meet built-environment best practice standards to match interior environment quality. However, more sensitive tools are needed to measure preschool activity and OLE characteristics using research evidence, to which the results reported here add strength.

Building on the progress in North Carolina, and with support from a major health foundation, a further step was taken to help *providers* understand the need for design and management intervention in the childcare landscape to improve quality to meet new state evaluation standards. NLI launched Preventing Obesity by Design (POD) in 2006 as a community-based design intervention program, implemented with providers to create regional model OLEs to set a new level of quality using "naturalization" as a cost-effective health promotion strategy. "Naturalize" ("to cause a plant or animal from another place to begin to grow and live in a new area"—Merriam-Webster) is a key concept because the vast majority of childcare centers in North Carolina could be considered land restoration sites. Creating habitats for plants and wildlife restores ecosystem quality while simultaneously providing children with a health-promoting environment, motivating higher levels of physical activity through self-motivated free play and hands-on learning experiences. Naturalization was selected not only because of the low cost (compared to manufactured equipment) but also in recognition of the growing evidence supporting the positive effect of green environments on child development (Kuo 2004, 2010). Green exposure offers a first step in developing positive environmental values (Wells and Lekies, 2006), which in the long run may filter into society at large and influence healthy environmental quality globally.

In 2011, a joint effort by DCDEE and NLI was launched to change regulator perception of the OLE. Supported by the growing evidence of the influence of the outdoor-environment on children's health, NLI conducted a 12-month training program in OLE best practice to help state licensing consultants understand the significance of outdoor quality in supporting health-enhancing behaviors. A post-program survey of the 205 participants indicated substantially increased understanding and a change of attitude towards outdoor learning environments. Those responsible for enforcing licensing rules began to limit their interpretation to specific, rule-based health and safety issues. DCDEE is now diligently working to develop new policies to support outdoor learning. As part of the review of the North Carolina Quality Rating and Improvement System (QRIS), outdoor learning is recommended as an area of specialization (North Carolina Division of Child Development and Early Education, 2012).

Results from almost sixty POD intervention sites suggest that a naturalization approach lowers costs; costs can also be spread over time compared to an exclusively manufactured equipment approach with high up-front costs. Children do not choose their preschool settings; yet they are places where increasing numbers of children spend the majority of their waking hours. Society has an obligation to ensure preschools are designed and managed to support positive health trajectories. A rich landscape can increase positive perceptions of child-development centers by all users (children, parents, teachers), which may help parents feel more relaxed about the long hours in which their children are enrolled, and encourage them to be more fully engaged in center-based activities. Such intervention offers a beneficial, early impact on healthy behavior, which may track into adulthood (Moore et al. 2003).

The North Carolina Institute for Medicine (NCIOM) statewide initiative, which established a broad-ranging *Taskforce on Early Childhood Obesity Prevention*, carried policy a large step forward. The final report (North Carolina Institute of Medicine, 2013) recognizes OLE design and management, including "edible landscapes" as key recommendations for promoting physical activity and healthy eating. As a Taskforce member advocating for built-environment design, NLI concurrently developed an evidence-based/informed "best practice assessment scale." Items include loop/double loop pathway, density of trees and shrubs, amount of shade, edible landscape, and diversity of behavior settings (sand, water, digging, social gathering, multipurpose lawns, decks, manufactured equipment, tunnels, portable and wheeled toys, natural loose parts, natural construction, and more). "Best practices" are derived from literature addressing the influence of environment on children's healthy behavior. For example, loop/double loop pathways support higher physical activity (Cosco, 2006; Cosco et al. 2010; Cosco et al. 2014), especially when combined with wheeled toys. The number of wheeled and portable toys and loose parts are evidence-based items (Greenman, 2005). Analysis of the pre-post evaluation data of shade on POD sites is underway, using methodology developed by the Swedish team and adopted by NLI. Results are likely to demonstrate that the OLE, as defined by best practice criteria, not only supports higher levels of physical activity but can be considered a proxy for strategic UV protection as specified by the U.S. Surgeon General (U.S. Department of Health and Human Services, 2014:47).

Steps forward

The comparative results of the transatlantic collaboration reported here have focused on understanding behavioral health impacts of outdoor environmental quality in childcare centers. Shared methods for coding landscape quality, environment-behavior, physical activity, and UV exposure will continue to support the potential for positive interventions in preschool outdoor environments that may affect multiple health outcomes for young children. Improving children's physical outdoor environments, with its visually tangible outcome may be seen as an effective policy direction and efficient use of scarce preventive health and early education resources. Combined with the previous research by each team, evidence-based policy impacts already achieved (such as the Swedish authorities and NLI professional development of regulators to help change perceptions of the value of naturalized OLEs) are important steps forward.

Further development of a battery of research tools (the majority of which appear to function across childcare contexts) will continue to create a more solid evidence base to aid built environment design of health-promoting outdoor settings for young children. Behavior mapping, a method for objectively measuring physical activity, sun exposure, and other behavioral and environmental attributes is now digitally based, making data gathering more efficient and cost effective. This makes possible the development of valid, reliable management tools to enable childcare providers to monitor outdoor environments more closely to ensure that health promotion goals are being met in the broader context of the individual center educational mission. Examples of uniting municipal health intervention programs that otherwise compete for resources and attention have been initiated (Altin et al. 2014).

In summary, studies that bring knowledge concerning the dynamics of active children's environments will continue to support policy change at state and local level and will support new standards of practice. Both Sweden and North Carolina thus far demonstrate effective strategies linking landscape design with public health within an environment-behavior paradigm, including the value of local knowledge communicated by children and staff. Continuing the momentum of transatlantic collaboration to create an evidence-based perspective on the quality of preschool outdoor environments, as a further step POD is evaluating the hands-on experience of children's gardening and exposure to fresh fruit and vegetables and the impact on home-based behavior.

Recognizing current limitations, further study is needed to explore requirements for high-quality preschool environments in arid regions or in areas with limited vegetation, such as coastal areas with constant salty winds, or for different seasons or climatic conditions at high latitudes. In these situations and for urban redevelopment sites denuded of indigenous vegetation, evidence-based landscape design and ecological restoration techniques have an important and increasing role to play in creating high-quality, best-practice settings where young children can thrive. Moderating factors include teacher discomfort with nature or negative perceptions of the natural world – factors that can be turned around through hands-on teacher training conducted outdoors in best-practice natural settings.

Evidence is accumulating to support policies that promote well-planned, evidence-based high quality outdoor childcare environments that may motivate both self-triggered sun protective behavior and physical activity in preschool children. More time outdoors in spacious, naturally diverse outdoor environments may also contribute to combatting "nature illiteracy" and generate the knowledge necessary to respond to new threats to the health of the natural world. In all countries, preschools and childcare centers have a new, community engagement mission to become agents of change, to demonstrate how designed spaces combined with innovative educational programs can support healthy child development. Best practice design, childcare licensing policies, and accreditation regulations can be seen as viable instruments to produce environmental change and support the healthy lives of millions of children. Eventually, child health and environmental health may go hand in hand.

References

Altin, Carolina et al. 2015. "Upgrading preschool environment in a Swedish municipality. Evaluation of an implementation process". *Health Promotion Practice* : in press.

Armstrong, Bruce K. 2004. "How sun exposure causes skin cancer: an epidemiological perspective." In *Prevention of skin cancer*. Edited by David Hill and Dallas R. English (Kluwer Academic Publishers): 89–116.

Björklid, Pia and Nordström, Margareta. 2012. *Child-friendly cities – sustainable cities*. Living conditions: the influence on young children´s health. Early childhood matters (Bernard von Lear foundation): 118: 44-7.

Boldemann, Cecilia et al. 2004. "Swedish pre-school children's UV-radiation exposure - a comparison between two outdoor environments". *Photodermatology Photoimmunolology Photomedicine* 20:2-8. doi/10.1111/j.1600-0781.2004.00069.x/pdf

Boldemann, Cecilia et al. 2006. "Impact of preschool environment upon children's physical activity and sun exposure". *Preventive Medicine* 42: 301-8.

Boldemann, Cecilia et al. 2011. "Preschool outdoor play environment may combine promotion of children's physical activity and sun protection, Further evidence from Southern Sweden and North Carolina". *Science and Sports* 26: 72-82. DOI:10.1016/j.scispo.2011.01.007.

Bränström, Richard et al. 2006. "Sun exposure and sunburn among Swedish toddlers". *European Journal of Cancer* 42(10): 1441-7. DOI: 10.1016/j.ejca.2006.02.008.

Cosco, Nilda. 2006. "Motivation to Move: Physical Activity Affordances in Preschool Play Areas". (Phd diss, University of Edinburgh). http://www.era.lib.ed.ac.uk/handle/1842/5904.

Cosco, Nilda et al. 2010. "Behavior mapping: A method for linking preschool physical activity and outdoor design". *Medicine and Science in Sports and Exercise* 42(3): 513-9. DOI: 10.1249/MSS.0b013e3181cea27a.

Cosco, Nilda and Moore, Robin. 2003. *Baseline Survey of Environmental Conditions of Outdoor Play Areas in North Carolina Childcare Centers.* Unpublished report. http://naturalearning.org/baseline-survey-environmental-conditions-outdoor-areas-north-carolina-childcare-centers Accessed May 24, 2014.

Cosco, Nilda et al. 2014. "Childcare Outdoor Renovation as a Built Environment Health Promotion Strategy: Evaluating the Preventing Obesity by Design Intervention". *American Journal of Health Promotion* 28(3):27-32. DOI: 10.4278/ajhp.130430-QUAN-208.

DeBord, Karen et al. 2005. "Preschool Outdoor Environment Measurement Scale (POEMS)". Winston-Salem, North Carolina: Kaplan, Inc. http://www.kaplanco.com/media/poems.pdf.

Faber Taylor, Andrea, Frances E. Kuo, and William C. Sullivan. 2001 "Coping with ADD: The Surprising Connection to Green Play Settings". *Environment and Behavior*. 33(1): 54-77. http://eab.sagepub.com/content/33/1/54.full.pdf+html.

Grahn, Patrik et al. 1997. "Outdoors at day care centers" (Swedish). Stad och Land, 145, Movium, University of Agricultural Sciences, Alnarp. http://libris.kb.se/bib/7436222.

Greenman, J. 2005. *Caring Spaces, Learning places: Children's Environments That Work* (2nd ed). (Redmond, WA: Exchange Press).

Gronholt-Olesen, Line, Olesen, Line Groenholt, Peter Lund Kristensen, Lars Korsholm, and Karsten Froberg. 2013. "Physical activity in children attending preschools." *Pediatrics* 132(5):e1310-8. DOI: 10.1542/peds.2012-3961.

Harvey, NC Harvey, N. C., Z. A. Cole, S. R. Crozier, M. Kim, G. Ntani, L. Goodfellow, S. M. Robinson et al. 2012. "Physical activity, calcium intake and childhood bone mineral: a population-based cross-sectional study". *Osteoporosis International* 23:121-30. DOI: 10.1007/s00198-011-1641-y.

Heft, Harry. 1989. "Affordances and the body: an intentional analysis of Gibson's ecological approach to visual perception". *Journal for the Theory of Social Behavior* 19(1): 1–30. DOI: 10.1111/j.1468-5914.1989.tb00133.x

ICNIRP: Guidelines on Limits of Exposure to Ultraviolet Radiation of Wavelengths Between 180 nm and 400 nm (Incoherent Optical Radiation). 2004. *Health Physics* 87(2): 171-186. http://www.ncbi.nlm.nih.gov/pubmed/15257218.

Janssen, Ian and Leblanc, Allana G. 2010. "Systematic review of the health benefits of physical activity and fitness in school-aged children and youth". *International Journal of Behavioral Nutrition and Physical Activity* 11:40. doi: 10.1186/1479-5868-7-40.

Janz, Kathleen F Janz, Kathleen F., Elena M. Letuchy, Julie M. Eichenberger Gilmore, Trudy L. Burns, James C. Torner, Marcia C. Willing, and Steven M. Levy. 2010. "Early physical activity provide sustained bone health benefits later in childhood". *Medicine and Science in Sports and Exercise* 42: 1072–78. doi: 10.1249/MSS.0b013e3181c619b2.

Karolinska Institutet and Center for Epidemiology and Public Health, Stockholm County Council. Criteria for preschool environment to promote physical activity and sun-protective behavior. 2013. http://www.folkhalsoguiden.se/upload/Barn-%20och%20ungdomar/Criteria%20for%20preschool%20environment%20to%20promote.pdf

Karsten, L. 2005. "It All Used to be Better? Different Generations on Continuity and Change in Urban Children's Daily Use of Space". *Children's Geographies* 3: 275-290. http://www.tandfonline.com/doi/pdf/10.1080/14733280500352912.

Kuo, Frances. 2010. Parks and other green environments: Essential components of a healthy human habitat. Ashburn, VA: National Recreation and Park Association. http://search.informit.com.au/documentSummary;dn=076241413812440;res=IELNZC

Kuo, Frances. and Faber Taylor, A. 2004. "A potential natural treatment for attention-deficit/hyperactivity disorder: Evidence from a National Study". *American Journal of Public Health* 94(9): 1580-6. http://www.ncbi.nlm.nih.gov/pmc/articles/PMC1448497/pdf/0941580. pdf

McCarney, S.B., 1995. The early childhood attention deficit disorders evaluation scale. School Version. Technical Manual. Hawthorne Educational Services, Columbia MO. 1995.

Mårtensson, Fredrika. 2004. "The landscape in children's play. A study of outdoor play in pre-schools". PhD diss., Swedish University of Agricultural Sciences, Alnarp, 2004. http://www.ped.gu.se/pedfo/fakopp/martensson.pdf.

Mårtensson, Fredrika, Cecilia Boldemann, Margareta Söderström, Margareta Blennow, J-E. Englund, and Patrik Grahn. 2009. Outdoor environmental assessment of attention promoting settings for preschool children. Health and Place, 15. 1149-57. doi: 10.1016/j.healthplace.2009.07.002.

Mårtensson, Fredrika. 2013. Guiding environmental dimensions for children's outdoor play, ed. Boldemann C, Socialmedicinsk tidskrift, 4: 659-665. www.socialmedicinsktidskrift.se.

Moore, Lynn L, Di Gao, M. Loring Bradlee, L. Adrienne Cupples, Anuradha Sundarajan-Ramamurti, Munro H. Proctor, Maggie Y. Hood, Martha R. Singer, and R. Curtis Ellison. 2003. "Does Early Physical Activity Predict Body Fat Change Throughout Childhood?" Preventive Medicine, 37(1): 10-7. http://www.sciencedirect.com/science/article/pii/S0091743503000483.

National Association for Sport and Physical Education. 2002. *Active start: a statement of physical activity guidelines for children birth to five years*. Reston, VA: NASPE Publications. http://journal.naeyc.org/btj/200605/NASPEGuidelinesBTJ.pdf

North Carolina Division of Child Development. 2009. *Child Care Center Handbook* (Chapter 3). <http://ncchildcare.nc.gov/pdf_forms/center_printercopy.pdf> Accessed May 25, 2014.

North Carolina Division of Child Development and Early Education. 2012. The NC Quality Rating and Improvement System (QRIS). Advisory Committee Executive Summary. Accessed February 10, 2014. http://ncchildcare.dhhs.state.nc.us/PDF_forms/QRIS-Advisory-Committee-Executive-Summary.pdf

North Carolina Institute of Medicine. 2013. *Promoting Healthy Weight for Young Children: A Blueprint for Preventing Early Childhood Obesity in North Carolina*. Morrisville, NC: North Carolina Institute of

Medicine.

Pagels, Peter. 2013. "The study of children's physical activity". Ed. Boldemann C, *Socialmedicinsk tidskrift* 4: 639-646. www.socialmedicinsktidskrift.se .

Parsons, Peter G, Parsons, Peter G., Rachel Neale, Penny Wolski, and Adele Green. 1998. "The shady side of solar protection". *Medical Journal of Australia* 168: 327-30. http://europepmc.org/abstract/MED/9577442.

Rapport, David J., Connie L. Gaudet, R. Constanza, P. R. Epstein, and Richard Levins, eds.1998. *Ecosystem Health: Principles and Practice.* Oxford: Blackwell Science.

Raustorp, Anders, Peter Pagels, Cecilia Boldemann, Nilda Cosco, Margareta Söderström, and Fredrika Mårtensson. 2013. "Accelerometer measured level of physical activity indoors and outdoors during preschool time in Sweden and the United States". *Journal of Physical Activity and Health* 9(6): 801-8. http://journals.humankinetics.com/jpah-back-issues/jpah-volume-9-issue-6-august.

Reznik, Marina, Judith Wylie-Rosett, Mimi Kim, and Philip O. Ozuah. 2013. "Physical Activity During School in Urban Minority Kindergarten and First-Grade Students". *Pediatrics* 131: e81. DOI: 10.1542/peds.2012-1685.

Robinson, Leah E Wadsworth Danielle D, Peoples Christina M. 2012. "Correlates of school-day physical activity in pre-schoolers". *Research Quarterly for Exercise and Sport* 83(1): 20-6. http://www.tandfonline.com/doi/pdf/10.1080/02701367.2012.10599821.

Sallander, Ellinor, Ulf Wester, Emil Bengtsson, and Desiree Wiegleb Edström. 2013. "Vitamin D levels after UVB radiation: effects by UVA additions in a randomized controlled trial". *Photodermatology Photoimmunology Photomedicine* 29: 323-29. DOI: 10.1111/phpp.12076.

Sandseter, Ellen. 2009. "Affordances for Risky Play in Preschool: The Importance of Features in the Play Environment". *Early Childhood Education Journal*, 36: 439-46. DOI 10.1007/s10643-009-0307-2.

Sääkslahti, Arja, Pirkko Numminen, Väinö Varstala, Hans Helenius, Anne Tammi, Jorma Viikari, and Ilkka Välimäki. 2004. "Physical activity as a preventive measure for coronary heart disease risk factors in early childhood." *Scand J Med Sci Sports.* 14(3): 143-9. http://onlinelibrary.wiley.com/doi/10.1111/j.1600-0838.2004.00347.x/pdf.

Söderström, Margareta et al. 2004. "The outdoor environment of day care centers. Its importance to play and development" (Swedish). *Ugeskr for laeger* 166: 3089-92. http://europepmc.org/abstract/MED/15387307.

Söderström, Margareta et al. 2013. "The quality of the outdoor environment influences children's health – a cross-sectional study of preschools". *Acta Paediatrica* 102: 83- 92. doi: 10.1111/apa.12047.

Tanha, Tina et al. 2011. "Lack of physical activity in young children is related to higher composite risk factor score for cardiovascular disease". *Acta Paediatrica* 5: 717-21. DOI: 10.1111/j.1651-2227.2011.02226.x

Tudor-Locke, Catrine, Robert P. Pangrazi, Charles B. Corbin, William J. Rutherford, Susan D. Vincent, Anders Raustorp, L. Michaud Tomson, and Thomas F. Cuddihy. 2004. "BMI-referenced standards for recommended pedometer-determined steps/day in children." *Preventive Medicine* 38: 857-64. http://www.sciencedirect.com/science/article/pii/S0091743504000064.

U.S. Department of Health and Human Services. *The Surgeon General's Call to Action to Prevent Skin Cancer*. Washington, DC: U.S. Dept of Health and Human Services, Office of the Surgeon General; 2014.

Wells, Nancy M and Lekies, Kirsti S. 2006. "Nature and the life-course: Pathways from childhood nature experiences to adult environmentalism." *Child, Youth and Environments* 16 (1): 1-25. URL: http://www.jstor.org/stable/10.7721/chilyoutenvi.16.1.0001

Wester, Ulf and Josefsson, Weine. 1997. "UV-Index and Influence of Action Spectrum and Surface Inclination." In: *Report of the WMO-WHO Meeting of Experts on Standardization of UV-indices and their Dissemination to the Public* Les Diablerets, Switzerland, 21-24 July. World Meteorological Organization, Global Atmosphere Watch Report No 127, 63-66.

Weiss, Ram, James Dziura, Tania S. Burgert, William V. Tamborlane, Sara E. Taksali, Catherine W. Yeckel, Karin Allen et al. 2004. "Obesity and the metabolic syndrome in children and adolescents". *The New England Journal of Medicine*350(23): 2362-2374. DOI: 10.1056/NEJMoa031049.

WHO, WMO, UNEP, ICNIRP. 2002. *Global solar UV-index – a practical guide*. Available at: http://www.who.int/uv/publications/globalindex/en/. Accessed May 2014.

Notes

[1] A UV threshold limit and its possible wavelength dependence for skin malignancies (melanoma) still remain to be established. Though there may be no "safe UV dose" considering skin cancer risk, there are guidelines for avoiding acute effects (e.g. photoceratitis, erythema) from UVR during one day (ICNIRP 2004). These guidelines formulated by the International Commission on Non-Ionizing Radiation Protection (ICNIRP) specify threshold values, which for erythemally effective solar UVR mean doses less than half or a third of a minimal erythemal dose (MED) for sun sensitive persons (1 MED = 2 standard erythemal doses "SED", i.e. 200 Jm^{-2}). Some UVB-radiation (shortwave UVR) is needed for the skin to form vitamin D in sunlight. One SED (100 Jm^{-2} erythemally effective UVR) normally is sufficient for vitamin D acquisition if the exposed skin area is adequate (Sallander et al 2013).

[2] The Environmental Code in Swedish law stipulates that extended time in the outdoor environment of an institution or enterprise is "to supply sufficient protection against disturbances so that the stay there will not imply inconveniences for people's health." Occupational safety law stipulates that safety inspections be carried out at certain intervals at workplaces, schools, and preschools. Safety inspection content is to a large extent settled at local level and is dependent on the type of workplace or educational institution.

[3] "Ecosystem health is an integrative field exploring the relations between human activity, social organization, natural systems, and human health. Its focus is the human condition at all levels, from the community, to the regional, to the global." (Rapport et al. 1998, p. xi.)

CHAPTER SEVEN

MAKING SENSE OF SUSTAINABILITY: BALANCING TECHNOLOGY, USER SATISFACTION, AND AESTHETICS

MARIE-ALICE L'HEUREUX

Introduction

Architects in the early twentieth century thought they could improve the human condition through design. By applying mass-production principles and efficient design to city planning and housing, they hoped to overcome urban overcrowding, the scourge of disease, and the perceived moral lassitude among urban workers. Many cities and countries adopted these principles in order to create (minimal) dwelling standards to house people more efficiently and effectively (Teige 2002).

Conditions among the poorly housed did improve, especially in industrial countries; however, the indiscriminate application of modernist principles across the landscape created over-concentrations of poverty, interpersonal alienation, and a lack of identity and engagement among residents. Architects, especially in the United States' post-WWII euphoria, largely abandoned the social aspects of design and focused on the aesthetic characteristics of modernism—glass facades detached from structure; structure independent of spatial organization; the separation of function vertically and horizontally; machine precision and repetition.

In the 1970s, provoked by OPEC's (Organization of Petroleum Exporting Countries') oil embargo, and the subsequent increase in energy prices, architects started to address energy efficiency in buildings as an economic issue.[1] Prior to 1972, energy articles in architectural journals focused on nuclear energy. In the 1970s and 1980s, economic arguments held forth, although some architects and planners started to recognize the need to consider the environment more carefully. In the late 20th century, architects were again challenged to address societal problems through design, this time to mitigate the impact of the built environment on global climate change.

Buildings account for around 41% of the primary energy consumption in the United States; therefore, improving their efficiency could substantially reduce their contribution to the quantity of greenhouse gases in the atmosphere, the primary contributor to global climate change (U.S. Department of Energy 2012). Given the legacy of past environmental crises, the current political climate in the United States, and the long-range and uncertain nature of potential solutions, it is very difficult to create the national will to tackle climate change (or global warming) effectively (Damon and Kunen 1976). Indeed, many scientists feel we have already gone beyond the Earth's ability to absorb the carbon we have already produced. Major climatic disruptions are, thus, inevitable (Meadows et al. 1972; Meadows, Meadows, and Randers 1992; Meadows, Randers, and Meadows 2004). In the view of these scientists, we should focus on mitigating these future effects by creating more diverse and flexible solutions (Symposium 2012). In other words, by creating a more resilient built environment that people could embrace. Others acknowledge the threat but see the solution in technology and design. They highlight the amount of energy wasted in the generation, distribution, and consumption systems as an opportunity to create technological solutions and efficiencies at the manufacturing level that effectively by-pass the need for getting consensus among people to change behavior.

In this chapter, I argue that architects need to address and become more knowledgeable about global climate change and the importance of going beyond energy standards by engaging all building users in the process. Creative architects *can* design buildings that are carbon neutral *and* functional, structurally rational *and* beautiful. I review the contribution of environment behaviorists to environmental challenges and the goals of energy-and-sustainability standards in design. I discuss the role of architectural education and the profession in promoting sustainability and conclude with a number of case studies of student design-and-built projects and the challenge of introducing sustainable principles into real-world contexts when aesthetic decisions often trump functional ones. This study demonstrates that aesthetics, behavior, *and* technology all need to be engaged for projects to be successful from both a community and a climate change perspective.

Since Ancient Roman times, architects have considered functionality, structural stability, and aesthetics (represented in the Vitruvian triad of *Utilitas*, *Firmitas*, and *Venustas*) (Collins 1965, 22) to be fundamental to their mission. In recent years, however, the reward system embodied in architectural publications and the Pritzker Prize has prioritized dramatically beautiful and innovative buildings over functional ones. Although buildings that "fall down" are relatively rare in the West, buildings that do not meet the needs of their users are, unfortunately, easy to find. Thom Mayne's award winning San Francisco Federal Building (2007) received the lowest user-satisfaction score (twelve percent) among twenty-two federal buildings studied in 2010 (Fowler et al. 2010, 65). Although the building was built on a brownfield site and proved to be energy efficient, it only achieved a Silver LEED (Leadership in Energy and Environmental Design) rating because it failed to incorporate many non-energy related features and used many "decorative" features—such as a cascading exterior metal skin that neither shaded nor insulated the building.

LEED rated or Energy Star buildings that are ostensibly more energy efficient than earlier buildings have not necessarily reduced the built environments' overall carbon footprint since LEED has focused on a broad range of building issues that do not necessarily reduce energy use or increase user satisfaction (Janda 2011). Architects have also received points for innovation, indoor air quality, reusing materials, and more recently, regional priorities—all important considerations. Yet, to achieve carbon neutrality, architects need to go beyond LEED and solve the Vitruvian triad by engaging building users and solving problems at the local, neighborhood, and city scales (Gehl 2010).

Environmental psychology versus design and technology

Man can hardly even recognize the devils of his own creation
—Albert Schweitzer (Carson 1962, p. 6).

In the 1970s, in the face of growing concerns about environmental problems, a team of ecological psychologists became concerned that the field of psychology focused too much on the impact of given environments "on man's behavior" while ignoring "the effect of man's behavior on the environment" (Maloney and Ward 1973, 584). They reasoned that the "ecological threat" was related to overpopulation, over-consumption, and over-pollution—in other words, to "maladaptive behaviors" (Maloney and Ward 1973, 583; Malthus 1817). From this perspective, it is a serious fallacy to think that technological changes alone can solve environmental problems; rather, peoples' thoughts and behaviors must change as well (Schipper et al. 1989; Destatte 2010). Sociologists have to recognize how people understand complex issues before they can find ways to encourage people to change their thinking or act in line with their beliefs (Kempton 1993).

Since the 1970s, psychologists, environmental behaviorists, and sociologists have contributed a plethora of studies on human-environment relationships that have helped urban planners and architects make design decisions (Stern and Gardner 1981; Winett and Geller 1981; Geller 1995; Geller, Willett and Everett 1982; Osbaldiston and Schott 2012). An ongoing discussion among researchers is whether individual attitudes (e.g., ideas about the environment, sustainability, and equity) matter more or less than context (e.g., household type, dwelling, and location) to explain resource consumption (such as water, energy, housing, carbon-intensive travel, and the choice of domestic appliances) (Newton and Meyer 2012). They also have come to realize that attitudes do not directly predict a person's actions. It is not sufficient to ask, *Do you support public transportation?* Better to ask, *Would you use public transportation to travel to work most days?* This makes the desired behavior concrete by introducing a time and a context dimension (Jones 1996). Most studies also focus on only one aspect of the human-environment relationship, such as the motivation to adopt pro-environment behaviors such as recycling (Oskamp et al. 1991), while what is needed is a more nuanced method to understand how human characteristics and activities interact to influence behavior (Cranz 1993; Kibert 2004; Fowler and Christakis 2010; Hards 2011; Hannigan 2014).

In contrast to the behavioral psychologists, the architect William McDonough argues that the environmental crisis is a *design* problem. He distinguishes between eco-efficient designs that simply "make the old destructive system a bit less so" and an "eco-effective" approach that rethinks design problems to reduce the overall ecological footprint (McDonough and Braungart 2002, 62-63; Braungart and McDonough 2007; for more on the ecological footprint, see Wackernagel 1996).

McDonough's ideas resonate with those of physicist Amory Lovins and the sociology-trained lawyer L. Hunter Lovins, who launched the Rocky Mountain Institute (RMI) in 1979 in order to promote ecological values. Lovins and Lovins recognize that people cannot continue consuming resources and polluting the environment as they have in the past. They also think that resources can be used more effectively (by design) so that the necessities and conveniences of modern life can be accommodated more efficiently without fossil fuels. In 1999 they co-authored *Natural Capitalism* with environmentalist Paul Hawken that accounted for the value of the ecosystem. They used an economic argument noting that using oil, which at the time was mostly imported, costs much more than investing in alternatives to it, and they called for "radical resource productivity" (doing more with less) from extraction to end-use and for biomimetic production that turns waste into value (Hawken, Lovins and Lovins 1999, 10). They argue, for instance, that using high-efficiency fans and low-friction ducts saves in construction and in operating costs. An even more innovative approach, using computation fluid dynamics to move air silently and passively through the building, contributes to net-zero energy use (Hawken, Lovins, and Lovins 1999, 99). The later *Climate Capitalism* (Lovins and Cohen 2011) further promotes the idea that businesses and companies, and thus the environment, will benefit from investment in renewable energy and energy-efficient strategies in buildings and neighborhoods. Lovins and Cohen argue, for instance, that employees in structures that are "delightful to be in" are more productive and that students enjoying optimally day-lighted classrooms progressed faster in math and reading (2011, 100). If these principles are applied across the production of goods and services from housing to agriculture, then through efficiencies and the adoption of new fuels, we could maintain our lifestyle while reducing the negative impact of behavior on the environment, "*not at a cost, but at a profit*" (Hawken, Lovins, and Lovins 1999, 243; emphasis in original).

Compared to *Limits to Growth* (Meadows et al. 1972), a study that first sounded the alarm about the over-consumption of natural resources, the works discussed above are infused with optimism and make very seductive arguments. We *are* very wasteful of energy and other resources at the national level. McDonough, Lovins, and the others promote new ways of using technology, such as highly insulating glass and ultra-strong lightweight materials to create efficient systems. They do not advocate changing our behavior or lowering our standard of living so much as devising new ways of thinking in order to use existing resources more effectively—in ways that will still allow us to move from place to place and communicate easily with one another. In the view of people motivated by technological innovation, corporate self-interest rather than governmental regulation will produce the necessary changes. They argue that through *design* we can overcome the negative impacts generated by burning fossil fuels and over consumption (Becerik-Gerber, Gerber, and Ku 2011).

The Rocky Mountain Institute never considered the social and behavioral aspects of adopting new technologies until its most recent work *Reinventing Fire* (Lovins and Rocky Mountain Institute 2011), and even then, only to a very limited extent. In RMI's view, people will change behavior and waste less energy if they have the right feedback (Lovins and

Rocky Mountain Institute 2011, 93-94). The Institute gives multiple examples of successful energy-use reductions. This rosy picture is belied by the most recent Intergovernmental Panel on Climate Change (IPCC) publication that finds that the "total anthropogenic GHG [greenhouse gas] emissions were *the highest in human history* from 2000 to 2010" (IPCC 2013, 5, emphasis in the original). Despite many efforts to reduce carbon emissions and to create sustainable buildings and processes, world-wide emissions have increased because of increasing population and economic development. It is not possible for the world population to achieve the same level of lifestyle that we have in North America without any adjustment to our own lifestyles and expectations. If our lifestyles become more energy and resource efficient, will we simply consume more? (Jevons 1866; Khazzoom 2008). The recent (Fall 2014) drop in energy prices and the related drop in the sale of new hybrid vehicles combined with an increase in the purchase of new trucks and SUVs, demonstrate that Americans would probably consume more (Glinton 2014). Unless we understand that our incremental behaviors contribute to the environmental problem, is change possible (Hardin 1968)?

Architectural standards of sustainability in education and practice

> But architecture is more than aesthetics...
> Form must facilitate function.
> —Edward Feiner, GSA head, 1981-2005 (Dart 2005).

The architectural profession as a whole did not start to focus seriously on environmental issues until 1989, when the foundation was laid to create the Committee on the Environment (COTE) within the American Institute of Architects (AIA) (COTE 2014). This group consists of architects and engineers who work for private firms, national research laboratories, and other similar organizations. COTE promotes and disseminates information to the profession, the building industry, and the academy about creating energy-efficient, healthy, and safe environments. COTE defines "true sustainable design" as "beautiful, humane, socially appropriate, and restorative." It also emphasizes the importance of multiple dimensions in the design process:

> The sustainable design process holistically and creatively connects land use and design at the regional level and addresses community design and mobility; site ecology and water use; place-based energy generation, performance, and security; materials and construction; light and air;

bioclimatic design; and issues of long life and flexibility (COTENotes 2006, 12).

These dimensions, as I show below, parallel the breadth of issues included in developing sustainable standards for architecture, but they do not specifically mention reducing greenhouse gases or the use of fossil fuels—the major contributors to climate change. Nor do they advocate engaging end users in the process. Such broad definitions allow architects to continue to work as they always have, since most architects would argue that this "sustainable design process" (COTENotes 2006, 12) describes their own way of working and designing regardless of global climate change or constricted resources. Consequently, they are often satisfied with achieving the *appearance* of sustainability (i.e., a LEED rating or meeting some of the goals) rather than trying to achieve net-zero carbon in their projects. COTE led the AIA to adopt the 2030 Challenge, created by the architect Edward Mazria in 2002, which calls for buildings to be fossil-fuel free and carbon neutral by the year 2030 (Mazria 2003).

A similar problem exists in schools of architecture. The five collateral organizations that oversee the profession and education of architects (the American Institute of Architects [AIA]; American Institute of Architect Students [AIAS]; Association of Collegiate Schools of Architecture [ACSA]; National Architectural Accrediting Board [NAAB] and the National Council of Architectural Registration Boards [NCARB]) agree that sustainability is a "core issue of architectural education" (Wright 2003, 102). Studies have shown, however, that students and many professionals have a very narrow grasp of sustainability and sustainable development (Kagawa 2007; Moe 2007). Architectural educators might promote sustainability, but few courses are offered to support this interest (Boake 1995; Boyer and Mitgang 1996; Fleming 2002; Allen 2012). In a 2005 study of ecological design programs in the United States and Canada, Sandra Leibowitz Earley shows that few schools of architecture have an emphasis in sustainability according to the following criteria: more than one person teaches in the area and more than two courses are taught in that subject area (Earley 2005).

In a 2012 search of ACSA-Arch *On-line Guide to Architecture Schools*, I found that out of 137 schools of architecture, a total of 107 schools listed a specialization in Sustainability (89 schools) and/or Environment/Sustainability (95 schools).[2] Out of the 107 schools, I randomly selected twenty-one (20%) and investigated online the extent to which sustainability is emphasized in the curriculum and among the teaching staff, using the same criteria Earley used in her study.[3] In 48% (ten) of the schools, the courses and research of the faculty supported the claim that sustainability was a specialization; in 52% (eleven schools), there was not enough evidence to support even a mild claim to a specialization on sustainability. Many school representatives would argue that sustainability is actively taught in the design studio and that this is not evident in the course descriptions. Nonetheless, this is a pretty poor showing since with little evidence of research in this area or the production of energy efficient buildings among the design instructors, it is difficult to understand how they would have sufficient expertise to adequately teach sustainability. A 300-year history of architectural education shows that environmental issues were marginal in schools of architecture until very recently (Leslie 2012). Professors and students still rarely evaluate designs based on energy-efficient criteria (McLennan 2004; Brukman 2012; Salama and Wilkinson 2007). Even professionals who are very committed to both community interests and sustainability are not always successful in realizing buildings that would mitigate atmospheric carbon. The 2014 (draft) version of the *NAAB Conditions for Accreditation* eliminated any mention of zero-carbon strategies that existed in the NAAB's 2009 version (NAAB 2009, 24). The NAAB 2014, however, makes Stewardship of the Environment one of its five perspectives and it argues for "the ethos of sustainable practices" (NAAB 2014, 11). In the 2009 version, that perspective was entitled "Architectural Education and the Public Good" and states that students should "acquire the knowledge needed to address pressing environmental, social, and economic challenges through design, conservation, and responsible professional practice" (NAAB 2009, 11).

Researchers have suggested a number of strategies to help architects and future architects design more sustainably. The architect Kiel Moe argues that our definitions of sustainability limit us and that students should be taught "technics...through the history and philosophy of technology" (2007 p. 28). Some studies urge greater reliance on technology (Becerik-Gerber, Gerber and Ku 2011). Others have shown that technological solutions are favored over basic design strategies even though they are less effective at achieving the goal of zero carbon (Fleming 2002). Architects continue to design buildings and garner awards, but little work is done to understand how the completed buildings actually perform environmentally and socially.

The United Nation's 1987 *Brundtland Report* (which defined sustainability as "development that meets the needs of the present without compromising the ability of future generations to meet their own needs") only refers to "aesthetic reasons" in the context of a justification for "species conservation" (*Report* 1987).[4] Energy efficient buildings until very recently had a reputation of being uni-dimensional and not aesthetically appealing or "modern" among architects. In response to this negative view of energy-efficient buildings, COTE and the Living Building Challenge, two sustainability-rating organizations, have included "beauty" as a desirable characteristic—buildings should after all uplift the spirit of residents and users (Living Building Challenge 2014). LEED grants design innovation points for features that are exceptionally sustainable or innovative. COTE also gives annual awards to outstanding examples of sustainable buildings and has produced hundreds of case studies. For many architects, the aesthetics of buildings is a necessary component of sustainability. But they need to be more than simply aesthetically pleasing, since, as Jacques Herzog notes, only "beautifully *made* buildings" can be truly sustainable (Guy 2012, 560, emphasis mine).

Fig. 7-1. Heifer International, Little Rock, Arkansas, is LEED Platinum certified. Guy and Farmer would designate it as *eco-technic* because it uses conventional building methods to address global climate change. Source: Author, 2014.

In examining a substantial number of design approaches to sustainability, Simon Guy and Graham Farmer identify six sustainable logics of architecture that they characterize as *competing* with each other: *eco-technic*, integrating global environmental concerns with "conventional building design strategies" (Fig. 7-1); *eco-centric*, buildings attuned to their context with a minimal ecological footprint (Fig. 7-2): *eco-aesthetic*, a redefinition of aesthetics that is "nature focused," transforms our consciousness of nature, and is expressed as "non-linear organic;" *eco-cultural*, dwelling adeptly in a given physical and cultural bioregion (Fig. 7-3 and 7-4); *eco-medical*, a "natural and tactile environment" that promotes well-being for individuals; and *eco-social*, focused on

individuals within participatory communities (Guy and Farmer 2001, 142-
44).

Fig. 7-2. Earthship Biotecture, near Taos, New Mexico, by Michael Reynolds,
would be classified *eco-centric* because of its response to context and low
ecological footprint. Earthship buildings have been built around the world and are
self-sufficient and "off the grid." They predate LEED and are more energy efficient
than most certified buildings. Source: Author, 2010.

Architects who want to design in ways that reduce the carbon footprint
of their buildings and occupants thus encounter an array of standards
created by a variety of actors—from the private sector and non-
government associations to local, state, and federal governments (Moore
and Engstrom 2005). Several categories of programs differ in their
approaches to sustainability, depending on the goals of the regulating
organization. Some advocate for and support the creation of a carbon-
neutral built environment (e.g., 2030 Challenge, Zero Carbon Building
(ZCB); and *Passivhaus*/Passive House); others focus narrowly on energy
conservation (Energy Star); some are certificate-based programs that
define sustainability or "green" much more broadly (LEED, Green Globes,
and the Living Building Challenge); and others are traditional building
codes and standards such as IECC (International Energy Conservation
Code), ASHRAE (American Society of Heating, Refrigerating & Air
Conditioning Engineers) 90.1 (the current minimum standard); ASHRAE
189.1 (for High Performance Buildings), and California's Title 24 Energy
Code, to name only a few.

Fig. 7-3. This *eco-cultural* building responds to the architecture of Southern Methodist University and uses a variety of landscape strategies (native wildflowers, green trellises, and landscaped berms to hide the parking) to achieve LEED Platinum. The main entrance to George W. Bush's Presidential Library, Dallas, Texas. Robert A. M. Stern, Architects. Source: Author, 2014.

The advocates of each of these standards promote the idea that following their guidelines will result in buildings that are healthy and sustainable. But they do not necessarily mitigate the worst effects of global climate change—especially if we consider population growth, urban expansion, and development in the Third World. Most of these are comparative standards that claim to reduce the consumption of energy by a percentage compared to "building as usual" or by exceeding the minimum standard by a certain percentage (Energy Star). But these claims are hard to support unless the entire life cycle of the building and its operations (including the embodied energy in materials used to construct and equip it) are taken into account (McDonough and Braungart 2002, K. Fowler et al. 2010). Very few post-occupancy evaluations (POEs) compare base-line values with modeled values and actual consumption data (K. Fowler et al. 2010).

Fig. 7-4. William J. Clinton Presidential Center in Little Rock, Arkansas, initially received a LEED Silver rating that was upgraded to Platinum through LEED Operation + Management v2.0 in 2007 with 69 of 85 points. Similar to the Heifer International building it could be considered *eco-technic*. It also attempts to build on Clinton's "Bridge to the 21st Century" metaphor and its context on the Arkansas River also includes some *eco-cultural* aspects. Designed by James Polshek. Source: Author, 2014.

Many of the building rating systems also rely solely on technological aspects of resource use and do not account for the variable human-behavior aspects of consumption. Any given building varies greatly in energy performance depending on the behavior and context of its inhabitants (Sonderegger 1978). Many of the promoters of these programs have agendas other than reducing the consumption of fossil fuels and the production of greenhouse gases. Architects also interpret these standards differently. As I showed earlier, Heifer International in Little Rock, Arkansas, (by Polk Stanley Rowland Curzon Porter Architects, Ltd.) (Figure 7-1) and Earthship near Taos, New Mexico (Figure 7-2) are both recognized as *sustainable* yet represent completely different approaches to sustainability. The former is an office building with expansive glazing, sophisticated heating and cooling systems, high-tech materials (such as permeable concrete), and a LEED platinum rating NC 2.2 with 52 points. The latter is partially buried, passively heated and cooled, built with recycled materials (such as used tires), equipped with a water-recycling center, and is not LEED rated. The housing units are also smaller than average homes, ranging from 900-1500 square feet compared to the 2010 national average of 2169 square feet.

The concepts of sustainability and unsustainability are socially constructed based on the values ascribed to global climate change, nature, technology, development, and equity. The range of solutions that architects are developing to create "green" or "sustainable" buildings is a testimony to the multiple ways that architects understand and translate these ideas into built form. These multiple interpretations and understandings of the meaning of sustainability, the role of technology, and attitudes about nature translate into significantly different solutions, most of which actually increase the carbon footprint, since all new buildings regardless of their performance are net carbon producers compared to not building anything at all. This creates a wicked problem for architects that is almost insoluble but, nonetheless, needs to be addressed.

Aiming for beauty and energy efficiency in a design-build studio

Anyone who has researched sustainability and the myriad issues surrounding it understands that there are no easy answers. Nonetheless, as architects, if we believe that global climate change is an ethical and social justice issue we should do our utmost to mitigate the impact of our work on the environment. Educating and training architects to design buildings that satisfy the Vitruvian triad of *firmitas*, *utilitas*, and *venustas* in a sustainable way is a challenge. As Tom Spector notes in *The Ethical Architect*, Vitruvius treats the triad as irreducible and does not acknowledge the possibility of conflicts among the three ideals (2003, 36). As any architect who has practiced knows, however, the conflicts among them are not easily resolved.

In this final section, I use a number of award-winning projects created by the design-build course, known as Studio 804, at the University of Kansas to link theoretical ideas about sustainability with the reality of trying to create sustainable buildings. Studio 804, according to its publication, is "a student led process that creates prefabricated architecture that thoughtfully responds to global problems of density and sustainability" (*Schemata XVII* 2008, n. d.). Dan Rockhill is the powerhouse behind the studio and the projects reflect his design vision and commitment to train students to build innovative projects using new processes and incorporating recycled and donated materials. Although some university-based design-build programs, such as Yale's (which dates from 1967) are based in the first year of the graduate program, Studio 804 is the culmination of the degree.[5]

These examples illustrate the difficulty of realizing "sustainability" by simply paying lip service to it or following guidelines without verifying outcomes or involving the client to establish what is needed. The imperatives of teaching and the desire among both professors and students to explore innovative and expressive design ideas seem to prioritize *venustas* over *utilitas* although an appropriately focused course on affordable and sustainable housing could be effective. Structural stability is a given, but detailing for energy performance, maintenance, functionality, and user satisfaction are often sacrificed to "delight." As studio 804 has moved from affordable housing to university buildings, the functional, maintenance, and cost issues have become less detrimental to the client, but making beautiful buildings seems to still be prioritized over function rather than allowing them to be balanced and reinforce each other.

Tenants to homeowners

When Studio 804 celebrates its 20th anniversary in 2015, it will have built twenty projects. Three of these are houses for Tenants to Homeowners (TTH) in Lawrence, Kansas: 216 Alabama (2000), 1603 Random Road (2001), and 1718 Atherton Court (2003). At the time, the Studio 804/TTH partnership seemed a perfect match, since TTH itself embraces innovative ideas to create affordable, accessible, and energy efficient housing and Studio 804 has a desire to build energy efficient projects for the community, reusing local materials, and experimenting while educating students. Each of these projects won some kind of design, affordability, and/or sustainability award. Indeed, 216 Alabama garnered seven awards including First Place in the ACSA Hollow Steel Tube competition; Best Practices in Affordable Housing from the City Design Center at the University of Illinois, Chicago; and a Y2K Roadmap to Green Buildings from the Mid-America Regional Council (MARC). Another building type, the 5-4-7 Arts Center (listed as "Sustainable Prototype" in the LEED database) memorializes the date that the town of Greensburg, Kansas, was destroyed by an F5 tornado (May 4, 2007) (Fig. 7-5). It was the first LEED Platinum building in Kansas and the 13th project created by Studio 804.

Fig. 7-5. Memorial in Greensburg, Kansas, with the remnants of the Big Well Museum and the Pallasite Meteorite sign, five months after an F5 tornado devastated the town. Source: Author, 2007.

The ideal client for many architects is one that gives them the program, and then allows them to resolve it without interference. The client for Studio 804's EcoHawk project, completed in 2013, had this attitude and is delighted with the results.[6] Creating housing for low-income residents, however, requires attention to the fine-grained features of daily life and the maintenance and utility costs. Alan Bowes, the Director of Tenants to Homeowners when Studio 804 built the first house in 2000 was interested in creating more contemporary design solutions for their affordable housing. Generally, low-income projects cannot afford quality design services—so the prospect was enticing. Since much of the materials and labor would be donated, this allowed the projects to also be more affordable. Donated materials, however, create many challenges, and do not necessarily meet energy standards. Although TTH provided Studio 804 with a program of spatial needs and the accessible and energy-efficient requirements, one student admitted that, "The most difficult aspect is you don't know your [specific] client... [you] end up designing for a concept." Another student added that "without specific clients...you lose a sense of a particular [design] direction."[7] Ultimately, the students did not achieve TTH's goal of allowing the residents to become homeowners, since each of the three houses had major utility cost, maintenance and livability issues and TTH ultimately reclaimed ownership to complete the repairs.[8]

At 216 Alabama, students sided the buildings with Okoume panels, a strong lightweight wood from Gabon, Africa, usually used as marine plywood. It is very susceptible to rot, but boat hulls are monolithic with no exposed joints and coated in epoxy, so it works well in that application. Students I interviewed said that it was a controversial choice because the class wanted to be sure that Okoume was being sustainably harvested. The 4'-0" x 8'-0" sheets were cut into 2'-0" x8'-0" horizontal strips for the house and left at 4'-0" horizontal strips on the garage. Although the students sealed the joints, used flashing, and double-and-triple-coated both sides of the panels, they were unable to prevent moisture from entering the joints and the richly red-gold panels soon rotted. TTH had to replace them in a few years with Hardie board siding (Figures 7-6a and 7-6b).

Issues of privacy were also a concern in the houses because of the placement and arrangement of windows. In the 216 Alabama house, the link between the house and the garage was designed as a transparent glass entry with sliding glass doors facing east and west, which was visible from the street—an appealing modernist solution. In the Random Road house, the bathroom was enclosed in translucent panels which, when lit from inside, made residents visible and understandably uncomfortable.

Fig. 7-6a. Looking east at 216 Alabama built in 2000 shortly after completion used with permission of Studio 804. Source: Dan Rockhill.

Fig. 7-6b. Similar view in 2012. The Okoume marine plywood was replaced with Hardie board when the original material rotted. The original sliding glass doors in the entry between the house and garage were replaced with a conventional solid door and panels for privacy and the driveway has been reconfigured. Source: Author, 2012.

Student builders admitted that "we did not really design a house that people would live in...it had a neat effect, made good pictures." Another said, "We were designing for ourselves...trying to do something for ourselves."

The 1718 Atherton Court house incorporated many passive solar features and used recycled materials, such as "industrial steel windows," as much as possible. It also had many maintenance and heating and cooling issues from the start. TTH spent $15,000 in repairs in the first 4 months of occupancy since the recycled steel-frame windows did not provide adequate insulation, the HVAC system was not properly sized, the 20+ glass water-filled tubes along the south wall (about 1'-0" diameter and 42" high that were to store heat in the day and release it in the evening) "leaked" and were removed. They were not only ineffective but consumed valuable space in the living room.

Tenants to Homeowners provided the architectural studio with feedback about the projects every year, but the suggestions were not systematically implemented. At the time TTH did not grasp that innovation and creativity come at a cost and that Studio 804 students needed more guidance. Although Studio 804 and TTH had overlapping needs and could have developed a fruitful partnership, the requirement for affordability and low maintenance conflicted with pedagogical needs and the students' desire to use recycled material and to create innovative beautiful homes that they themselves would be proud to own. Consequently, this was the last TTH house that Studio 804 built. TTH has been building Energy Star but conventionally-designed projects since then. This is not unusual in design-build programs. Many of the early projects built through Yale's School of Architecture have been demolished or have needed extensive renovation (Hayes 2007, 36, 44, 51, 57).

5-4-7 Arts Center

Dan Rockhill approached Greensburg, Kansas, officials soon after the F5 tornado demolished the town. He was interested in having Studio 804 contribute to the rebuilding and appreciated the emerging emphasis on energy-efficient standards. The decision to build every public building to LEED Platinum standards, however, did not translate very well into the private sector. The Arts Center Director and artist, Stacy Barnes had limited input into the design of the building and its features because of the nature of Studio 804's design-build process and Rockhill's feeling that user-or-community input unnecessarily slows down the process, which is very tight given the academic calendar. City leaders also argued that involving the public in design decisions would be "tedious and inordinately time-consuming for the public" (Hoxie, Berkebile and Todd 2012, 73). Consequently, some decisions made in Greensburg were not approved by the general public and did not involve community consensus.

The 5-4-7 Arts Center (Figure 7-7) was designed and built in sections in Lawrence, and transported 325 miles to Greensburg—a feat that took a week to negotiate. Students then completed the construction on-site over the next three months. The Arts Center, inaugurated on the first anniversary of the May 2007 tornado, is architecturally striking with its double skin of tempered glass that extends from just above grade to above the roofline. The glass panels are suspended a few inches from a layer of reclaimed yellow pine from the Sunflower Army Ammunition Plant near Lawrence. The three (600 kWH) wind turbines express the 5-4-7 Arts Center's sustainability, while its glass façade and narrow elongated shape celebrate its twenty-first-century design sensibilities. It received an Honorable Mention in the Life Cycle Building Challenge and an AIA Education Honor Award.

Although Director Barnes appreciates the Arts Center's innovative qualities and recognizes the incredible labor of love the students poured into the project, she told me that she would have made different trade-offs in the $150,000 building if she had been asked. For instance, the shower and changing room, which had to be provided to earn the LEED point for the bicycle rack, consume valuable space but are never used, cost resources to purchase and install but cause confusion for users: people using the combined toilet and sink area have accidently turned on the shower. Barnes would have preferred that that LEED point had been achieved by mitigating light pollution with the selection of more appropriate lighting. The exterior lights are light-weight metal plates, one of which blew off in the first strong wind. Greensburg is an ideal place for night-sky viewing and is the home of the famous Brenham Pallasite Meteorite that was found nearby in 1949 and is housed in the Big Well Museum, the other major Greensburg attraction that lies directly south of the Arts Center.

Fig. 7-7. The 5-4-7 Art Center, Greensburg, Kansas, designed and built by Studio 804 of the University of Kansas was completed in May 2008 and is LEED Platinum. View looking north. The door on the right (east side) was often mistaken for the entrance since it is the closest to the street. The sign of white letters is visible on the western end of the south façade was added by the owner in 2013. The six exterior lights and three 600-watt wind turbines are also visible. The (horizontal) header of the pivoting façade is on the right side of the south facade. Source: Author, 2014.

The pivoting front façade that creates a canopy and opens the interior exhibition space to the exterior is never used except to impress visitors. Barnes would have preferred better access to the lower level since art classes are held there and supplies and exhibition materials often need to be carried up and down the single narrow stair. There is also no stair or ladder access to the roof, which is a "green roof" planted with sedum and equipped with solar panels. This lack of access makes maintenance unnecessarily difficult.

Building	Square footage (SF) and source of information.	Yr. data collected	KWH	kBtu /sf/ yr EUI	Bldg. type average CBECS EUI	Water use gallons/ year according to owner
Greensburg City Hall	4700 NREL	2012 2008-12	51680	41	49	36,000
	4700 owner	2013	56620	45	52.16	8,000
5-4-7 Art Center	1672 owner	2008-11	8580	17.5	69.8	3,020
	1670 NREL	2008-12		13.6		

Table 7-1. Current and projected LEED/ National Renewable Energy Laboratory (NREL) ratings based on projected and actual energy consumption. Arts Center data for the Energy Use Intensities (EUI=kBtu/sf/yr) are from the client for the period spanning from May 28, 2008 to April 29, 2011. The actual consumption data provided by the client differs from the energy use reported by NREL. Also, it is unclear what Commercial Building Energy Consumption Survey (CBECS) data for typical buildings was used by NREL.

The building is not as energy efficient as expected. The solar panels, geothermal system and three 600-watt wind turbines were supposed to provide 44 percent of the on-site renewable energy, but the actual amount of energy that the Arts Center has returned to the grid is only 15 percent of the overall usage (2.6kBTU/sf/Year) according to NREL reports in the 5-year energy consumption figures for the Greensburg projects NREL 2012, 2). However, according to the detailed energy data from 2008-2011 that Barnes gave me, the average electric usage during that period is 8580 kWH/year (29,276 kBTU/year), which translates to 17.5kBTU/SF/year as compared to NREL's calculation of 13.6kBTU/sf/year (Table 7-1).[9] It is still less than the average for the building type (24.2 kBTU/sf/year). The numbers would probably be better if the calculations used the entire building area of approximately 3300 square feet and if the environmental system had been commissioned and balanced. The original design and LEED submissions do not include the lower-storage area, about half the building area, so neither LEED nor NREL counts this space.

Conclusion

Many architects have adopted the language of sustainability and will design to LEED standards if the owner, time, and budget allow. But the need is so much greater as the Living Building and 2030 Challenge developers recognize. The world's entire ecosystem is in dire need of focused, concerted action—a veritable sea change in thinking and action must take place on every front. Political antagonisms have made reasoned discussion on global climate change impossible. Individuals and groups representing every effected field must face the seriousness of this challenge and seek genuine rather than ersatz solutions.

Training students of architecture to design and build in a sustainable way needs to include meeting the needs of the people who will use those environments. Although some of the features of sustainability may conflict with each other, such as reusing and recycling local materials and using energy efficient products, students also need to be trained to make the right ethical design decisions. Beauty is a necessary component of architecture, but simply the desire to create innovative or fanciful forms does not relieve the architect of the responsibility of making a building that is functional and affordable for its users and energy efficient and sustainable for the environment.

References

Allen, Stan. 2012. "1990-2012: The Future Is Now." In *architecture school: Three centuries of educating architects in North America*, edited by Joan Ockman and Rebecca Williamson, 202-229. Cambridge: MIT Press.

Becerik-Gerber, Burcin, David J. Gerber, and Kihong Ku. 2011. "The pace of technological innovation in architecture, engineering, and construction education: Integrating recent trends into the curricula." *Journal of Information Technology in Construction (ITcon)* 16: 411-432. http://www.itcon.org/2011/24.

Boake, Terri Meyer. 1996. "A survey of sustainability and passive design curriculum development in schools of architecture" in Judith Kinnard & Kenneth Schwartz, ed. *84th ACSA Annual Meeting and Technology*

Conference Proceedings. Washington, DC: Association of Collegiate Schools of Architecture.

Boyer, Ernest L., and Lee D. Mitgang. 2007. *Building community: A new future for architecture education and practice*. Princeton, NJ: The Carnegie Foundation for the Advancement of Teaching, 1996.

Braungart, Michael, William McDonough, and Andrew Bollinger. 2006. "Cradle-to-Cradle Design: Creating healthy emissions: A strategy for eco-effective product and system design." *Journal of cleaner production* (15) 13: 1337-1348. doi: 10.1016/j.jclepro.2006.08.003.

Brukman, Eden. 2012. "Drawing From Nature: Envisioning a World of Living Sites, Buildings and Communities." Paper presented at the Making It Real, Green Energy Conference, International Living Future Institute, Kansas City, Missouri, May 10.

Carson, Rachel. 1962. *Silent Spring*. Boston: Houghton Mifflin Co.

Collins, Peter. 1965. *Changing Ideals in Modern Architecture 1750-1950*. Montreal: McGill University.

COTE. 2014. http://network.aia.org/CommitteeontheEnvironment/Home/.

COTENotes. 2006. "A Sustainability Strategy Takes Shape." Newsletter of the Committee on the Environment. (Fall): 73-78. www.aia.org/aiaucmp/groups/aia/documents/pdf/aiab091249.pdf.

Cranz, Galen. 1993. "Environmental Power in Human Transitions: Sustainable Development and Environmental Design Research," in *Power by Design* edited by Roberta Feldman, Graham Hardie, and David Saille, 27-31. Chicago, IL: EDRA 24 Proceedings.

Damon, Paul E., and Steven M. Kunen. 1976. "Global Cooling?" *Science* 193 no. 4252 (August 6): 447-453. doi:10.1126/science.193.42 52.447.

Dart, Bob. 2005. "Top Federal Architect Refined U.S. Landscape; Before His Retirement, Feiner Shifted Design of Public Buildings from Dull to Dramatic." *Austin American-Statesman* (February 27): A17.

Destatte, Philippe. 2010. "Foresight: A Major Tool in Tackling Sustainable Development." *Technological Forecasting and Social Change* (77)9:1575-1587. doi: 10.1016/j.techfore.2010.07.005.

Earley, Sandra Leibowitz. 2005. *Ecological Design and Building Schools: Green Guide to Educational Opportunities in the United States and Canada*. Oakland, CA: New Village Press.

Fleming, Rob. 2002. "Survivor Studio@Philadelphia University: Promoting Sustainability in the design studio through collaborative game playing." *International Journal of Sustainability in Higher Education* (3)2: 146-54.

Fowler, James H., and Nicholas A. Christakis. 2010. "Cooperative Behavior Cascades in Human Social Networks." *Proceedings of the National Academy of Sciences* (107)12: 5334-5338. doi: 10.1073/pnas.0913149107.

Fowler, Kim M., Emily M. Rauch, Jordan W. Henderson, and Angela R. Kora. 2010. *Re-assessing Green Building Performance: A Post Occupancy Evaluation of 22 GSA Buildings.* PNNL-19369. Richland, WA: Pacific Northwest National Laboratory.

Gehl, Jan. 2010. *Cities for People.* Washington, DC: Island Press.

Geller, E. Scott. 1995. "Integrating Behaviorism and Humanism for Environmental Protection." *Journal of Social Issues* 51: 179-95.

Geller, E. Scott, Richard Willett, and Peter B. Everett. 1982. *Preserving the Environment: New Strategies for Behavior Change.* New York: Pergamon Press.

Glinton, Sonari. "As Gas Prices Drop, Hybrid Sales Shift into Low Gear," *All Things Considered*, National Public Radio, October 17, 2014. http://www.npr.org/player/v2/mediaPlayer.html?action=1&t=1&islist=false&id=356949485&m=357004650

Guy, Simon. 2012. "Introduction: Whither 'Earthly' Architectures: Constructing Sustainability." In *Sage Handbook of Architectural Theory,* edited by C. Greig Crysler, Stephen Cairns and Hilde Heynen, 555-572. London: Sage Publications.

Guy, Simon, and Graham Farmer. 2001. "Reinterpreting Sustainable Architecture: The Place of Technology." *Journal of Architectural Education* (54)3: 140-148.

Hannigan, John. 2014. *Environmental Sociology.* 3rd ed. Abingdon, Oxon: Routledge.

Hardin, Garrett. 1968. "The Tragedy of the Commons." *Science: New Series* (162)3859 (Dec. 13): 1243-1248.

Hards, Sarah. 2011. "Social Practice and the Evolution of Personal Environmental Values." *Environmental Values* 20: 23-42.

Hawken, Paul, Amory B Lovins, and L. Hunter Lovins. 1999. *Natural Capitalism: Creating the Next Industrial Revolution.* Boston: Little, Brown & Co.

Hayes, Richard W. 2007. *The Yale Building Project: The First 40 Years.* New Haven, Yale University Press.

Hoxie, Christina, Robert Berkebile, and Joel Ann Todd. 2012. "Stimulating Regenerative Development through Community Dialogue." *Building Research and Information* (40)1: 65-80.

IPCC (Intergovernmental Panel on Climate Change). 2013. "Summary for Policymakers." In *Climate Change 2013: The Physical Science Basis.*

Contribution of Working Group I to the Fifth Assessment Report of the Intergovernmental Panel on Climate Change, edited by Thomas F. Stocker, Dahe Qin, Gian-Kasper Plattner, M. Tignor, S.K. Allen, J. Boschung, A. Nauels, Y. Xia, V. Bex and P.M. Midgley. Cambridge, UK: Cambridge University Press. http://report.mitigation2014.org/spm/ipcc_wg3_ar5_summary-for-policymakers_approved.pdf.

Janda, Kathryn B. 2011. "Buildings Don't Use Energy: People Do." *Architectural Science Review* (54)1: 15-22.

Jevons, William Stanley. 1866. *The Coal Question; An Inquiry Concerning the Progress of the Nation, and the Probable Exhaustion of Our Coal Mines.* Second ed. rev. London: Macmillan.

Jones, Alice. 1996. "The Psychology of Sustainability: What Planners Can Learn from Attitude Research." *Journal of Planning Education and Research (*16)1 (Fall): 56-65.

Kagawa, Fumiyo. 2007. "Dissonance in Students' Perceptions of Sustainable Development and Sustainability: Implications for Curriculum Change." *International Journal of Sustainability in Higher Education* (8)3: 317-338. doi: 10.1108/14676370710817174

Kempton, Willett. 1993. "Will Public Environmental Concern Lead to Action on Global Warming?" *Annual Review Energy Environment* 18: 217-45.

Khazzoom, J. Daniel. 2008. "Economic Implications of Mandated Efficiency Standards for Household Appliances." *The Energy Journal* (1)4: 21–40. doi:10.5547/issn0195-6574-ej-vol1-no4-2.

Kibert, Charles J. 2004. "Green Buildings: An Overview of Progress." *Journal of Land Use & Environmental Law* (19)2: 491-502.

Leslie, Thomas. 2012. "Environmental Technology, Sustainability." In *Architecture School: Three Centuries of Educating Architects in North America,* edited by Joan Ockman and Rebecca Williamson, 306-12. Cambridge: MIT Press.

Living Building Challenge. 2014. http://living-future.org/lbc

Lovins, Armory B. and Rocky Mountain Institute. 2011. *Reinventing Fire: Bold Business Solutions for the New Energy Era.* White River Junction, VT: Chelsea Green Publishing.

Lovins, L. Hunter and Boyd Cohen. 2011. *Climate Capitalism: Capitalism in the Age of Climate Change.* New York: Hill and Wang.

Maloney, Michael P., and Michael P. Ward. 1973. "Ecology: Let's Hear from the People: An Objective Scale for the Measurement of Ecological Attitudes and Knowledge." *American Psychologist* 7: 583-86. Doi: 10.1037/h0034936.

Malthus, Thomas Robert. 1817. *An Essay on the Principle of Population; or, A View of Its Past and Present Effects on Human Happiness with an Inquiry into our Prospects Respecting the Future Removal or Migration of the Evils Which it Occasions*. Fifth ed. London.

Mazria, Edward. 2003. "It's the Architecture, Stupid." *World and I.* May/June: 48-51. http://search.proquest.com/docview/235839746?accountid=14556.

McDonough, William and Michael Braungart. 2002. *Cradle to Cradle: Remaking the Way We Make Things*. New York: North Point Press.

McLennan, Jason F. 2004. *The Philosophy of Sustainable Design: the Future of Architecture*. Kansas City, MO: Ecotone.

Meadows, Donella H., Dennis L. Meadows, Jørgen Randers, and William W. Behrens III. 1972. *The* Limits to Growth*: A Report for the Club of Rome's Project on the Predicament of Mankind*. New York: Universe Books..

Meadows, Donella H., Dennis L. Meadows, and Jørgen Randers. 1992. *Beyond the Limits: Confronting Global Collapse, Envisioning a Sustainable Future*. Post Mills, VT: Chelsea Green Pub. Co.

Meadows, Donella H., Jørgen Randers, and Dennis L. Meadows. 2004. *The Limits to Growth: The 30-year Update*. White River Junction, VT: Chelsea Green Pub. Co.

Moe, Kiel. 2007. "Compelling yet unreliable theories of sustainability." *Journal of Architectural Education*: 24–30. doi:10.1111/j.1531-314X.2007.00105.x

Moore, Steven A. and Engstrom, Nathan. 2005. "The Social Construction of 'Green Building' Codes: Competing Models by Industry, Government and NGOS" in *Sustainable Architectures: Cultures and Natures in Europe and North America*, edited by Simon Guy and Steven A. Moore, 51-70. New York: Spon Press.

NAAB (National Architectural Accrediting Board). 2009. *2009 Conditions for Accreditation.* Washington, DC.

—. 2013. *2014 Conditions for Accreditation First Draft.* Washington, DC. August 29.

Newton, Peter, and Denny Meyer. 2012. "The Determinants of Urban Resource Consumption." *Environment and Behavior* (44)2: 107-35. doi:10.1177/0013916510390494.

Osbaldiston, Richard and John Paul Schott. 2012. "Environmental Sustainability and Behavioral Science: Meta-Analysis of Proenvironmental Behavior Experiments." *Environment and Behavior* (44)2: 257-99. doi:10.1177/0013916511402673.

Oskamp, Stuart, Maura J. Harrington, Todd C. Edwards, Deborah L. Sherwood, Shawn M. Okuda, and Deborah C. Swanson. 1991. "Factors Influencing Household Recycling Behavior." *Environment and Behavior* 23: 494-519. doi:10.1177/0013916591234005.

National Renewable Energy Laboratory (NREL). 2012. *Rebuilding It Better: Greensburg, Kansas, High Performance Buildings Meeting Energy Savings Goals.* US Department of Energy: Golden, CO.. www1.eere.energy.gov/office_eere/pdfs/53539.pdf

Salama, Ashraf M. A., and Nicholas Wilkinson. 2007. *Design Studio Pedagogy: Horizons for the Future.* Gateshead, UK: Urban International Press.

Schemata XVII Studio 804_8. 2008. Lawrence, KS.: School of Architecture Design and Planning, University of Kansas.

Schipper, Lee, Sarita Bartlett, Dianne Hawk, and Edward Vine. 1989. "Linking Life Styles and Energy Use: A Matter of Time?" *Annual Review of Energy* 14: 273-320. doi: 10.1146/annurev.eg.14.110189.001421

Sonderegger, Robert C. 1978. "Movers and stayers: The resident's contribution to variation across houses in energy consumption for space heating." *Energy and Buildings* (1)3: 313-324. doi: 10.1016/0378-7788(78)90011-7.

Spector, Tom. 2001. *The Ethical Architect: The Dilemma of Contemporary Practice.* New York: Princeton Architectural Press.

Stern, Paul C., and Gerald T. Gardner. 1981. "Psychological Research and Energy Policy." *American Psychologist* (36)4: 329-342. doi:10.1037/0003-066X.36.4.329.

Symposium. 2012. "Perspectives on Limits to Growth: Challenges to Building a Sustainable Planet," Co-sponsored by the Club of Rome and the Smithsonian Institution's Consortium for Understanding and Sustaining a Biodiverse Planet presented in the Rasmuson Theater, National Museum of the American Indian at the Smithsonian Institution on March 1. www.si.edu/consortia/limitstogrowth2012.

Teige, Karel. 2002. *The minimum dwelling: The housing crisis, housing.* Trans. Eric Dluhosch. Cambridge, MA: MIT Press.

U.S. Department of Energy. 2012. *2011 Buildings Energy Data Book.* Buildings Technologies Program Energy Efficiency and Renewable Energy by D&R International, Ltd. March. http://buildingsdatabook.eren.doe.gov/docs%5CDataBooks%5C2011_BEDB.pdf.

Wackernagel, Mathis. 1996. *Our Ecological Footprint: Reducing Human Impact on the Earth.* Gabriola Island, BC: New Society Publishers.

Winett, Richard A. and E. Scott Geller. 1981. "Comment on Psychological Research and Energy Policy." *American Psychologist* (36)4: 425-426. doi: 10.1037/0003-066X.36.4.425

Wright, James. 2003. Introducing Sustainability into the Architecture Curriculum in the United States. *Journal of Sustainability in Higher Education* (4)2: 100-105. doi:10.1108/14676370310467131.

Notes

[1] For instance, the entire April 1980 issue of *Progressive Architecture* was dedicated to "Energy Conscious Design,'.

[2] http://apps.acsa-arch.org/guide_search/ consulted July 28, 2012.

[3] I listed the schools is alphabetical order and selected school ranks that ended in 0 or 7 (so 7, 10, 17, etc.)

[4] According to the Report, "The diversity of species is necessary for the normal functioning of ecosystems and the biosphere as a whole. The genetic material in wild species contributes billions of dollars yearly to the world economy in the form of improved crop species, new drugs and medicines, and raw materials for industry. But utility aside, there are also moral, ethical, cultural, aesthetic, and purely scientific reasons for conserving wild beings." (Report 1987, 20).

[5] In 2013-14, Studio 804 undertook the design and construction of The Forum, a new gathering and education space for the School of Architecture, Design, and Planning at the University of Kansas which extended into a third semester.

[6] From a meeting with Dr. Christopher Depcik on September 22, 2014.

[7] Phone interviews of 1-1.5 hours, were conducted with 4 students from each of the three projects in August 2012.

[8] See http://studio804.com/projects/projectsPage.html for images and plans of the projects.

[9] I thank Stacy Barnes for giving me this data, in the form of printouts of the bills from May 2007 through our meeting in 2011. As an independent researcher, I have found this data very difficult to get. I also thank Greensburg's current Mayor, Bob Dixson, who authorized the City Administrator, Ed Truelove, to give me the consumption data for City Hall and the Public Works Building—which he did as yearly totals for energy and water for 2012 and 2013. Unless the data for particular buildings can be studied, it is impossible to know if modeled energy and water consumption is achieved or not. This feed-back loop is critical to improving the sustainability of buildings and should be part of the public record.

CHAPTER EIGHT

SOCIAL FACTORS IN THE AGE OF SOCIAL MEDIA: TRANSDISCIPLINARY CO-DESIGN WITH THE PINOLEVILLE POMO NATION

YAEL V. PEREZ, RYAN SHELBY, DAVID EDMUNDS, ANGELA JAMES AND ALICE M. AGOGINO

Introduction

In the last five decades, scholarship in environmental psychology has highlighted the centrality of users to the design process. Moreover, sustainable building measures, such as those created by the American Institute of Architects, include criteria for social and cultural factors. These measures, however, did not significantly change the design tools and methods used in practice. Co-design—a methodology that is predicated on the recognition that local people and users are key participants, with significant contributions to offer to and throughout the design process—is still not commonly deployed in architectural enterprises. With the goal to identify tools and technologies to facilitate co-design, this study investigates the design-methods and social-factors literature to extract recommendations regarding the role of local people in the design process from its very early stages. The recommendations for face-to-face and mediated methods for co-design in the literature are tested through a case-study in which a group of University of California, Berkeley faculty and students design sustainable homes with the Pinoleville Pomo Nation (PPN), a Native American Nation located two hours' drive north of Berkeley. We conclude with a suggested framework for leveraging existing digital social media into a platform for co-design.

The architectural-design process starts by studying the place where the building will be situated. Kalay (2004) refers to this early stage of design as an "exploration of the problem to be solved." According to Kalay, this process includes understanding the context of the project, which contains physical, social, economic, political, and cultural aspects. All of these are man-made or people-related aspects, except the physical context which may also include natural elements that are not social products.

Though social factors have become increasingly important with the growing awareness that social and cultural aspects are part of sustainable design,[1] the methods for understanding the social context remain unsettled. Liane Lefaivre and Alexander Tzonis (2003) use the term "critical regionalism" to describe a bottom-up approach to design "that recognizes the value of the identity of a physical, social and cultural situation" (11). On a more metaphoric level, Burns and Khan (2005) claim that "Design does not simply impose on a place. Site and designer engage in a dialogic interaction" (XV). Hence, this chapter focuses on bottom-up methods that facilitate the site-designer dialog by incorporating the local community, with their expertise on the local site, culture, and needs, as part of the design team and identifying technologies to support this co-design process as part of a sustainable design approach.

Approaches to learning about the people in the place

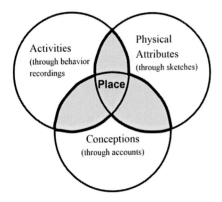

Fig. 8-1. Mirroring the elements of place (Canter, 1977).

While there is general agreement about the importance of understanding social and cultural attributes of place, there are different recommendations for best achieving this understanding as part of the design process. Canter recommends three methods—sketching, accounts, and recordings—to comprehend the place through the three essential elements of place, which are physical attributes, activities and conceptions (Fig. 8-1). In Canter's (1977) own words: "Sketches mirror the physical attributes, accounts the conceptual, and behavior recordings the activity components" (161). Rapoport (2005) advocates a similar focus on the social in his recommendations for architects, by encouraging them to look at people's lifestyle. According to him, lifestyle should "be seen as the outcome of choices about how to allocate resources, not only economically but also time, effort, involvement, etc." (96). To learn about people's lifestyle, Rapoport suggests using customers' information gathered to aid product marketing.

Lynch and Hack (1984), supporting a similar perspective of the subjective nature of place, give an extensive list of the elements that planners should consider before designing, including soil, plants, water, animal behavior, human behavior, and more. They then detail the tools that can be used in this foundational evaluation, from maps and wind-tunnels to demographic analysis and observations.

While the 1980s' literature focused primarily on on-site data collection methods, current debates center more on the analytical process. Site analysis, according to Ellis (2005), is a method that helps designers to express the local character in the design. O'Donnell (2006) argues, conversely, that methodological site analysis creates generic buildings. She suggests using abstract diagrams rather than descriptive analysis for understanding the particular environment, arguing that the resulting "decontextualization" will yield an integrated, sustainable architectural solution.

Alexander (1964), in his early search for rational methods to produce the optimal building, claimed that representations and diagrams are key to the architectural solution. A decade later he (Alexander, Ishikawa, and Silverstein 1977) developed the Pattern Language in which architecture is decomposed to generative grammar components that can be tailored together to fit each project and should be implemented through a participatory process with users (Alexander et al. 1975). However, even as "the medium of representation" becomes increasingly more sophisticated, representation, for example representation of people, always unavoidably selects and transforms the information, including some aspects and leaving others out (Kalay 2004). It is therefore important to examine which medium of representation fits the co-design needs. Since participatory design or citizen participation, as Arnstein (1969) suggests, encompasses eight different levels from citizen control to (citizen) manipulation we choose the term co-design as a partnership between professional designers and local users that focuses on empowering the users, as experts on their locality and needs. Choosing the term co-design aims to distinguish the design process from participatory processes that abuse the term "participation," an abuse which Arnstein labels as "tokenism" and "non-participation," but is often associated unrightfully with terms such as "participatory design" and "citizen participation."

People, users and co-design in practice

Despite the variety of scholars emphasizing the need for local, emic understanding of place for design purposes, direct interaction that goes beyond the clients into groups of users and local communities is a mostly uncommon architectural practice. As Cuff (1989) puts it "The connections between places and individual behavior and perception are well established, both in the academy and in the minds of designers. The weaker link is between places and groups, societies, or culture" (101). A political change that empowers local groups through budget allocation, design restrictions or design controls, together with appropriate tools and methods to support a non-hierarchical design process, would offer ways for design to reinforce the link between place and local groups.

Alexander, working on the design of the school of music building at the University of Oregon, supported collaboration with users and recommends a process of reaching consensus in the co-design team (Alexander et al. 1975). Nevertheless, due to the nature of the project he worked on, a university campus building, set in a hierarchal environment, the design team he managed was ingrained with top-down approaches and his representative user-group was a relatively homogeneous group of only academics though at different levels: the dean, two faculty members, and a student, working together with two designers from Alexander's crew (Alexander et al. 1975). Therefore, in his experiment it was probably easier to reach decisions with a consensus process, as he recommends, than it would be with users of different cultures, disciplines, and socio-economic backgrounds. This chapter expands the thinking of co-design by presenting a project in which the design team, consisting of Native American clients and UC Berkeley faculty and students, designed together culturally-sensitive housing while transcending cultural, social, and professional differences. These differences offered an opportunity to identify and evaluate design methods and tools that support the co-design process, with the assumption that those effective in these extreme conditions could be useful to a broad variety of other case-studies.

Research problem: Supporting top-down approach with bottom-up solutions in US Native American country

Hindering the implementation of socially sensitive design recommendations are a range of factors including time, costs, and unquantifiable benefits. In his book, *Social Design*, Sommer (1983) suggests that "time will tell whether professional education and research without politics (social design) or politics and legislation without research (consumer movement) is the more successful strategy for improving product quality and increasing accountability within industry and the professions" (167). We contend that increasing professional accountability and incorporating social factors in practice necessitates both the political top-down approach through regulations and laws as well as the academic grounding through research and professional education.

In our case study, the political is a top-down approach, which includes changes in building policies to empower local communities and to provide them with freedom to make their own design decisions at the local scale. In 1996, the U.S. department of Housing and Urban Development (HUD) passed the Native American Housing Assistance and Self-Determination Act (NAHASDA), which allows Native-American nations to use federal funds to self-compose their housing solutions as opposed to imposing on them pre-designed HUD houses[2]. Particularly for small tribes in Northern California, this change in top-down paradigm is empowering tribal citizens to directly influence their own housing solutions. It provides them with an opportunity to identify bottom-up methods, which can facilitate community driven design, supported by professional designers. This change was the starting point of our co-design project with the PPN.

The PPN's search for a way to use the federal funds to create housing that will support their needs for self-sustainability and unique cultural needs, led them to CARES (Community Assessment for Renewable Energy and Sustainability), a group of UC Berkeley professors and students engaged in developing methods to help communities choose among the variety of sustainable solutions appropriate for them and make more informed decision in the path for a culturally-sensitive, sustainable future[3].

The PPN brought to CARES its current design needs for developing a variety of sustainable, culturally sensitive housing projects. These projects were developed over several semesters using different co-design methods drawn from product design and architecture. The goal of the projects reflects both a bottom-up and the top-down approach: the direct goal was to build better tribal housing for the PPN while defining the PPN's prototype house to represent the tribes' design needs at different levels. To support that top-down change, another political goal was to advocate tribal needs for culturally-appropriate and sustainable housing in-front of federal agencies (Edmunds et al. 2013). At the same time, the academic goal of the project, which is the focus of this chapter, was to identify and experiment with co-design methodologies and supporting technologies that could conciliate the top-down and bottom-up approaches.

Research method

In this community-based, case-study research project we gather knowledge from interactions between professional designers (architects and engineers) and PPN citizens that spanned over three years. During that time, the designers and citizens worked on three projects:

- The co-design of a concept house and supporting engineering systems,
- The co-design of a low income clustered-housing neighborhood for PPN tribal members, and
- The co-design of two prototype houses on the PPN reservation and supporting engineering systems.

All the design projects focused on sustainable housing and the required supporting systems. On the designers' side were members of the CARES leadership team, as well as students from the College of Engineering and the College of Environmental Design. The PPN community was composed of the PPN Chair, Vice Chair, other elected council members, and other citizens. The co-design process aimed at understanding the unique needs of the PPN and developing, with tribal members, the appropriate housing solutions. While doing so, we explored appropriate design and communication methods, including discussions, workshops, meetings, and design-charrettes, and experimented with in-person and mediated tools such as phone, email, content management systems to support these methods.

The process started by discussing broad concepts such as sustainability and technology, including understanding their unique meaning for the PPN. It then became more project-specific: visiting current PPN citizens' houses, discussing current problems of the existing homes as they emerged during walk-through of the current housing, and establishing priorities for the tribal housing and sustainable living practices as part of collaborative workshops. Eventually, the process included a design charrette in which tribal citizens envisioned their housing solution guided by CARES members. As all authors of this paper, the CARES members and PPN representatives, are active participants in the design method we analyse, we situate this research between Participant Observation (DeWalt and DeWalt 2011), in which the researchers participated in the design activities while observing the process, and Participatory Action Research (Whyte, Greenwood, Lazes 1989) as PPN participants were active researchers by taking decision regarding the project and the methods used, rather than being blind participants.

Co-design through unmediated and mediated interactions: Findings

The design process of the prototype houses developed was in response to needs and restrictions coming both from the tribal leadership and from the academic counterpart; the project was part of design education of the UC Berkeley engineering students and architecture students. The workshop, organized as part of the co-design, aimed to familiarize the students with Native American culture and lifestyle as well as to attract native community members to actively participate in the process through discussions, sharing of experiences, and developing alternatives and solutions. We divide the in-person process into three parts before presenting the technologically-mediated interactions, which happened in between these different stages: (1) producing knowledge from cultural understanding of broad concepts, (2) producing knowledge from current tribal housing experiences, and (3) producing knowledge through design charrettes.

Producing social knowledge from cultural understanding of broad concepts

The first workshop with the PPN included a session in which we gathered subjective responses to the meanings of broad concepts such as 'technology' and 'sustainability' with PPN citizens. In the interaction between CARES members and PPN citizens, different terms were used interchangeably to describe the tribe's housing needs such as ecological, environmentally sensitive, sustainable, etc. During the workshop, four major aspects that frame sustainability for the tribe were identified: Cultural Sovereignty, Tribal Sovereignty, Economic Self-Sufficiency and Environmental Harmony (Shelby, Perez and Agogino 2012).

An important element of this stage of the process was the "situating" (Haraway 1988) of all participants, including engineers and architects. All participants expressed their own histories related to the project and their own aspirations for the work. This allowed for points of shared experience as well as points of difference to be identified. Doing so improved social relations across race, class, and educational barriers and possibly expanded the range of ideas put forward within the group. Moreover, the situating of all participants allowed the process to be transdisciplinary, setting the foundations for interaction and cross-fertilisation among different professions and the non-professionals. The expression of different subjectivities and epistemologies holds significance beyond the strictly interpersonal and allows each worldview to be situated in a socio-cultural matrix that constitutes the design team yielding a deeply rooted co-design process.

Producing social knowledge from current tribal housing experiences

To better translate the broad concepts of housing needs into design guidelines, PPN members participating in the workshop were divided according to age groups (elders, adults, and youth) to describe or illustrate their needs based on their experience from their current housing. Then, in the mixed group of elders, adults and youth the community identified five top priorities: (1) traditional building techniques, (2) energy generation and conservation, (3) exercise and recreation, (4) privacy, and (5) heating, cooling, and lighting. The CARES member acted as interpreters, helping to extract and organize the needs that were voiced. The full process of extracting the subjective sustainable priorities with the PPN is described in Shelby, Perez and Agogino (2012). This knowledge production was combined with meetings between CARES and PPN citizen on campus, often as part of the student's class. The switch of roles that happens when PPN citizens are coming as guests to campus and provide feedback was meaningful. It allowed the PPN citizens to experience their role as the local experts while exposeing them to the students' lives within the university and class setting, a switch from previous meetings in which citizens exposd their lifestyle to the students for the project's purposes.

In addition CARES members visited current tribal HUD houses, talked to their inhabitants while touring the house, and identified and discussed characteristics in the current housing that the inhabitants appreciated and those the inhabitants felt were inappropriate to their lifestyle. HUD-designed houses provided to the PPN are designed for the stereotypical American, nuclear family of four. When CARES members visited the houses on the Indian reservation the Native residents mentioned the kitchen was too small to serve the richer social activity involved in food preparation in Native American culture. According to some residents, the living rooms were not open enough to allow visual and oral communication between family members or to have social life in the main living space and in the kitchen. Rooms were too small and too few to fit the cultural need of often having extended family members residing together for long periods of time.

Fig. 8-2. PPN citizen presenting solutions for privacy. Source: Authors.

Producing social knowledge from current housing also included defining characteristics of the ideal house of PPN citizens. Thinking about the ideal house helped the community to bracket off, albeit momentarily, the constraints anticipated in imagining new housing solutions for them. In this part of the workshop, we focused on conceptualizing problems rather than looking for solutions that are set into a form. For example, some of the needs identified for a dream house included "fence," "block wall," and "bulletproof," when we discussed these needs further we found we could categorize them under "privacy and security." This opened up a greater variety of solutions and forms to be considered for achieving privacy (see Fig. 8-2). The CARES members mobilized higher order concepts as prosthetic devices (Bruner 1991) to enable the problem solving and planning to go beyond the concrete token level towards the more abstract, encompassing an open ended realm of possibilities (and solutions).

Producing social knowledge through design charrettes

As we moved forward into conceptual designs, social knowledge was produced through a design charrette. For the prototype house we prepared "cardboard plan pieces," and community members used them to produce their own design and formulate their own solutions, using placement of the form to prioritize needs and alternatives.

During the design process each of the participating members, which included architects, engineers and the local community, had to go through a process of detachment. It is often accepted that architects are strongly attached to their designs; their attachment is based on feelings of ownership towards their artistic creation and some level of detachment is needed to adjust to. But engineers also get attached to the optimized shape they produced and are reluctant to move from what they perceive as the optimum, called "design fixation" (Linsey et al. 2010). Moreover, users may also be attached to some specific forms, often things with which they are familiar. (This attachment could be positive, as in they keep using the forms they are familiar with, or negative, as with avoiding some forms). The discussions we had through words and visuals, and the process of attachment and detachment from suggested solutions are the premise of what the co-design in transdisciplinary teams is all about—a team with multi-disciplinary skills transcending their specific disciplines and fixations through discussions, leading to mutual understanding, and resulting in an agreed solution. The following example, of incorporating round shapes in the design of the homes, provides insight into the detachment process.

Round shapes

According to tribal belief, bad spirits live in corners, and thus straight corners should be avoided in PPN housing. This guideline created debates among the different disciplines. Architects explained the difficulty of building and living in round spaces, due to inefficiency of wall materials, complexity in creating openings, inefficiency in insulation quality, as well as the difficulty of organizing the interior space and furniture. Following some discussions with PPN members the CARES and tribal leadership organized a collaborative charrette.

Fig. 8-3. PPN citizen Debra Smith discusses design ideas with Leona Williams, PPN's chair. Source: Authors.

In this charrette, PPN members were provided different cardboard shapes cut to scale, varying in size and shape to represent the house footprint (squares, rectangles, circles and partial circles, each marked with the square footage it represented) and paper-cut furniture to scale, from which they produced a floor plan of a prototype house. During the activity, one member mentioned that while their culture supports rounded corners, it was hard for her to leave the "known space" of square corners and experiment with rounded shapes. While the architects assumed that direct interaction of tribal members with rounded shapes would convince them that curves are too difficult to handle, the PPN members developed a house plan that included two round corners: one that created the house's entry and another directly across, to create the kitchen. In addition, the design included a round space in the center of the house for socializing. In plan, the house was shaped like an eye, and the design resolved the desire for round spaces without complicating the insulation or furnishing (Figures 8-3 and 8-4).

Producing social knowledge through mediated interaction

In our collaboration with the PPN we aimed to sustain direct, face-to-face interaction as much as possible. This interaction was spread between locations at UC Berkeley and the PPN's reservation. Nevertheless, the 120 miles between the designers' location and the PPN's reservation made each of the visits challenging. Due to the four hours' drive required for each in-person interaction, we combined different activities into each visit, which was demanding, both for the community and for the designers.

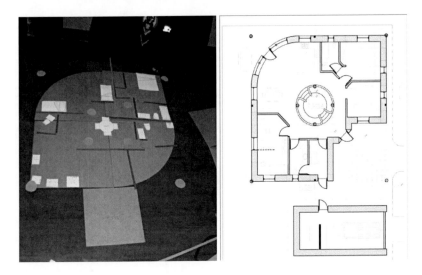

Fig. 8-4. The final design produced by PPN citizens during the design charrette (left) and the refined design as developed over several weeks afterwards (right). Source: Authors.

To compensate for the physical distance and increase interaction we tried different types of mediated interaction (Table 8-1). These included conference calls (phone calls using speakerphones with a few participants on both sides), emails with questions and answers, emails with attachments of case-studies or design alternatives, and later a dedicated website with a content management system (CMS) that allowed uploads, blogging, commenting and discussions. We used Drupal as our CMS. As the professional interaction between the CARES team and PPN citizens increased, we found ourselves adding each other to our Facebook pages, and while we did not use Facebook for direct professional interaction, we realized that it provided insight into Native American culture, both traditional and contemporary, and indirectly contributed to a shared understanding of culture and place.

Interaction Type	Goals	Characteristics
Conference call	Getting answers to specific questions. Discussion of design alternatives.	No anonymity; No diversity of media; High technological accessibility to those invited and attended.
Email	Getting answers and feedback from specific community representatives. Sharing drawings and photos.	No anonymity; High diversity of media; Good accessibility of email in this community.
Drupal (CMS)	Keeping the community informed on design progress of the Berkeley team. Getting feedback on design alternatives.	Good anonymity options; High diversity of media; Low accessibility to unfamiliar technology.
Facebook (no dedicated group page)	A mutual acquantance process between designers and community members. Gaining some knowledge on contemporary Native culture and lifestyle.	No anonymity, high diversity of media, high accessibility to Facebook within the community

Table 8-1. Types of mediated interactions used in the co-design process.

We used conference calls when the CARES team needed timely information or feedback from community members. Through this interaction we were able to discuss alternatives and get opinions from community representatives that allowed the CARES team to direct the design towards the community's chosen alternative. We participated in conversations in which we learned about energy use in houses and benefitted from feedback on previously sent designs. Conference calls were not public events open to all PPN citizens, but rather limited to PPN representatives. Usually, these were representatives of the tribal governance and those holding official relevant positions within the tribes' administration. Some representatives within this group were more active and influential than others.

Email was used to share drawings or to send out lists of questions to individuals or a group. It was our main form of communication with the PPN's Environmental Director and was very often used to send drawings produced by CARES to different members of the community whose email address we had. It was rarely used to get direct feedback from members of the community we sent it to, but the environmental director often collected responses in meetings with different members and shared these responses with us.

Similar to email, Drupal was used for spreading out information that could potentially allow a wider variety of members to have access to the information we posted. Rarely, however, did we receive comments on alternative designs via through the Drupal site. Most discussions started online then moved to and developed through targeted phone calls.

Project goals vs. people's goals

Beyond the different perspectives about design, our co-design team members differed in their goals. Architects and engineers are often evaluated by their design results—the building as the product—but the design process has great importance too, and is too often ignored. In his book, *Great Planning Disasters*, Peter Hall (1982) chooses disasters (e.g., the BART- Bay Area Rapid Transit system and Sydney's opera house) based on failures in the design *process*, such as poor financial planning or inadequate population studies, rather than on the architectural or engineered qualities or performance of the final product. In his analysis Hall identifies, among other important factors, the importance of the community's role in the design. He suggests either finding a way to get "more reliable, less biased information directly from the real public" or improving the "amount and quality of participation" (207).We found that identifying broader community goals, which lay beyond the building results, is key to improving the amount and quality of participation.

In bringing community participation to design projects, there is often imbalance in the motivations of the varied participants. While the designers are getting paid for their time, it is often assumed that the influence on the building is enough of a motivation for community partners. But community members have other commitments, which often make it hard for them to invest the time needed for design, even in projects which have great importance and influence on their lives. Motivating the community to spend their weekend on workshops, going over design ideas and sharing experiences, was one of CARES' main tasks. In this task we were depending on an "ambassador," a community representative devoted to the project and the community, who was being compensated for some of the time he invested in enabling this interaction. Our ambassador was the PPN's Environmental Director, a co-author of this article, who was not a tribal member but had worked for the PPN for five years. The ambassador answered most of our questions and referred us to others for more information when necessary. Moreover, through his understanding of both the community's and the designers' worlds he was able to shape our interaction in ways valuable not only to the design project but also for other goals the tribe would have, such as familiarizing youth with academic institutions to increase the number of them continuing to higher education, or expanding the collaboration to include grant writing to fund this and other projects to benefit both sides. Therefore, the strategy of combining a variety of goals and purposes into the design of the prototype homes made the homes a multi-purposes collaborative project—this paper, for example, is one of its fruits. These mutually beneficial interactions motivated participants and increased the amount and quality of collaboration with the community.

Conclusions

Each type of communication, whether direct or mediated, has different affordances which make it better suited for certain goals. Through this case study we learned that community participation thrives through the use of a range of communication methods and cannot be achieved through one existing communication technology. Based on this understanding, the technology chosen to mediate should enhance direct interaction with community members and should be diversified to provide different characteristics that suit the diversity of people. We identify three characteristics that are important for technologies to support co-design: (1) it should provide different communicative modalities (e.g. verbal–written and oral, visual–photos and drawings) to convey ideas and exchange information; (2) it should offer the choice of anonymity or different levels of exposed identity; and (3), it should be readily available and easy to use. Technologies that have these characteristics broaden the spectrum of people participating in the design process and offer a mediated alternative to support transdisciplinary co-design.

Co-design includes both interaction with form (design) and continuous interaction with the community (social interaction) in multiple platforms. We organize our interactions as a three-step process (Table 8-2).

Community interaction	Design interaction	Main face-to-face tools used / Supplemental technology used	Main required characteristics
Creating a mutual getting to know process. Discussion of broad concepts (such as culture, technology, sustainability).	Avoiding form.	Round robin sessions. / Facebook	• Reciprocal information change. • Racial/cultural diversity.
Discussion of current experiences and other case-studies.	Reacting to form.	Posters and post-it notes. Building visits with the community. / email blog posts video blogs	• Getting examples from the community. • Anonymity
Producing design ideas.	Interacting with form	Flip chart drawings in small groups. Design charrette. / Missing appropriate technology.	• Simple design tools that do not require professional or technical knowledge. • Producing unique pattern blocks, appropriate for the project that can easily be put together into a draft design.

Table 8-2. Defining co-design tools for community and design interactions.

To eschew biased co-design process and to allow all members of the design team, whether design professionals or not, to engage in the process with their expertise and exigencies, it is important to avoid interaction with form at the early stages of the process. A variety of activities could be useful for early exploration of the design problem. Table 8-2 lists the face-to-face and virtual tools we used as an example. In the first step of the process we found it helpful to use tools that facilitate reciprocal relationships between professional and non-professional designers and that situate all worldviews with the team in a socio-cultural matrix. This feature allows community members to learn about the designers as well as the designers learn about the community in the meeting. Since our work with the PPN community included racial differences, having designers from a variety of races, even if none were Native American, also contributed to achieving trust among participants in the co-design enterprise (Shelby and James 2009).

Step two includes discussions of current existing HUD housing and other case-studies. These may be the current built environment and conditions (whether housing or other buildings) or could be other built examples. This step allows members to quickly react to form and direct the design ideas produced in the next step towards their preferred form and solutions. In step three, when the co-design aims at interacting with form and coming up with a scheme, simple tools are needed. By this time some understanding of preferred form exists and professional designers can produce a simple mock-up toolkit with the appropriate shapes, which allow non-professionals to play with the patterns and give shape to design ideas. Using Christopher Alexander's pattern language system (Alexander, Ishikawa, and Silverstein 1977), the designer should produce the appropriate "pattern blocks" based on the interaction and the knowledge accumulated in the co-design team, which will allow the community to produce solutions with their own project's language. Existing design tools, even simple ones, are not equally conducive to such process. In our interaction with the PPN we used existing technology to complement our face-to-face interactions. Each tool we used, whether email, conference phones calls, or Content Management Systems, was selected only when the face-to-face was limited by geographical constraints or by the capabilities of the unmediated interaction.

Co-design, as a process that comprises both professional and non-professional players, is summarized in Figure 8-5. While designers use online technology such as Google Maps to learn about the physical attributes of a place, by harnessing other existing technologies, such as blogs, video blogs, and social-networks, into design projects they may better learn about the people.

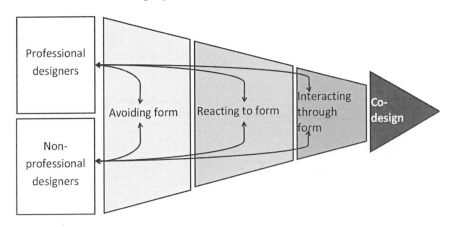

Fig. 8-5. Interaction with form in the process of co-design. Source: Authors.

Figure 8-6 shows how different existing online technologies can fit into Canter's definition of place. We identified three main characteristics for the mediated digital technologies to support co-design process: Anonymity options, diversity of media, and accessibility to the technology. Any one available technology still does not offer solutions encompassing all characteristics identified hence the ability of one digital, mediated technology to support co-design is still limited.

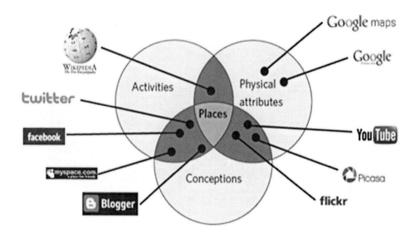

Fig. 8-6. Existing technologies that could teach designers about place based on Canter's definition. Source: Authors.

References

Alexander, Christopher. 1964. *Notes on the synthesis of form*. Cambridge: Harvard University Press.

Alexander, Christopher, Sara Ishikawa, Murray Silverstein, and Max Jacobson. 1977. *A pattern language: Towns, buildings, construction*. New York: Oxford University Press.

Alexander, Christopher, Murray Silverstein, Shlomo Angel, Sara Ishikawa, and Denny Abrams. 1975. *The Oregon experiment*. Oxford University Press.

Arnstein, Sherry R. 1969. "A ladder of citizen participation." *Journal of the American Institute of Planners* 35 (4): 216–24. doi:10.1080/01944366908977225.

Bruner, Jerome. 1991. "The narrative construction of reality." *Critical Inquiry* 18 (1): 1–21.

Burns, Carol, and Andrea Kahn. 2005. "Why site matters." In *Site Matters: Design Concepts, Histories, and Strategies*, vii – xxix. Psychology Press.

Canter, David V. 1977. *The Psychology of Place*. Architectural Press.

Cuff, Dana. 1989. "Through the Looking Glass: Seven New York Architects and Their People." In *Architects' People*, edited by Russell Ellis and Dana Cuff, 64–102. New York: Oxford University Press.

DeWalt, Kathleen M., and Billie R. DeWalt. 2011. *Participant Observation: A Guide for Fieldworkers*. Rowman Altamira.

Edmunds, D. S., R. Shelby, A. James, L. Steele, M. Baker, Y. V. Perez, and K. TallBear. 2013. "Tribal Housing, Codesign, and Cultural Sovereignty." *Science, Technology & Human Values* 38 (6): 801–28. doi:10.1177/0162243913490812.

Ellis, Cliff. 2005. "Planning Methods and Good City Form." *Journal of Architectural and Planning Research* 22 (2): 138–47.

Ellis, Russell, and Dana Cuff. 1989. *Architects' People*. First edition. New York: Oxford University Press.

Hall, Peter Geoffrey. 1982. *Great Planning Disasters*. University of California Press.

Haraway, Donna. 1988. "Situated knowledges: The science question in feminism and the privilege of partial perspective." *Feminist Studies* 14 (3): 575. doi:10.2307/3178066.

Kalay, Yehuda E. 2004. *Architecture's new media: principles, theories, and methods of computer-aided design*. MIT Press.

Lefaivre, Liane, and Alexander Tzonis. 2003. *Critical Regionalism: Architecture and Identity in a Globalized World*. Prestel.

Linsey, J. S., I. Tseng, K. Fu, J. Cagan, K. L. Wood, and C. Schunn. 2010. "A study of design fixation, its mitigation and perception in engineering design faculty." *Journal of Mechanical Design* 132 (4): 041003–041003. doi:10.1115/1.4001110.

Lynch, Kevin, and Gary Hack. 1984. *Site Planning*. 3rd edition. Cambridge, Mass: The MIT Press.

O'Donnell, Caroline. 2006. "Gibson, Giraffes, and Gibbons." *Anyone Corporation \ Log Journal for Architecture*, no. 8 (Summer): 21.

One Planet Living. 2014. "The Ten Principles." Accessed October 28. http://www.oneplanetliving.net/what-is-one-planet-living/the-ten-principles/.

Rapoport, Amos. 2005. *Culture, architecture, and design*. Chicago: Locke Science Publishing Co., Inc.

Shelby, Ryan, and Angela James. 2009. "Co-Productions of Environmental Science, Technology, and Indigenous Governance: The Pinoleville Pomo Nation – UC Berkeley Partnership to Co-Design Culturally Informed, Sustainable Housing." In . Minneapolis. http://www.ryanlshelby.com/uploads/1/9/8/6/1986376/ryan_shelby_09_naisatalk.pdf.

Shelby, Ryan, Yael Perez, and Alice Agogino. 2012. "Partnering with the Pinoleville Pomo Nation: Co-Design methodology case study for creating sustainable, culturally inspired renewable energy systems and infrastructure." *Sustainability* 4 (5): 794–818. doi:10.3390/su4050794.

Sommer, Robert. 1983. *Social Design: Creating Buildings with People in Mind.* Englewood Cliffs, N.J: Prentice-Hall.

The American Institute of Architects. 2014. "AIA/COTE2014 Top Ten Green Projects Entry Form." http://www.aiatopten.org/sites/default/files/pages/AIA_COTE_2014_T op_Ten_Entry_Form_Details.pdf.

US Department of Housing and Urban Development. 2014. "NAHASDA - HUD." *HUD > Program Offices > Public and Indian Housing > Indian Housing's Office of Native American Programs (ONAP) > CodeTalk Home > NAHASDA.* Accessed October 28. http://portal.hud.gov/hudportal/HUD?src=/program_offices/public_indi an_housing/ih/codetalk/nahasda.

Whyte, William F., Davydd J. Greenwood, and Peter Lazes. 1989. "Participatory action research: Through practice to science in social research." *American behavioral scientist* 32 (5): 513–51. doi:10.1177/0002764289032005003.

Notes

[1] Examples for emphasizing social and cultural factors as part of a sustainable design definition:

The American Institute of Architects (2014): Top Ten Green Projects: "Sustainable design recognizes the unique cultural and natural character of a given region."

BioRegional: One Planet Living Programme 10 Principles: principle number eight urges, "Valuable aspects of local culture and heritage must be maintained, enhanced or revived." (One Planet Living 2014).

[2] The Native American Housing Assistance and Self Determination Act of 1996 (NAHASDA) reorganized the system of housing assistance provided to Native Americans through the Department of Housing and Urban Development by eliminating several separate programs of assistance and replacing them with a block grant program. The two programs authorized for Indian tribes under NAHASDA are the Indian Housing Block Grant (IHBG) which is a formula based grant program and Title VI Loan Guarantee which provides financing guarantees to Indian tribes for private market loans to develop affordable housing. Regulations are published at 24 CFR Part 1000 (US Department of Housing and Urban Development 2014).

[3] For more details about CARES please visit:http://ppn.airjaldi.org/drupal/node/71

LIST OF ABBREVIATIONS

ACSA, Association of Collegiate Schools of Architecture
AIA, American Institute of Architects
AIAS American Institute of Architect Students
AIDA, Architectural design In Dialogue with disAbility
ASHRAE, American Society of Heating, Refrigerating & Air
    Conditioning Engineers)
BIM, Building Information Modeling
CARES Community Assessment for Renewable Energy and Sustainability
CBECS, Commercial Building Energy Consumption Survey
CED, College of Environmental Design
COTE, Committee on the Environment
DCDEE, Department of Child Development and Early Education
EBD, Evidence Based Design
EBS, Environment Behavior Studies
EDRA, Environmental Design Research Association
GHG, Greenhouse Gasses
GIS, Geographic Information System
HARYOU, Harlem Youth Opportunities Unlimited
HUD, Housing and Urban Development
IAPS, International Association for Person-Environment Studies
ICF, International Classification of Functioning, Disability and Health
IECC, International Energy Conservation Code
IHBG, Indian Housing Block Grant
LEED, Leadership in Energy and Environmental Design
MARC, Mid-America Regional Council
MIT, Massachusetts Institute of Technology
NAAB, National Architectural Accreditation Board
NAHASDA, Native American Housing Assistance and Self-Determination
    Act
NC, North Carolina
NCARB National Council of Architectural Registration Boards
NCIOM, The North Carolina Institute for Medicine
NIB, Neighborhood Improvement and Beautification
NLI, Natural Learning Initiative
NREL, National Renewable Energy Laboratory

NYRP, New York Restoration Project.
OLE, Outdoor Learning Environment
OPEC, Organization of Petroleum Exporting Countries
OPEC, Outdoor Play Environment Categories
PA, Physical Activity
POD, Preventing Obesity by Design
POE, Post Occupancy Evaluation
POEMS, Preschool Outdoor Environments Measurement Scale
POPS, Privately Owned Public Spaces.
PPN, Pinoleville Pomo Nation
PPS, Project for Public Spaces.
PS, Polysulphone
QRIS, Quality Rating and Improvement System
RMI, Rocky Mountain Institute
SEED, the Social Economic Environmental Design Network
TTH, Tenants to Homeowners
UC, University of California
UN, United Nations
US, United States
UV, Ultraviolet
UVR, Ultraviolet Radiation
WHO, World Health Organization
ZCB, Zero Carbon Building

CONTRIBUTORS

Alice M. Agogino is the Roscoe and Elizabeth Hughes Professor of Mechanical Engineering and is affiliated faculty at the Haas School of Business at the University of California at Berkeley. She directs the Berkeley Energy and Sustainability Technologies Lab, co-directs the Berkeley Institute of Design and is Chair of the Development Engineering Graduate Group.

Brad Bieber, MLA, Design Associate, Natural Learning Initiative, NC State University, Raleigh, NC, USA, designs and supports the implementation of sustainable outdoor play and learning environments for children and families that support healthy development. He also participates in research that informs design and facilitates professional development.

Cecilia Boldemann, PhD in community medicine, Associate Professor at the Department of Public Health Sciences, Karolinska Institutet, Stockholm, is research director of implementation projects dealing with the impact of everyday physical environment on health. She has a record as an advisor to expert committees of the WHO, and the Swedish government.

Nilda Cosco, PhD, Natural Learning Initiative, Research Associate Professor, College of Design, NC State University. She conducts research on impact of the outdoors on children's development and coordinates statewide projects (e.g. Preventing Obesity by Design). She holds a Ph.D. in Landscape Architecture, School of Landscape Architecture, Heriot Watt/Edinburgh University, Scotland.

Susanne Cowan is an Assistant Professor at the School of Architecture at Montana State University. She received her Ph.D. at University of California, Berkeley in the History of Architecture and Urbanism. Her research focuses on the relationship between urban design and the social conditions of cities, particularly regarding participatory democracy as a method for policy making. In her dissertation, Democracy, Technocracy and Publicity, Cowan explored how architects and town planners created a forum for democratic debate about new planning policies. She recently codirected an oral history documentary entitled "Design as a Social Act." In her current work, she is tracing how planning policies in de-industrializing cities have shaped urban decay and gentrification.

Galen Cranz is Professor of Architecture at the University of California at Berkeley, a Ph.D. sociologist from the University of Chicago, and a certified teacher of the Alexander Technique. She teaches social and cultural approaches to architecture and urban design, emphasizing user experience and ethnography as a research method. She wrote *The Politics of Park Design: A History of Urban Parks in America* (MIT 1982) and has since published "Defining the Sustainable Park: A Fifth Model of Urban Parks" in Landscape Journal (2004). *The Chair: Rethinking Culture, Body and Design* (1998) received the 2004 Achievement Award from the Environmental Design Research Association (EDRA). In 2011 she received EDRA's Career Award, its highest award. As a designer she has been part of several park design competition teams including Tschumi's Parc de LaVillette in Paris. She holds two US patents for body conscious bathtub and chair designs, and she has designed and built a residence for the elderly following universal design principles.

David Edmunds has a PhD in Geography from Clark University and was environmental Director at the Pinoleville Pomo Nation from 2007 to 2012. He is currently Track Director of Global Development Studies at the University of Virginia where he works on environmental issues as they intersect with culture, social relations, politics and community development.

Dominic L. Fischer is an assistant professor of Landscape Architecture at North Dakota State University and a senior associate landscape architect for Land Elements.

Karen A. Franck is a professor in the College of Architecture and Design at the New Jersey Institute of Technology where she also serves as Director of the Joint PhD Program in Urban Systems. She has a PhD in environmental psychology from the City University of New York. Over the years, Karen has written about a wide range of topics: collaboration between clients and architects in *Design Through Dialogue* (2010); designing for human needs in *Architecture from the Inside Out* (2007); possibility and diversity in urban life in *Loose Space* (2004)*;* relationships between food, architecture and the city in two issues of the journal *Architectural Design (AD)*; types in architecture and design in *Ordering*

Space (1994)*;* and alternative housing in *New Households, New Housing* (1989)*.* Her most recent book is *Memorials as Spaces of Engagement* (2015).

Emily Golembiewski co-leads the West Coast strategy practice of AECOM, a 50,000 person public company in the Fortune 500. She works across building types, including sports venues, museums, cities and offices. Recent projects include the SFMOMA expansion, Sacramento Kings arena and a ground-up development in Northern Brazil. Her projects have been published in Forbes and CIO and she lectures at Berkeley and Stanford on research methods. She serves on the board of the Oberlin Dance Collective, and is on the membership committee at SFMOMA. Emily curated a gallery at UCLA on alternate modes of architectural discourse and was part of the early team for 826LA's time travel supply store.

Ann Heylighen, PhD, is professor in the Research[x] Design group of the Department of Architecture at the University of Leuven (KU Leuven) in Belgium, where she teaches design theory and conducts research on disabled people's spatial experience as a source of design knowledge. She studied engineering/architecture at KU Leuven and ETH Zürich (Switzerland), conducted research at KU Leuven, Harvard University and UC Berkeley. She was awarded several grants, including a Starting and Proof-of-Concept Grant of the European Research Council.

Angela James is a Native American from Northern and Coastal Pomo decent. Angela serves as the Vice Chairperson on the Tribal Council for the Pinoleville Pomo Nation and she is also the director of the Tribal Historic Preservation Office.

Georgia Lindsay is a Visiting Assistant Professor in the Environmental Design Program at the University of Colorado Boulder, where she is also the department's Honors Council Representative. She received her PhD in Architecture from the University of California, Berkeley. Her research focuses on the user perspective on architecture, especially in cultural buildings such as museums and in LEED buildings. Her dissertation turned the Bilbao Effect critique back on US cities, using the Denver Art Museum as a case study, finding that the iconic architecture used to increase international visibility also changed curators' and patrons' relationship with art. She is currently working on a book about the user perspective in contemporary museum design, due out in 2016.

Marie-Alice L'Heureux, AIA, started her career as an architect in 1978 after graduating from McGill University in Montreal. She worked as a research assistant in the Energy and Environment Division at the Lawrence Berkeley Laboratory from 1993-1996 and earned a doctorate in architecture from the University of California, Berkeley in 2002. Her research focus has been on the politics of the built environment, social justice, and sustainability. She has published on the built environment of the former Soviet Union, especially Estonia, and has been writing and publishing articles on urban infrastructure and ideology in cities in the United States and Canada. She is an Associate Professor in the School of Architecture, Design, and Planning at the University of Kansas where she has taught since 2003.

Fredrika Mårtensson, PhD, Associate Professor in environmental psychology at the Swedish University of Agricultural Sciences at Alnarp in Sweden with research on schoolground greening, health promoting preschool settings and children´s everyday mobility. She is an expert on outdoor play behavior and has developed a tool for environmental assessment.

Ayda Melika is a Ph.D. candidate in the History of Architecture and Urbanism at University of California, Berkeley. She received her M.S. in Environmental Design and Urbanism in Developing Countries and her M.Arch. in Cultural Landscapes. As a documentarian her films focus on socio-cultural and political aspects of design and the spatial manifestations of collective activism. Ayda's most recent co-directed trilogy, "Design as a Social Act", documents how the spirit of the civil rights protests of the 1960s and 70s shaped the growing emphasis on the social research in environmental design.

Robin Moore, Dipl.Arch, MCP, Hon. ASLA, is Professor of Landscape Architecture and Director of the Natural Learning Initiative, North Carolina State University, Raleigh, USA, and past president of the International Play Association. His books include *Natural Learning, Play For All Guidelines*, and *Childhood's Domain: Play and Place in Child Development.*

Lusi Morhayim is an architectural researcher. She received her PhD at University of California, Berkeley. Her research lies at the intersection of social and environmental sustainability and politics of space. Her primary research focuses on grassroots communities' right to the city demands, particularly bicycle and pedestrian movements' role on urban social and spatial justice in San Francisco, CA. Her research interests include right to the city, health and architectural design, bioclimatic design and post occupancy evaluations. She has taught architectural research and theory classes at the University of California, Berkeley and Academy of Art University in San Francisco, CA and design at the Yildiz Technical University in Istanbul. Prior to teaching she practiced architecture.

Peter Pagels, M.Sc. University Lecturer in Sports Science and Physical Education at Linnaeus University Kalmar, and PhD student at the Department of Public Health Sciences, Karolinska Institutet, Stockholm.

Yael Valerie Perez holds a PhD. in Architecture from UC Berkeley. Her research focuses on technology to bridge international designers and local communities. She has co-founded CARES, Community Assessment of Renewable Energy and Sustainability and has design experience from Israel, India and USA.

Anders Raustorp, Associate Professor Physiotherapy (RPT) and Physical Education, University of Gothenburg and Linnaeus University Kalmar. He held a central position in developing Physical Activity on Prescription in Swedish Health Care System and introduced pedometry in Scandinavian research on children and adolescents.

Ryan Shelby is an energy engineering advisor for USAID's Powering Agriculture and Power Africa initiatives. He holds a Ph.D. in Mechanical Engineering from UC Berkeley and co-founded the Community Assessment of Renewable Energy & Sustainability (CARES).

Margareta Söderström, GP and associate professor at the University of Copenhagen, Denmark. Her research theme concerns common infections in families. Child nurseries are one important setting for research. Her focus has changed from a pathological to a salutogenic approach to infections which formed the base for an interdisciplinary cooperation.

Ulf Wester, M.Sc. is a physicist, formerly at the Swedish Radiation Safety Authority, a national regulatory government authority in Stockholm. He is an expert within the science of health physics concerning ultraviolet radiation from the sun and its measurement and has a record as member/consultee of CIE, ICNIRP, IEC and WHO.

INDEX